'Almost Like a Dream'

A Parish at War
1914–19

'Almost Like a Dream'

A Parish at War

1914–19

Letters from the Front published in the
Parish Magazine of St Michael's, Derby

Edited by
Michael Austin

MERTON PRIORY PRESS

First published 1999

Published by Merton Priory Press Ltd
67 Merthyr Road, Whitchurch
Cardiff CF14 1DD

ISBN 1 898937 33 8

© Introduction, Biographical Notes and other editorial matter
Michael Austin 1999

The editor has assigned his royalties from this publication
to the Royal British Legion and Derby Cathedral

Printed by Hillman Printers (Frome) Ltd
Handlemaker Road, Marston Trading Estate
Frome, Somerset, BA11 4RW

To the men of the parish and congregation
of St Michael's, Derby
who did not return
from the Great War
1914–18

and

to the memory of
Harry Roger Rolfe

'The taking of one trench stands out in
my mind more than anything else,
and I don't think I shall ever
forget it, perhaps because I saw two of
my best friends killed almost by my side.
We failed to take the trench the first time
and were in "no man's land" unable to move
either way. During that time I was buried
by a shell and hit by a piece of shrapnel
in the finger, it was not much, I managed
to get in four wounded men after a great
struggle. I was left 2nd in command
of the company, and for a part of
time commanded it ...

... There is a lot more I could say but I cannot
remember everything just now, it still seems
almost like a dream.'

2nd Lieut. Robert Barker
in a letter dated 15 July 1916,
describing the assault on Fricourt,
the Battle of the Somme.

Capt. Robert Barker MC was killed in action
on Sunday 13 October 1918 aged 24.

CONTENTS

LIST OF ILLUSTRATIONS

Between pages xxi and xxxvi

1   The front page of St Michael's parish magazine for December 1913, showing the interior of the church as the servicemen would have known it.

2   *Left:* St Michael's, with St Alkmund's in the background, from the tower of All Saints, *c.* 1890. *(Derby Museum and Art Gallery) Right:* Canon Harry Roger Rolfe, *c.* 1917. *(Mr David Bewley)*

3   St Michael's in the 1930s. The War Memorial was placed over the door early in 1921. *(Derby Museum and Art Gallery)*

4   Two views of St Michael's Lane, *c.* 1890, that on the left taken from St Michael's churchyard. Several servicemen lived here. *(Derby Museum and Art Gallery)*

5   Jimmy Hill's cap held aloft to attract enemy fire. *(British Library, LD4 Daily Mirror, 'On the lookout for the enemy', 6 Oct. 1914, p. 6)*

6   The members of the Bewley family who served. *(British Library, LD22 Daily Graphic, 'All in their country's service', 2 Nov. 1916, pp. 6–7)*

7   *Left:* Mrs Henrietta Bewley with her son Cecil. *(Mr Gordon Bewley). Right:* Alec Bewley. *(Mr David Bewley)*

8   Joseph Bewley (on the right) in Durban. *(Mr David Bewley)*

9   Arthur Ollerenshaw (left) and his brother-in-law Henry Lowe, who was killed on 1 July 1916, the first day of the Battle of the Somme. Arthur saw him die. *(Mr Frank Lowe and Miss Barbara Lowe)*

FOREWORD

In November 1960 I became vicar of St Andrew's, Derby. I found in the vicarage a bound volume of parish magazines for the small parish of St Michael's, Derby, by then long since cared for by the clergy of its near neighbour the Cathedral Church of All Saints, of which I subsequently became a residentiary canon. The priest who had built St Andrew's and who had become its first incumbent one hundred years earlier, John Erskine Clarke, had been vicar of St Michael's, hence the connection. This volume covered the period 1912–20. A quick glance through it suggested that it contained a unique record of the experiences of the many young men from the parish and congregation who went to war. The vicar of St Michael's at the time was Canon Harry Roger Rolfe. He and members of his congregation wrote regularly to 'our lads' and every month throughout the war Rolfe published in his parish magazine their letters to him, to their Sunday school teachers, their families and their friends.

These letters are reproduced here. The text of the letters and editorial and other material relating to the war is taken from the St Michael's parish magazines as it stands. I have made minor adjustments to punctuation and presentation to achieve clarity and uniformity. My own editorial notes have been kept to a minimum.

What follows is inevitably an incomplete record. Other than for a comparatively small number it has not been possible to trace the personal details and service records of the 224 men mentioned in the magazines. This would have been an almost impossible task as many men are mentioned only by name, and then often without their full first names, and with no note of number, rank or regiment. In any case many regiments did not record the names of soldiers below the rank of warrant officer. Further, the Ministry of Defence holds only some 20 per cent of service records in their original form, since the rest were damaged by fire in 1940. For these reasons it has so far not been possible to produce further information. Much more research, time and good fortune might have traced more men. The attempt will continue.

The book is arranged in three parts. The introduction tells briefly of the parish, congregation and priest that these men knew so well. This is followed by the letters as Harry Rolfe had edited them. Finally, there is a biographical index of the servicemen arranged so that readers interested in a particular man can readily find references to him in the letters. Additional personal and service information is to be found here. The general index relates to both the introduction and the letters.

I acknowledge the great help that I have received from Ted Aspley, Margaret Bidmead (Keeper of Archives at the Royal Naval Submarine Museum, Gosport), Peter Blatherwick, John Plenderleith for his generously given technical support, the staffs of the Imperial War Museum, the Public Record Office, the Royal Naval Museum in Portsmouth, the Royal Air Force Museum, Hendon, Lambeth Palace Library and Derby Local Studies Library. The Bishop of Derby and the Provost of Derby have given me much encouragement and support. Cliff Housley, curator of The Sherwood Foresters Museum in Nottingham, gave me much of his time and made his wide knowledge and his database readily available to me. I owe an important debt to Philip Riden of Merton Priory Press. I am indebted also to Jessica Bomford of the *Derby Evening Telegraph*, to my cousin Mrs Pat Hillman, and to Ann, who had to cope with yet another enthusiasm which has absorbed her husband. Above all I am deeply grateful to those relatives of servicemen whom I have been able to contact and who responded so readily to appeals for information and made precious photographs available to me for publication with the letters.

Considerable effort has been made to trace the families of all the men whose names feature here significantly, but it was an almost impossible task. I apologise for any inadvertent infringement of copyright. I hope that relatives I have been unable to contact and who read this book will feel that their very courageous young men have again been rightly honoured, eighty years after their dreadful war ended. For this reason also my royalties have been assigned equally to The Royal British Legion and Derby Cathedral.

For those who wish to set the letters in the wider context of the events and personalities of the First World War the accounts by John Keegan and Martin Gilbert and (for the memories of ordinary soldiers) Lyn Macdonald are exceptional. For the responses of the Church of England to the war see Alan Wilkinson's excellent study, *The Church of England and the First World War*, first published by SPCK in 1978 and reissued in paperback by SCM Press in 1996.

A PERSONAL POSTCRIPT

One of my three uncles Frank was my mother's brother, Frank Ridgwell. He served in the army in the First World War. Throughout my childhood he and his wife Gladys kept a grocer's shop in the East End. I remember them well. They were always very kind to me. My mother told me Uncle Frank's story. It was one of extraordinary heroism, confirmed much later (as I learned while preparing these letters for publication) in a very condensed, graphic but understandably reserved account that he wrote for his grandchildren when he was 81.

Frank Ridgwell volunteered in 1915. In the trenches he kept a sick friend warm and alive by rubbing dubbin on his chest. Although he was suffering from trench fever he was posted to a shell-hole in No-Man's Land to observe enemy movements. He was dazed. An officer accused him of sleeping on duty. He was court-martialled and sentenced to death. He was reprieved, given a suspended sentence of five years penal servitude and immediately sent back to the trenches as his platoon was short of men. He volunteered for hazardous duty to obtain remission of part of his sentence, narrowly escaping death on one 'walk back over the top between machine-gun fire' to escort a ration and ammunition party, one bullet passing through his pay book (and a photograph of one of his sisters) in one tunic pocket and a second piercing his cigarette case in another. He was recommended for an award for bravery in the field. Although he never received any award above a Certificate of Honour his prison sentence was quashed. On 25 March 1918 he was taken prisoner and was subsequently badly treated in captivity, spreading dubbin on crusts and eating horse flesh to keep alive. In October he escaped, living rough in civilian clothing as he made his way to the coast until the Armistice. He was arrested and interrogated by the British military police, put into khaki and shipped home. He left the Royal Fusiliers as he had joined the regiment, as a private.

As a child I knew something of this story and accepted it without question though, as I grew to adulthood, I supposed that it had gained much in my imagination.

In preparing these letters for publication I routinely consulted Gerard Oram's *Death Sentences passed by Military Courts of the British Army 1914–1924*. Not one of the 224 men whose names are recorded here is to be found in Oram's list, but my Uncle Frank's name is. F.H. Ridg[e]well of 24th Royal Fusiliers, Sportsman's Battalion, was condemned to death on 10 February 1916 for 'sleeping'. The death sentence was not confirmed but the final sentence was that he serve five years penal servitude.

This book is as much a tribute to Frank Ridgwell as it is to the young men from Derby who fought beside him on the Western Front at, as he and they record, Grenay and Bethune and on the Somme. It is a tribute also to those of their comrades upon whom the sentence of execution was carried out, in the hope that one day soon their unjust and dreadful sentences will be annulled and their honour restored.

Fiskerton, Notts.   Michael Austin
June 1999

THE PARISH

In 1856 a remarkable man, John Erskine Clarke,[1] assistant curate of St Mary's, Lichfield, became vicar of St Michael's, Derby. He had not been in his new post for many months when, on 17 August 1856:

> during the sermon on that Sunday forenoon, the preacher and congregation were startled by a strange rumbling sound, in a second or two it was repeated more loudly, and some who were in the church saw stones falling from the top of the chancel gable, happily they fell outwards and the ceiling of the chancel was not even broken. But those who saw the falling stones thought the whole church was coming down and rushed for the door. One gentleman in springing over the end of his pew threw down a glass lamp-shade, and this crash made the panic more general and all fled in confusion. Mothers ran eagerly to the gallery fearful for their children, forgetful of themselves. But, by God's mercy, no one was hurt.[2]

A rebuilt and enlarged St Michael's, designed by H.I. Stevens, was opened on 8 April 1858. Its predecessor had been very small, and the new building was still very modest in size. This was the parish church that the servicemen of 1914–18 knew well. It contained 430 sittings, a large number in such a relatively confined space. Clarke insisted that all these seats should be free and unappropriated, in contrast to the other medieval parish churches in the town in which pew-renting was the norm. There the poor were accommodated (if they were accommodated at all) on seats in areas away from the view of those who held them-

---

[1] John Erskine Clarke, Wadham College, Oxford, B.A. 1850, M.A. 1853; deacon 1851, priest 1852; assistant curate St Mary, Low Harrogate; St Mary, Lichfield; vicar, St Michael, Derby 1856–66; P.C. St Andrew, Derby 1866–72; Preb. Lichfield 1869–72; chap. to Bishop of Rochester 1877–91; vicar of Battersea 1872–1909; St Luke, Battersea 1901–14; Proc. Conv. Rochester 1880–1905; Hon. Chaplain Queen Victoria 1895–6, Chaplain in Ordinary 1896–1901; Hon. Chaplain to King Edward VII 1909–10; Hon. Chaplain to King George V 1910; Hon. Canon Winchester 1875–1905; Hon. Canon Southwark 1905.

[2] J.E. Clarke, *The Story of St Michael's Church, Derby: the Old and the New* (Derby, 1857), pp. 8ff.

selves to be their social superiors or, as in some other Derbyshire churches, on benches facing the well-to-do members of the congregation as a warning that there, but for the grace of God, went they. In fact all but two of the pews in the former St Michael's had been free but these free seats had been appropriated by usage over a long period and were not available to all-comers. In the new church, Clarke insisted, all must be allowed freely to sit where they chose regardless of economic or social status.

The principle that class distinctions in society should not be reflected in seating arrangements in churches was very important for John Erskine Clarke. In a leaflet that he distributed around the parish when the new St Michael's opened for worship he said this:

ST MICHAEL'S NEW CHURCH

TO THE POORER PARISHIONERS
AND OTHERS WHOM IT MAY CONCERN

My Friends,

I wish to say a few words to you about our new Church. I am sadly afraid that we have made the Church so beautiful that smart people will come, and fill up the places meant for you—and so I wish you to know that if it is so, it is your fault, not mine.

My wish and hope is that St Michael's should be a Church for the Poor, and if the poorest worshipper is not treated with the same respect as the richest it will be altogether against my instructions and desires. And I hereby invite the poorest and neediest to come and put in their claim to their share of the Church.

I know that many of you have not such clothes as you would like to come to Church in but till you have better I say, Come in such as you have. The Church is not built for showing off people's fine clothes, but for praying to God, for praising Him, and for learning something of that world where there is no more sin nor trouble (because there is no sin), and where poverty never pinches, and labour never wearies. Wherefore, I urge you to come in such clothes as you have, however poor they may be; make them as clean as you can and come. You may freely enter any seat if you are regularly at Church, in good time, you will find that seat will be left for you, and will become as much your own as if you paid for it, for others will leave it for you.

> Begin at once to come to your Parish Church. You cannot make
> a start at a better time ... Begin to come and keep on coming—on
> Sundays and when the Church is open in the week ...

Another handbill announced that 'Handicraftsmen or labourers will be as
welcome in fustian as if they were in broadcloth, and their wives as
welcome in cotton gowns as if they were in silk ones'.

These handbills indicate the character of the parish, the smallest of the
five medieval parishes in Derby and socially and economically the most
deprived. Its population declined from a peak 1,064 in 1841 to 520 in
1901 and this at a time when the population of the town as a whole was
growing rapidly, consequent above all on the coming of the railway in
1839. The effect of the physical and social change effected by the
railway is illustrated by the fact that in the 1870s the locomotive and
carriage sheds of the Midland Railway Company occupied an area as
large as the whole of pre-railway Derby.[1] By 1851 half the population
of Derby over 20 years of age had been born outside the borough. Many
of the newcomers consisted of 'Yorkshire and Tyneside men with their
rude energy, broad outlook and ready tongue' who 'were regarded with
suspicion by old residents of Derby, jealous lest the even tenor of the
town be upset'.[2] More than these in number were the Irish navvies and
labourers, speaking only Irish, who congregated in Derby's worst slums,
the courts and alleys in the Walker Lane district of St Michael's parish
and served by the Pugin-designed St Mary's Roman Catholic church
opened in 1839 close to St Michael's. Clarke, and his neighbour at All
Saints, E.W. Foley, were active in raising funds to relieve distress. In
1861 Clarke intervened in a trade dispute, chairing a meeting of striking
Derby ribbon weavers and urging the establishment of a cooperative mill.
These two clergy were among the few in Derby who protested at the
social and economic conditions suffered by that still new phenomenon,
the industrial labouring poor.

Not the least of these evils was housing. The brick hovels they lived
in had neither drainage, sanitation nor running water. They surrounded
open cesspits. It was said in 1849 that the ground itself was 'saturated
with all that was offensive'. In one court off St Helen's Street the hovels
were next to a slaughter-house around which lay blood and offal 'making

---

[1] E.C. Vollans, 'Derby. A Railway Town and Regional Centre', *Trans. Inst. British Geographers* (1949), 107.

[2] G.J. Pratt, *Midland Railway Memories* (Derby, 1924), p. 25 of 1st series, 'Personalities of other days', reprinted from *Derby Evening Telegraph*.

a stench not to be endured'.[1]

It was to serve this area that John Erskine Clarke rebuilt St Michael's in 1858. His egalitarian principles and welcome to the poor attracted very considerable numbers from 'the railway end of the town' who passed the pew-rented St Peter's, St Werburgh's and All Saints on their way to St Michael's and for whom Clarke built St Andrew's in 1866, becoming its first incumbent. The fifth medieval parish church in Derby, St Alkmund's, stood between St Michael's and Pugin's new St Mary's.

The worst of the slums surrounding St Michael's had been cleared well before the First World War, yet the character of the parish as a socially deprived area had not changed. In 1913 the vicar, Harry Rolfe, could report that its population had declined to 373 at the last census in 1911 and that with the exception of shops in Queen Street and Irongate it 'consisted of very poor houses, many of which ought not to be inhabited'. The continuing memory of John Erskine Clarke,[2] and the readiness of the parish church to welcome all regardless of social class had not changed either. Rolfe noted that 'the congregation is mainly composed of working people ... gathered from all parts of the town [and] would, including the children, more than fill the church twice over'.[3] The physical appearance of the parish remained depressing. Alexander Fisher, the sculptor of the parish's war memorial, wrote in 1920 that 'it [a crucifix] should be in ... a place for all men to see "who pass by", and especially in a district where there is so little to be seen of a beautiful and ennobling kind, that brings with it the only message that will help and relieve the sufferings of our daily life'.[4]

Harold Roger Rolfe[5] became vicar of St Michael's in 1885. He came to a church that had embraced what at the time would have been regarded as high church practices. At 'Little Mickel's' altar lights, unleavened bread and a mixed chalice were used at least from the 1870s.

---

[1] W.A. Richardson, *Citizens' Derby* (Derby, 1949), pp. 200–1, quoting a sanitary inspector's report. For a full account of social conditions in Derby, and the reaction of the clergy, not least J.E. Clarke, see M.R. Austin, 'The Church of England in the town of Derby, 1824–85' (Unpublished M.A. thesis, University of Birmingham, 1966).

[2] *St Michael's Church Magazine*, Sept. 1916. Clarke had suffered a stroke.

[3] *St Michael's Church Magazine*, Jan. 1913, Statement at the Bishop of Southwell's visitation, 12 Dec. 1912.

[4] *St Michael's Church Magazine*, June 1920.

[5] Lichfield Theological College 1872, assistant curate Beighton (Derbys.), 1874–7, assistant curate of Staveley (Derbys.) 1877–84, vicar of Misson (Yorks., but in the diocese of Southwell from its formation in 1884) 1884–5. He died in 1924 while still vicar of St Michael's.

The priest took the eastward position and, by the 1890s, was robed in a plain linen chasuble, but no cope. During the incumbency of Rolfe's predecessor, H. Howard Twist (1876–81), white stoles embroidered with crosses had been introduced. Twist's assistant curate, R.W. Cooke, was brave enough to say at a public meeting in 1878 that, while he never heard confession, if a penitent came to him he would not send him away but would rely on the office of the Visitation for the Sick (the prayer book office which allows for auricular confession) for his authority. He left the hall 'amid the laughter, groans and hisses of the audience'. Yet neither Twist nor F.J. Lyall at St Luke's (where, it was said, could be 'enjoyed ... the purest English catholic ritual in town') were attacked for these practices. In Derby Ferris Utterson at St Anne's was the only Anglican priest in the highly charged religious atmosphere of the 1870s to incur real censure for what were held to be his ritualistic practices and Romanising theology.

Harry Rolfe therefore came to a parish church which had for some years been moderately Catholic in religious practice. It was also resolutely Anglican in religious conviction. Rolfe himself was described as 'perfectly orthodox' in 1893.[1] He was anxious to maintain a high conception of the authority of the Church and the centrality of the sacraments within a reformed Catholic tradition in such a way as not to cause offence, still less to be thought to be of a Romanising tendency. So while, for example, he was strongly opposed to the disestablishment and disendowment of the Church in Wales,[2] flew the Union flag from the tower 'on special days connected with the State', and used the Book of Common Prayer and no other, he gradually acquired and used sets of eucharistic vestments, called the eucharist 'the Holy Sacrifice', and urged prayers for the departed. When Bishop King of Lincoln was prosecuted by the Church Association in the famous ritual case in 1888 Rolfe said a eucharist for him ('for Bishop King' appears at least once in the service register at that time) and he frequently invited Ferris Utterson to preach at St Michael's. At the same time Rolfe, inheriting the tradition of John Erskine Clarke, though perhaps not as passionate an advocate for the poor, was alert to the social needs of his parish. As one of several examples it was reported that at the George Yard Mission 'a good but unpretending work is being carried on Sunday by Sunday in the large lodging-house by members of the Church of England Working Men's Society'.

---

[1] C.J. Payne, *Derby Churches Old and New* (Derby, Frank Murray, 1893), p. 109.

[2] *St Michael's Church Magazine*, Jan. 1912 et seq.

Worship, as he remembered it in the 'small, plain and unpretending' St Michael's, was described in a letter to Rolfe from a homesick serviceman in France at the time of the patronal festival in 1917. For festal evensong there would be twelve candles on the altar with 'the Cross bearer and the choir standing before it in the form of a cross singing the final clauses of the Te Deum, and you at the Altar facing East, in the position as an intercessor between your people and their God'. He regretted though that, 'here are not to be found the incense and cope, as perhaps some of us would like'.[1] Rolfe was available every Saturday evening and at other times by appointment and throughout Holy Week 'to help anyone, who feels the need, to make a good Communion' but never called this Confession. Citing the 1640 Canons of the Church of England he encouraged members of his congregation to bow towards the altar on entering and leaving church but never to reverence it on rising from the altar rail. In these and in other matters of external observance Rolfe recommended that charity towards others should be the key. It would be better to omit outward acts of devotion, he said, than to distract the thoughts of some 'weaker brethren'.[2] This, he said, was simply a matter of church manners. He invited the Superior of the Society of the Sacred Mission in Kelham to preach. He recommended to his congregation books by Charles Gore and E.B. Pusey and hymns by John Mason Neale. Throughout the war, and notably on the first anniversary of the Armistice, he celebrated a requiem eucharist (not 'Mass') for those who had fallen. He supported the practice of praying for the dead by citing Scripture and Anglican practice but to make his resolute Anglicanism plain he rejected the title 'Father'.[3] This was Anglican Christianity as Harry Rolfe practised it and taught it to the many young men from his parish and congregation who enlisted in 1914.

On the declaration of war Rolfe had been vicar of St Michael's for 29 years. His attitude to it was typical of those who, while avoiding jingoism, were unquestioning in their belief that, as Rolfe wrote in September 1914, 'our cause is just'. He told the children that 'our Country just now is out on the biggest and most difficult task she has had in all the long and wonderful course of her history'. He had no doubt that to go to war with Germany was a young man's clear duty. In September 1914, naming the first 25 men who had enlisted, he wrote: 'I trust that there will be many more who will hear their country's call in

---

[1] *St Michael's Church Magazine*, Oct. 1917.

[2] Ibid., Sept. 1918.

[3] Ibid., Aug. 1920.

her hour of peril and emulate their example'. 'In this war of right against wrong', he wrote in October, 'every young man should seek to know his duty and when he knows it, face it even unto death'. He printed in full Rudyard Kipling's *Hymn before Action* with the lines, 'Jehovah of the Thunders/Lord God of Battles, aid!'. Rolfe was clear that the God of the Bible was on the side of 'our lads'. Yet he knew that war results in wounding, tragedy and death and tried to comfort those who felt that their prayers for the safety of these young men had not been answered.[1] He never shielded the congregation from the horrors of war. The letters he published from servicemen told of these horrors only too powerfully. In September 1917 he published extracts from a sermon by C.B. Mortlock,[2] a chaplain in the Army who had recently been invalided out of the service, in which he inveighed against the 'brutalizing [of] the national character by investing the horrors of warfare with a romantic glamour ... It is stupid, false, dishonouring and wicked, and I know that many soldiers stay away from church because they are afraid of hearing more of it'. Rolfe reproduced in his parish magazine *After the Battle* by E.M. James, E.W. Hornung's *Wooden Crosses*, and Owen Seaman's *Pro Patria*. To a reader today this verse may seem sentimental and trite and does not stand comparison with the major war poets, yet it was hugely popular and captured the mood of those at home. Those at war and facing its terrors would have their experiences and feelings expressed and interpreted much more sharply and perceptively through the poetry of the men who served alongside them.

Harry Rolfe wrote of the Armistice that Monday 11 November 1918 was a never to be forgotten day, 'for then the fighting ceased and a prospect of a righteous peace was assured. It is a matter of great thankfulness that generally the thought of God and His goodness was in the minds of the people'. Although the services to commemorate the end of the war were, he said, 'of a festal character', their emphasis was more one of thankfulness that the war had ended and less of triumph that victory had been achieved. This was the tone that Rolfe had maintained from the beginning.

---

[1] Ibid., Sept. 1914.

[2] Charles Bernard Mortlock, Jesus Coll. Camb., B.A. 1913, M.A. 1918; curate Batcombe with Upton Noble (diocese of Bath and Wells); St Mary-le-Bow 1915–16; TCF 1916–17; Perm. Offic. St Silas, Kentish Town 1918–20, St John's, Great Marlborough St 1920–7; curate St Mary le Strand, Westminster 1927–33; Proc. Conv. London 1931–45, Chelmsford 1945; vicar of Epping, 1936–47; rector of St Vedast, Foster Lane with St Peter, Cheapside 1947–67; Canon and Treasurer of Chichester 1950–67. Editor of the Anglican weekly *Challenge* 1914–16.

St. Michael's, Derby.

DECEMBER, 1913.

Clergy: { Rev. CANON H. R. ROLFE, *Surrogate*, St. Michael's Vicarage.
{ Rev. J. E. STALEY, M.A., St. Michael's Churchyard.

All the seats in the Church are free and unappropriated, and the Church is
open during the day for private prayer.
All cases of sickness should be made known at once to the Clergy.
The Vicar can usually be seen in Church on Saturdays from 7.0 to 8.0 p.m.,
and at other times by appointment.

Services:

HOLY EUCHARIST.—Every Sunday—7.0, 8.0,
and 11.10 a.m. On Saints' Days, Tuesdays and
Thursdays, 7.30 a.m.

MATINS. — Sundays, 10.30 a.m. Saints' Days,
8.0 a.m. Mondays and Saturdays, 7.30 a.m.
Tuesdays and Thursdays, 8.0 a.m. Wednesdays
and Fridays, 10.30 a.m.

EVENSONG.—Sundays, 6.30 p.m. Week Days—
Mondays & Fridays, 5.0 p.m. Other days, 8 0 p.m.

SCHOLARS' SERVICE alternate Sundays, 2.30 p.m.

SERMONS and ADDRESSES—Sundays, 11.0 a.m.
and 6.30 p.m. Wednesdays, 8.0 p.m.

INTERCESSION.—Saturdays, 8.0 p.m. For
Foreign Missions—3rd Sunday, 7.45 p.m.

BAPTISMS on First Sunday of the Month at
3.15 p.m., and at Evensong on Week Days.
Due notice must be given to the Verger.

LITANY.—Every Sunday. Wednesdays & Fridays,
10.30 a.m.

CHURCHINGS before any Service, notice being
given.

SPECIAL SERVICES announced in Church.

1. The front page of St Michael's parish magazine for December 1913, showing the
interior of the church as the servicemen would have known it.

2. *Left:* St Michael's, with St Alkmund's in the background, from the tower of All Saints, *c.* 1890. *(Derby Museum and Art Gallery) Right:* Canon Harry Roger Rolfe, *c.* 1917. *(Mr David Bewley)*

3. St Michael's in the 1930s. The War Memorial was placed over the door early in 1921. (*Derby Museum and Art Gallery*)

4. Two views of St Michael's Lane, *c.* 1890, that on the left taken from St Michael's churchyard. Several servicemen lived here. (*Derby Museum and Art Gallery*)

ON THE LOOKOUT FOR THE ENEMY.

5. Jimmy Hill's cap held aloft to attract enemy fire. *(British Library, LD4* Daily Mirror, *'On the lookout for the enemy', 6 Oct. 1914, p. 6)*

THE DAILY GRAPHIC, THURSDAY, NOVEMBER 2, 1916.

ON WAR SERVICE AT HOME AND ABROAD:

THE ROLL OF A SINGLE FAMILY.

ALL IN THEIR COUNTRY'S SERVICE; A SPLENDID FAMILY RECORD.

This is the record of these ten brothers and sisters:—1. Miss F. Bewley, St. John Ambulance Brigade, V.A.D.; 2. Second-Lieut. A. Bewley, 17th Sherwood Foresters; 3. Miss S. Bewley, S.J.A.B., V.A.D.; 4. Sergt. E. Bewley, Army Pay Corps; 5. Miss G. Bewley, S.J.A.B., V.A.D.; 6. Private G. Bewley, R.F.C.; 7. Trooper O. Bewley, Derbyshire Imperial Yeomanry; 8. Lance-Corpl. C. Bewley, Derbyshire Imperial Yeomanry; 9. Sergt. T. Bewley, R.A.M.C.; 10. Petty Officer J. Bewley, R.N.A.S., died at Nairobi, East Africa.

6. The members of the Bewley family who served. *(British Library, LD22 Daily Graphic, 'All in their country's service', 2 Nov. 1916, pp. 6–7)*

7. *Left*: Mrs Henrietta Bewley with her son Cecil. (*Mr Gordon Bewley*). *Right*: Alec Bewley. (*Mr David Bewley*)

8. Joseph Bewley (on the right) in Durban. (*Mr David Bewley*)

9. Arthur Ollerenshaw (left) and his brother-in-law Henry Lowe, who was killed on 1 July 1916, the first day of the Battle of the Somme. Arthur saw him die. (*Mr Frank Lowe and Miss Barbara Lowe*)

10. Sam Whitaker (second row back, marked with a cross). (*Mr John Whitaker*)

11. *Left:* Sam Whitaker. *(Mr J. Whitaker) Right:* Herbert (left) and John Lowe, who landed on Suvla Beach, Gallipoli, together. Herbert was killed; John survived. *(Mr David Lowe)*

12. Royal Engineers Camp, 1913. A postcard sent by Sam Whitaker (far left foreground) to Nell Lovelock. (*Mrs J.A. Whitaker*)

13. _Left:_ Harry Cocker, killed in action, 4 April 1917. _Right:_ Wilfred Burrows and his fiancée Grace Bland, February 1916. _(Mr John Burrows)_

14. Capt. Robert Barker MC, killed in action, 13 October 1918. *(Mr Robert Owen)*

Throughout the war Harry Rolfe organised practical support for those who had enlisted. Letters, cards, money and parcels were sent regularly. In December 1915, for example, fifty parcels were sent to servicemen overseas—a practice which continued throughout the war and into 1919. Initially they were of the value of 5s. each and were supplied by a local grocer. Scarves, socks, toffee and, most importantly, candles as well as food were sent, though soldiers reported that very late delivery of these parcels resulted in food being wasted. By January 1918 money was being substituted for parcels for, as one serviceman reported, 'we think that it is better than a parcel which may never reach you'. Money to the value of 10s. was sent to those overseas and those in hospital, and 5s. to men training in Britain. A note in July 1917 details the value and contents of food parcels sent to prisoners of war. Three parcels were sent each month for six months to the value of 7s. each. Sunday school prize-winners gave up their prizes as a contribution to the cost. Harry Rolfe travelled the country to visit wounded servicemen in hospital. Members of his congregation wrote, knitted and prayed. Harry Rolfe mobilised his parish to support the servicemen. Any criticism of them was challenged immediately. In July 1915 Rolfe's assistant priest, J.E.S. Hackforth, later to be chaplain to local Army units,[1] vigorously defended their moral probity:

> Some months ago the statement went abroad that our soldiers— brave fellows as they are—had been guilty of immorality and every other vice. When these statements were put to the test it was found they were wicked slanders and no proof whatever could be found to substantiate these charges.

However, Hackforth was not ready to accept exaggerated claims made for them without similar verification:

> There has recently gone forth the statement of the miraculous visitation of angels to our men at the front,[2] and this statement also is on enquiry found to be at third and fourth hand and verification so far has been extremely doubtful. It is not that we disbelieve in angelic visitations at all, nor that we claim that these

---

[1] Hackforth wrote an article, 'The Soul of the Army', for the March 1918 magazine on the role of army chaplains in Derby.

[2] A reference to the claim that soldiers retreating from Mons in Aug. 1914 had been saved by angelic visitation: the myth of the 'Angel of Mons'.

visions are purely subjective, but these statements are 'uncertain', indefinite, and cannot be substantiated: we ask that there should be definite statements above all things, for at the present time there are too many 'uncertain voices' abroad and we are inclined to believe none.

The number of servicemen that the congregation supported was considerable. St Michael's had attracted to its choir, Men's Institute, football team, Sunday school and Scout troop boys and men from all over Derby. By the end of 1914 Harry Rolfe had listed 41 men from the congregation who were in the armed services. A few had been regular soldiers for a few years or were reservists rejoining their regiments or were Territorials but the majority had responded to Kitchener's appeal of 7 August 1914. Some had joined the Comrades Corps which became the 4th Company of the 12th Battalion of the Sherwood Foresters and among the first to form part of Kitchener's New Army of volunteers. By May 1915 50 communicants had enlisted in a number of regiments. In June Rolfe noted that more than one hundred belonging to St Michael's were on active service. By November that year 30 members of the Men's Institute had enlisted, 80 per cent of those eligible. Eight of the 1913–14 Sunday school football team had volunteered, together with brothers of the other three. Of these eight two were to be discharged seriously wounded, one wounded, one become seriously ill and one killed in action. By October 1916 twelve who had played for the football team had enlisted. By May 1917 eight Sunday School teachers had enlisted and two had been killed in action.

At home, Rolfe effectively mobilised his congregation. The Sunday school children gave up their prize money (willingly or not) to support the work of the Belgian Relief Committee, the Sherwood Foresters' prisoners of war committee, the Khaki Prisoners of War Fund and the Red Cross. The Scout troop, it was said in September 1914, 'had been actively engaged in work which, though we are not permitted to mention it in detail, is important and useful' (acting as orderlies in the military hospital in Mill Hill Lane and other 'Public Service Duties') and by March 1915 some of the older members had been enrolled in the Scouts Defence Corps and had been taught 'the use of the rifle'. By May 1917 one woman teacher was working in the War Office and another had become a nurse. Of these and other women Rolfe wrote: 'Time fails to tell of the war work, either direct or indirect ... which is being done by our present teachers; how one is making tanks, and one is supervising parcel packing for prisoners of war, another making aeroplanes, and another looking after the welfare of workers in a huge munition factory'.

By February 1916 threats of Zeppelin raids forced evening services to held at an earlier time. Two months later the military requisitioned the building in which the Sunday school assembled, forcing a few classes to be held 'at Mrs Bloomer's' and the remainder to meet

> at the Hostel in Full Street, where the Secretary has kindly done all that is possible for our comfort, but where the climatic conditions are truly British in their variability, only we go one better than the British Isles at the Hostel for you can experience every variety of climate simultaneously.

In fact the political affairs of the wider world had had an impact upon the parish much earlier. In August 1913 the choirboys had enjoyed their annual outing to Cleethorpes—an enjoyment enhanced by 'two unusual and exciting incidents':

> In the morning our respected choirmaster [later to be commissioned in the Army] was arrested and taken by the police before the Superintendent of the Grimsby Dock (in which the Admiralty have an interest) for the crime of using a camera, but happily he was able to prove that 'he was no spy' and was graciously permitted to take photographs. The second incident occurred on our homeward journey, when some ladies, presumably suffragettes, did their best to capture one of our leading boys and, but for the intervention of the Vicar, would have taken him off the carriage on which they were travelling. The danger was averted and all of us reached Derby in safety at about 11.15 p.m.

Together with the choirmaster, Thomas Wragg, eight former members of the choir are known to have enlisted. One was gassed, one was severely wounded and discharged, and five were killed in action.

This was the congregation from which 146[1] young men had enlisted and to which almost one in four did not return, and this was the 'small, plain and unpretending'[2] church and the 'dear old vicar' remembered

[1] 224 men are noted by Harry Rolfe in the parish magazine. Of these, 146 were listed on the St Michael's Roll of Honour as connected to St Michael's by the end of the war, though several names seem to have been omitted, apparently inadvertently, including two killed in action.

[2] Sixty years later the Council for the Care of Churches was to say of St Michael's that it was of 'very slender merit architecturally speaking' with a 'gloomy' interior.

with great affection by them. They formed a very tightly-knit group. They were bound together by ties of long friendship. Their families' names are to be found time and again in the marriage and baptism registers, the monthly lists of those who had died, the lists of the Sunday school prize-winners, the Scouts, members of the Men's Institute, the choir, and contributors to one cause or another. Five of them, Norman Powell, George Froggatt, Tom Longdon, John Marshall and Fred Wright, had been confirmed together on 16 March 1915.

These men were bound together even more closely by kinship and, as the war progressed, they and their families were further united by great suffering. Brothers and cousins enlisted, not only the seven Bewley brothers but also the Downmans and the Whitakers, the Powells and the Greensmiths, the Bakers and the Fletchers and the Nortons, the Fosters and the Hallsworths and the Robinsons, the Lambtons and the Lowes and the Harrisons and the Marshalls and many more. Brothers-in-law enlisted. As an example of kinship made deeper by shared suffering we may take the three Lowe brothers who enlisted, Harry, Herbert and John, and their brothers-in-law. Arthur Ollerenshaw had married Lizzie Lowe, and George Wheatcroft's sister Susan was married to John. The tragedy of war struck that family several times. Of the three Lowe brothers Harry was killed on the first day of the Battle of the Somme, 1 July 1916. His brother-in-law Arthur witnessed his death. Herbert was killed in the Gallipoli landings in August 1915. John and Herbert had landed at Gallipoli and been trapped on the beach together. John reached safety but Herbert was killed. Their brother-in-law George Wheatcroft was killed at Arras in April 1917. Arthur Ollerenshaw was so seriously wounded in June 1917 that he was discharged from the Army. The war devastated many other families. Albert Powell and his younger brother Norman were both killed. Both parents died in the sixteen months that separated the deaths of their sons. Mrs Oakley, the Powells' neighbour in St Michael's Lane, lost her son Charles. Of the two Whitaker brothers who enlisted together in August 1914, Sam survived and Jack was killed. Of the two Downman brothers Theodore was taken prisoner and Bernard was killed. Of the two Lambton brothers who enlisted George survived and Henry was killed. Of the five men from the congregation who joined the RAMC one was gassed, one was wounded, and the other three were killed. There are other stories like these. Such was the terrible impact of the Great War on a closely-knit town centre community.

Many of the men who went to war were to claim, with evident sincerity, that the religious disciplines and teaching they had received together at St Michael's were of great importance to them as they struggled to survive the boredom, the loneliness and, far worse, the dreadful horrors of the war they so vividly described in their letters. Their families who suffered at home were to say the same.

The men who returned were to find that the way of life, the national mood and the church that they had left had been fatally undermined by the appalling war in which they had fought with such courage. They could not know that their sons and daughters were to be conscripted for that extension to the Great War which broke out in 1939. Within a few years of the end of their sons' and daughters' war the parish of St Michael's had virtually ceased to exist as a residential area, the congregation had inevitably declined and its church declared redundant (in 1977). It is now in secular use, sympathetically converted to house an architectural practice.

These young men did not claim then, and would not want claimed for them now, that they were more courageous than any one else, or more patriotic or even more religious. Their stories are not exceptional by the extraordinary criteria of courage, loyalty and sheer dogged determination which are the only positive and lasting legacies of their war. They said then that they were only doing their duty to their God and their country. This they had been taught at St Michael's and this they did. However, the war had not been in progress long before their confident certainty that God was unequivocally on their side came under strain. Could God be asked to sanctify a cause that was being prosecuted with so much attendant horror? Faced with this most intractable and troubling of dilemmas the men from St Michael's understandably took shelter behind the pronouncements of ecclesiastical authority.[1] It was a dilemma of which their chaplains were only too aware, as we can deduce from C.B. Mortlock's impassioned censure. Their children were largely to ignore a Church which seemed to them to have no answer to the moral and religious predicament that had troubled their fathers so much.

The letters that follow are from ordinary soldiers and sailors. Of the few officers here no-one who worshipped at St Michael's achieved a rank above captain. Their letters are inevitably reticent. Letters home very rarely told in detail of the terrors of the war. It was said of fallen comrades that they had died 'cleanly' and instantly. The reality all too often was horrifyingly different. Yet these men rarely questioned why they were fighting. They fought, suffered, and died following the orders of senior army commanders who were often at best incompetent, frequently driven by self-interest and all too ready to place blame for their own failures on the courageous young men they were not worthy

---

[1] See Caleb Fletcher, July 1915.

to lead in this tragic and unnecessary war. If for no other reason these letters should be read again after an interval of eighty and more years and, so it now seems, from another world, and why these young men, and their families that waited and worried and wept at home, should never be forgotten.

THE LETTERS

The month of publication is given at the head of each section. As it is frequently difficult to tell where servicemen were when they wrote home, the notes in italics are a guide to events in the areas where it is known that men from St Michael's were serving at the time. They necessarily relate to the month in which letters were written, not the month of the magazine's publication. For this reason the notes refer, in the main, to the previous month, though readers will occasionally need to look further back for relevant references.

SEPTEMBER 1914

4 August: Britain declares war on Germany.
*12 August: The first troops of the British
Expeditionary Force land in France.*
22–23 August: Battles of Namur and Mons.
24 August–7 September: Allied forces retreat from Mons.
30 August: Germans take Amiens.

The Vicar's Letter

MY DEAR FRIENDS,

There is but one subject in the minds of all of us to-day—the War. Soldiers and sailors, reservists and recruits are hurrying to withstand England's foes. Many of the young men of St Michael's, whose names are given elsewhere, who have been confirmed and made their communion at our Altar have gone or are going to the front. I trust that there will be many more who will hear our country's call in her hour of peril and emulate their example. May God bless and keep them.

The call to us who remain at home is a call to prayer. Those whose religion is a living reality know what prayer can do. All God's power is at the disposal of those who pray. We must pray for victory because our cause is just—we must pray that the war may result in a lasting peace. We must pray for all our soldiers and sailors, and for our brave allies that God may watch over them by day and by night, and protect them

1

from the danger of the enemy and bring them safely back to their Homeland. The wounded, the dying and the dead also claim our prayers, besides those who are in anxiety and sorrow at home. I trust that everyone belonging to St Michael's, men, women and children, will *really* pray, both at our services in Church and at home. I would ask you each day at 12 noon to offer a short prayer from your hearts, the bell of St Michael's rings out then as a reminder.

Our Bishop in writing to his clergy says 'How often we have felt disappointed at the little use made of the House of Prayer at all times. Now we can make a new start. Again, how we have deplored the neglect of Sunday morning! Cannot we now win back Sunday morning for God and make the Blessed Sacrament a reality. At the Holy Communion we shall specially mention the absent friends, the dying and the dead, so that with intelligence we share the intercessory work of the Great High Priest. Remember the power of the prayers of the little ones.'

I much regret that one consequence of the War is the postponement of the Mission, which should have taken place in November. All the Incumbents in the Town agree that postponement is right and the Bishop approves of their decision. But I hope that our Missioner will be able to come next year or whenever the War is over.

Commending you, and all for whom we pray to God's mercy and protection.

I remain, yours in our Blessed Lord,

Sept. 2nd 1914   HARRY R. ROLFE

Soldiers & Sailors belonging to St Michael's

CONFIRMED

Henry Cox	John Whitaker
Arthur Roe	Gordon Hunt
Oscar Bewley	Herbert Lowe
Eric Hardy	Peter Hudson
Laurence Hallsworth	Caleb Fletcher
Harry Curzon	Harry Jackson
Bert Harrison	James Hill
Henry Lambton	Richard Harrison
George Lambton	William Plant
Sam Whitaker	Reginald Plant

SCHOLARS

William Foy   John Hughes
                George Hutley

PARISHIONERS

Ferdinand Butler   Sam Timson

Many others have been commended to our prayers.

OCTOBER 1914

*3–4 September: German forces cross
River Marne and occupy Rheims.
5–12 September: First Battle of the Marne.
14 September: Allied forces recapture Rheims.
15–18 September: Battle of the Aisne.
26–28 September: Battle of River Niemen.*

Soldiers & Sailors belonging St Michael's

In addition to the names of those published last month we are glad to append the following.

COMMUNICANTS

George Bewley   Albert H. Dean
Joseph Bewley   Harry Coulson
Cecil Bewley   Arthur Collard
Theodore Bewley   Harry Eyre
Kenneth Stiven   Ralph Cholerton
Harry Ashby   Archibald J. Elvidge
                Frank Browne

The total is thirty-three; these include two Servers, three Sunday School Teachers and one Choirman.

In this war of right against wrong every young man should seek to know his duty and when he knows it, face it even unto death.

NOVEMBER 1914

1–4 October: First battle of Arras.
12 October: German forces take Ghent and Lille.
17 October–16 November: Battle of River Yser.
15 October–21 November: First Battle of Ypres. During this battle
and its immediate aftermath 24,000 British
and 50,000 German servicemen died.
The [German] Western Front: 'From the air it had a drably uniform
appearance, a belt of disturbed earth, ravaged vegetation and
devastated buildings some four miles across. Later, as the power of
artillery increased and local infantry fighting conferred advantage to
one side or the other, the zone of destruction would widen. What
would scarcely change for the next twenty-seven months was the
length of the front or the geographical trace which it followed'
(John Keegan, The First World War *(Hutchinson, 1998), 198)*

List of Soldiers and Sailors on Active Service

In addition to the names already published we must add to our Sunday
Scholars the names of Samuel Wood, Henry Lowe, John Lowe, George
King and William Adams. There are beside these several whose friends
are closely connected with St Michael's, their names we would also wish
to record and to remember in our prayers.

Owen Parry-Jones	Richard Hope
Edward Parry-Jones	George A. Cotton
Laurence Stuart-William	Reginald Bland
Robert Foster	Charles L. Woolley
William A. Moreton	John Greensmith
Percy Robinson	Ernest Smith
Herbert Herbert Stepney	Basil Greensmith
Guy Herbert Stepney	George Greensmith

Charles Cantrill

Camp Life

Shoreham
Sunday

Dear Vicar,

You ask me for a few details of our life at Shoreham that you may use. There are at least 20,000 men here all under canvas, although huts are being erected with all speed for accommodation during the winter. We are in a beautiful large park about a mile or so from the sea. The life, of course, is rather rough, but that is what one expected. We have plenty of clothing, blankets and food.

Those of us who joined the Comrades Corps, which was a happy idea on someone's part, have formed the 4th Company of the 12th Battalion of Sherwood Foresters. Col. Godley[1] is in command of the Battalion, and Major Gordon[2] is in command of our Company, and we all like him immensely. We are getting on famous with our drills, etc., and appear to give satisfaction. We have been measured for a new uniform and shall not be sorry when it arrives, although the one which we are now wearing is alright for practising skirmishing in. A Recreation Tent has been opened for the use of the Battalion, where one can read newspapers, magazines, etc., or write letters. It is also now possible to get a hot bath, which is a privilege greatly appreciated.

You ask me about the welfare of the spiritual side of the life. Well! there is a Chaplain who conducts a service on Sunday mornings. There are special services for members of the Church of England, Wesleyans and Roman Catholics. What the members of all the 'isms' do, I do not know, but I think they go Church of England. There is a Celebration on Sunday mornings, but it is at an inconvenient time, and so I have not been able to attend yet.

'Letters' is a magic call, when at least one representative from each tent flocks round the corporal who calls out the names, eagerly waiting to hear his name or the name of someone in his tent called, as a recipient of a letter or a parcel. Through the kindness of friends at home parcels containing cake, cigarettes, tobacco, or other equally welcome articles are not infrequently received, and are the cause of many treats in what is ordinarily a life in the rough. Still we rub along very happily, whether

---

[1] Francis Clements Godley: The Sherwood Foresters. Retired with rank of Brevet Col. in 1907. In command of training Reserve Brigade in first World War. Brigadier-General, 21 April 1917. *Source: The Sherwood Foresters Museum.*

[2] J.H.S. Grant Gordon: Major, 12 Battalion The Sherwood Foresters, 1 Oct. 1914. Disappears from the Army List in July 1916. *Source: The Sherwood Foresters Museum.*

it be drill or route marching, and we are all hoping to be ready for the front in a few months' time. We have been inoculated, in two doses, as a guard against any fever which might arise under these conditions of living. We are getting over the second dose to-day, but it has not been at all serious. We shall be glad when we commence to learn to shoot. We are hoping to be home for a few days at Xmas.

The 'Come to the Cook-house door boys' bugle call will soon be going now for dinner, so I had better close, the more so because I can think of nothing more to write about at this moment.

HENRY B. COULSON

DECEMBER 1914

15 October–21 November: First Battle of Ypres.
5 November: Britain and France declare war on Turkey.
The Western Front now relatively static: trench warfare.

Letters from the front

The Vicar has received several letters last month from our lads at the front, he is sure that our readers will like to read extracts from them. The first is from Harry Curzon, a communicant, whose widowed mother is a regular attendant at St Michael's. He is in the King's Royal Rifles, a regiment which has been specially commended in a recent despatch from Sir John French.[1] Curzon is well known to many in the town as the Champion Middle-weight Boxer in the Army. His letter is dated Nov. 24th, in it he says, 'I am going on all right and in the best of health and all the boys are the same. We are having pretty bad weather and very cold. I am very pleased to tell you that I been promoted sergeant for gallantry.' (We understand that he was made corporal and, within thirteen days, sergeant for conspicuous bravery in the field, for which Mrs Curzon understands he may receive the V.C. in due course).[2] 'We are back for well earned rest. Thanks for thinking of all the boys and myself, you may be sure we are doing our best. Give my best wishes to all at St Michael's.'

---

[1] C-in-C B.E.F. Replaced by Sir Douglas Haig in December 1915.
[2] See Feb. 1915 for the citation for the award of DCM.

The second letter is from CORPORAL JAMES C. HILL, the portrait of this lad is to be seen in the *Daily Mirror* for Oct. 7th, as one of a British outpost on the look out for the enemy. One of the men is holding Jimmy's cap aloft on his bayonet trying to draw the enemy's fire. He writes on Nov. 20th: 'Many thanks for your most welcome letter, which I received quite safe on Nov. 9th, it was the first mail we have received for a fortnight. We have been in the trenches 3 weeks at a stretch. We find it very cold at night time and we have had snow here to make it colder. Our only drawback was that we could not wash or shave regular. I have been in one or two warm corners and had a few hair's breadth escapes, one bullet passing through my coat, God alone must have saved me. Another time a piece of shell struck me on my left shoulder, but it must have been spent out, yet it hit like a steam hammer, made a slight cut in my jacket and bruised the shoulder, it took the use out of my arm for a day or two.

Now I am all right and still smiling. We have been as close as 300 yards from the German trenches, of course we were in trenches too. It is good to know that St Michael's have so many fighting for their country and I am sure they will all be proud to see their names on the Roll of Honour which you have in the Church. I also read about Miss Bewley's brothers joining the service and think it grand. Mrs Glesson sends me the Church Magazine every month, which I look forward to very much. Kindly remember me to all friends and members of the Church, hoping this will find you in the best of health as it leaves me.'

The third letter is from SAPPER SAM WHITAKER and is shorter, but interesting as coming from the fighting line. It is dated Nov. 22nd. 'I must thank you very much for writing to me and feel very much ashamed for not writing to you before. I am very pleased to see that St Michael's has not forgotten me, I feel honoured that my name should be hung up in the Church where I was taught to love and fear my Master and Maker. When it is possible we have Sunday services here and they are fine. I am not much of a hand at writing letters, so I am afraid you must excuse so short a letter, but it will let you know that I am still alive and well, so I will try to write more next time.'

JANUARY 1915

Stagnation on the Western Front.
Large British garrison now in Egypt, now a Protectorate.
By the end of 1914 the British Expeditionary Force of 100,000 had
suffered 90 per cent casualties, of which 30,000 had been killed.

Letters from our Soldiers

The Vicar has received during the past month, several letters from St Michael's lads who are at the front or preparing to go. SERGEANT J.C. HILL has not written a letter but sent a post card dated Dec. 13th, to say he is going on well. SERGEANT H. CURZON writes Dec. 18th: 'I am in the best of health and quite happy, it is no use worrying, when you are here it is up to everyone to do his best and all the boys are all right and still eager. Yes, Vicar, I have had a few exciting and narrow escapes, everyone has, we have been in a few, tight corners but we generally smarten the Germans up, we have lost heavily but they have lost nearly 10 to 1, and we are too good for them, I see they have started to bombard the East Coast of England,[1] it will make some of the young men of England think and join the Army and come out here. Thanks for parcel, we get plenty of warm clothing, they look after our needs very well, remember me to all St Michael's friends.'

SAPPER WHITAKER also sent a letter dated Dec. 16th. He says, 'I saw last month's magazine and the letters in it from H. Curzon and J. Hill, they seem to be having a rough time of it. Myself being with Headquarters, I have had a more lenient time than my comrades in the trenches, but still they seem happy through it all and sing all the time they are marching to and from the trenches ... I hope by the grace of God to be able to meet all the men of St Michael's after the war is over.'

The following interesting letter comes from BOMBARDIER A. ELVIDGE who is stationed at Bulford: 'Please accept my apology for not having written ere this, but I was promoted to the rank of Bombardier in charge of Battery Office, soon after the Brigade was quartered here and I have had my time well occupied in consequence. This place—Bulford—is situated in the bleakest part of Salisbury Plain, but the camp, which contains some 50,000 men, is a marvel of military organisation. The first arrivals had a certain amount of discomfort to contend with for the first 3 weeks, but nowadays the troops are well clothed and fed and there are few complaints. Of course slackers were found in plenty but no quarter is given to men of that calibre now. It is somewhat difficult for an "amateur"[2] to describe this military business, particularly artillery, but the raw recruits took the greatest pains in

---

[1] Four German battle-cruisers shelled Scarborough, Whitby and Hartlepool on 16 December 1914, killing forty civilians and wounding many more.

[2] A volunteer responding to Kitchener's appeal in August 1914.

everything that was shown to them, with the result that there are many Batteries here on the high road to efficiency much sooner than was expected. So far I have not been fortunate enough to discover any other fellows hailing from Derby, in these ranks, but am not in the least surprised, for one hears nothing but the broadest Lancashire from morning until night, the majority of the men have been drafted from the depot at Preston.

It is almost three months since I saw the lights of Derby, but I am looking forward, with no small sense of excitement, to the Christmas furlough. Rumour has it that all leave has been suspended for the festive season, and I am very concerned. One of the most striking things about the troops is the good fellowship and Christian feeling that is existent. The Church Parade on Sunday morning particularly in this Battery is a sight that does one's heart a great amount of good and particular care is taken to obtain the religion of each man. The Officers are quite a sporting crowd, and throw in their lot in anything the men take up. Football is the popular pastime, naturally, and large and enthusiastic crowds attend the various "inter-battery" matches.

Altogether on the Plain there are over 100,000 men, and the conditions generally are perfect. I am not in the least anxious to leave the life because it is invigorating and has already made men of hundreds of fellows who were "slackers" in civil life.'

FEBRUARY 1915

*In January German forces ordered to fortify
their front line, the Western Front.
8 January–5 February: Fighting in the area of
La Bassée and around Soissons.*

Our Soldiers

We heard with pride that SERGEANT H. CURZON will receive the grant of the Medal for Distinguished Conduct in the Field. The record is thus officially set forth:

'Sergeant H. Curzon (7820) 2nd Batt. K.R.R.C. For gallant conduct on October 31st, (then a private) in attempting to carry a wounded officer under heavy rifle and machine gun fire, and again on November

7th at Klein Zillebeke,[1] when he obtained valuable information as to the enemy's movements. Has been conspicuous for coolness and gallantry on all occasions.' It is evident that Sergeant Curzon has done his duty nobly and his example should spur on many a lad who has not yet enlisted. We are glad that he has been granted a short leave of absence, which, after his varied experiences, he most sorely needed. He is now staying in the town with his mother and will not go back to the front until February 15th. At an interview with the Vicar he gave graphic descriptions of the conditions of war at the present time and though not saying much about himself, it was evident that he has been thoroughly trusted by his superior officers and, needless to say, he experienced many hair breadth escapes, but he says that he has only done his duty. We should like to give the Sergeant a little present from St Michael's people to show their appreciation of his gallantry, the Vicar will be pleased to receive donations towards this object.

The Vicar has had several communications from SERGEANT J.C. HILL. On January 14th he writes: 'We are having some awful weather, raining all the time, it makes the ground so heavy, the trenches are too awful for words, in a communication trench which we had to pass through to get to the firing line the water was above our waists, but the trench in the firing line was not quite so bad only being up to knees in mud and water. These trenches are the worst I have been in, in this position we had to stand 24 hours, then we were relieved by another company and rested for three days and then took our trenches again, this went on for twelve days. We are all looking forward for Kitchener's Army to come out and take the strain off us a bit. Last Sunday we had a Church Service in a farm yard about one mile behind the firing line, which we attended ready dressed for action.' He had also sent a letter dated January 1st, in which he said: 'We spent Christmas Day in the trenches and it was very quiet, only sniping going on, on both sides. One of their snipers hit one of our chaps in the head while he was handing pudding over the trench to the chaps on our right.'

Extracts from a letter from PETTY OFFICER JOE BEWLEY, a motor driver of the R. Naval Air Service. 'We have left Sheerness and are now in London. Our Squadron is almost complete, and we are now on Active Service. A Corps consists of 14 Squadrons and each Squadron has three sections and there are about 60 men in a squad. The cars are of the latest pattern and very fine, with revolving turret, and we are now efficient in working the guns. I belong to No 1 Squadron, A Section, and the leading

---

[1] Ypres Salient.

car of the section is known as the "Flagship" and the head officer rides in it. We were all anxious as to who would be chosen to drive this car and you will be pleased to know that they have honoured me in making me driver of the "Flagship". My officer is a nephew of the late Lord Roberts.' In this letter Bewley stated that they anticipated going over to France very shortly: however, owing perhaps to the state of the roads and also the possibility of raids by the enemy on our coasts, the Aerial Service is still in this country patrolling the points which are considered likely to be raided.

MARCH 1915

In February fronts in Palestine and Gallipoli established.
8 January–5 February: Fighting in the area of
La Bassée Canal and around Soissons.

Our Soldiers

Our readers will have read in the local newspapers an account of the presentation made to SERGEANT CURZON at the Hippodrome, on Friday, Feb. 12th. Several members of the congregation sent contributions towards the purse of gold which was given him. On Thursday, February 18th, the Sergeant kindly presented proficiency badges in connection with our Troop of Boy Scouts. He has now been sent to Winchester where at present he is in hospital for an injury which had not been properly attended to. We all wish him a speedy recovery and 'good luck' wherever he may be.

So far as we know, the first of our young men to be wounded has been TOM DUFFY, who was in the Men's Bible Class. Mr Robert Hudson has received several letters from him from which we publish extracts. On Feb. 7th he wrote as follows: 'Derby seems to have created a record in recruiting; still, I think, we shall want more, yet it cheers one up to know that so many from Derby have answered their country's call. Well, Sir, we are going along A1, we have been out here since the commencement and have been in the thick of the fight every time. Thank God we both (SERGT J. C. HILL is with him) have been fortunate enough to escape injury, myself once, but Jim several times, but nothing to hurt, though very near—a bullet passing through his coat and a bruise on the shoulder from shrapnel—but we still keep smiling, although we have suffered much this last six weeks with the cold, and in the trenches where we are up to our waists in mud and water. But we live in hope and always trust in God, looking on the bright side of things but if the worst comes to the worst and we have to go under, you will know we died fighting.'

Then on the Saturday following, Feb. 13th, PTE DUFFY wrote from Netley Hospital: 'Just a line to let you know that I have been wounded, it occurred about an hour after posting my last letter to you, so you see I've travelled much in a week, or less, for I arrived here on Thursday night. It occurred at a village this side La Bassee, called Voilaines. We have been in the trenches four days and on the sixth we had a glorious battle, the Artillery commenced shelling about 2 p.m., and continued until 4 p.m., we had about 70 guns going, it ended in making a charge by the Guards while we were holding the enemy on the left of La Bassee canal, they were on the right 100 yards distant, we succeeded in taking two trenches and the brickfields, the first trench was no trouble but the second cost us about 100 men to their 1,000, so we didn't do bad, did we?

Of course we could take La Bassee to-morrow if we wanted it, but you see the enemy are situated on the far side and in the town are about 5,000 people, so if we were to shell it only the innocent would suffer.

Well, Sir, a week tomorrow we were relieved for 24 hours to get a rest, I wrote your letter that morning and posted it, the day was quiet until about 3 p.m., when the French Artillery started another duel, this lasted for an hour and me and my friend (Sergt Jim Hill) had just finished tea, he was staying a little further down the village from me, so I told him to go in case we had to stand to. I've thanked God a thousand times since then, for he had not gone two minutes when a shell from the enemy came through our roof and burst behind me, wounding ten of us very bad, but we hope to be well soon and back to it again. I was hit in the thigh and shoulder, the latter is not much, but the thigh I'm afraid will take some time. After being treated in various hospitals I was put on a Hospital Ship for England and arrived at Southampton at 8 p.m., on Feb. 12th, and again in Hospital here by 9.15. The first time I have been in bed since I left Derby. Hoping this will find you all at St Michael's in the best of health and spirits, as it leaves me, only for my wounds. I will close,' &c., &c.

Private Duffy is, we are glad to learn, going on well and hopes soon to be sent to Derby for a short time.

Several more of our lads have now gone to the front, whilst many are still training in England.

APRIL 1915

10 March: 7th and 8th Divisions of the B.E.F. and the Meerut and Lahore Divisions of the Indian Corps begin the Battle of Neuve Chapelle (to 13 March).

Our Soldiers

The following letter has been received from SERGEANT J.C. HILL, which will give some idea of the terrible nature of the warfare now being carried on and also of the wonderful bravery of our lads.

March, 16th 1915

Dear Vicar, just a few lines to let you know I am still in the land of the living. We have had a rather exciting time since I last wrote to you. On the 10th inst. we attacked the German trenches. My Company was the first to go forward and in places the distance between our trenches and the German's was only 70 yards. But we had to get through our own barbed wire entanglements and theirs, a few got in the trench and had a machine gun, but they (the enemy) threw a bomb at them and smashed one poor fellow, a Sergeant of ours, to bits. It was absolutely impossible to get in the trench anywhere as they had machine guns on our right and left. Out of eight Sergeants who went into the attack only two remain, myself being one. God alone pulled me through. Altogether we lost 4 Officers, 6 Sergeants and about 83 men, so you may guess how we suffered. When we got back to our own trench there was one Officer left and us two Sergeants and we tried to gather the Company, or rather the remains, together and could only muster 21 all told, but about two hours after the attack we numbered 67, a lot had run in from the front where they had dropped in 'Jack Johnson'[1] holes and a small ditch for shelter from the German machine guns. Many stayed out all day and returned at night. The sights were awful. I know I dropped a few tears to see one's pals, who have been out here all the time, knocked over, it's nothing else but murder, but I suppose we should do the same to them. Well after the attack we went into the reserve trenches and one of our Companies relieved us. We are now in Bethune for a few days rest and

---

[1] For a description see footnote under October 1915.

repairing. The weather is much better now and I hope it will continue to be good. Kindly remember me to friends at St Michael's, wishing you all the best of health as I am still smiling.

Two of those who, in former years, were connected with St Michael's have met their deaths. The first was SERGEANT SAM FETTERPLACE who, before he enlisted several years ago, was a member of the choir and was confirmed in 1901. His sister writes to say that he got killed in action on Feb. 21st. He was binding up another soldier's wounds when he was shot in the head and killed instantly. The second was PRIVATE TOM WESTON, formerly in our band when first it was formed by Miss Taylor. He was 29 years of age and had been in the Hussars six years and one year in the reserves. He went out to France at the commencement of the war and was killed in the trenches on March 4th. The Major wrote respecting Tom Weston, that 'he was shot through the head and killed instantly. He was buried in the Churchyard of a village near by. He was a splendid fellow, always cheerful, and worked splendidly, and I can assure you that we have lost a good comrade. He was most popular with everyone.'

MAY 1915

22 April–25 May: German offensive leading to the Second Battle of Ypres. German forces first use poison gas successfully on the Western Front.
24 April: Battle of St Julien.
25 April: Anglo-French forces land at Helles and Anzac Cove, Gallipoli, in the Dardanelles.

Letters from the front

Many letters have been received from our lads in France and not a few speak of the Bishop of London's inspiring addresses during his recent visit to our soldiers in the field. We give this month some extracts from a recent letter sent to his mother from SERGEANT DISPENSER BEWLEY; he writes from somewhere in Belgium.

'We are now actually connected with the firing line and very near a well known place, but names must not be mentioned. We are stationed at a very large convent, part of which has been turned into a dressing station, one large hall and a smaller one have been turned into wards and are capable of holding about 250 cases. A Field Ambulance has been here for the past four months and has now gone, we have taken it over. We are not far off from the firing line so the wounded are brought straight from the trenches to this place where they are properly dressed and attended to and the next day are sent to the various base Hospitals. Our ambulances go up each evening to fetch them when it is dark as it is not safe to go in the day time, so most of the work here is done during the night. Our Chaplain comes in every morning to see the sick, he is a splendid man, and awfully nice to all the men, he always has a word with me in the mornings. When a fellow dies here, he comes and reads the Burial Service before he is buried and then he is laid in the convent ground here, and a wooden cross is erected with his name, etc., upon it.'

JUNE 1915

*6 May: German Supreme Army Command orders the Western Front
to be further reinforced with a second line of trenches.
9 May–19 June: Allied offensive, Artois, Western Front.
12 May: Windhoek, South-West Africa, taken by Gen. Louis Botha.*

Letters from the front

PTE LAURENCE HALLSWORTH wrote a most interesting letter home on May 12th, in it he says: 'I am quite well after my experience of 5 days in the trenches. The first three days were practically quiet and nothing occurred worth noting. But in the evening of the fourth day it was arranged at a certain time to blow up a portion of the enemy's trench which was a bit too near ours for our liking. About an hour before the time appointed a German aeroplane came over our trenches. After it had got well over the other side an English aeroplane suddenly appeared, as if from a cloud. It was high above the German and darting down with circling sweeps it hovered above it like a hawk, waiting for a favourable opportunity to dive. Then we saw three puffs of smoke come from our plane and the enemy's suddenly began to come down nose first. About half way down it managed to right itself, but only for a second, for again it started downward and crash it went to ruin. When we saw what our airman had done we gave him a rousing cheer, which I expect made the Germans wild, for they opened a terrific rifle fire and did all they could to fetch our airman down, but he went sailing over their lines at top speed and over ours to his headquarters. Well that was something come down, now for something going up. They moved every one out of our trench except the brave machine gunners. Well exactly at the appointed hour up she (the mine) went. "Great Scot"! I shall never forget it. If I tried for a week I could not explain it. It's all right on a ship to feel it going up and down, but when the ground on which you are standing goes up and down and about lifts you off your feet, it makes you feel funny. Well, I saw it go up and it didn't half go up, I should say 200 ft in the air, and then it commenced to come down, lumps of earth fell all round us. Directly after it went up we rushed to our gun and sent a stream of lead at the enemy, and just then the fun started. It was like a thousand furies let loose, for both our and the enemy's artillery suddenly went mad ... for an hour it lasted. They dropped several shells in our trench, a piece of one, which very nearly hit me and was hot when I touched it, I have saved. On the next evening the enemy had a go at the same game, but they only blew up a piece of earth about 25 yards long, which was nearer to their own trench than ours, and then we had another hot half-hour. We worked like madmen, I fired fifty rounds through my rifle in about five minutes,[1] it was so hot then that I could not hold it, so I put it down and continued loading rifles for other men, when I had done I was wet through with sweat. We are now billeted in a barn under which is a pigsty, we don't spend much of our time there, outside are beautiful fields. At night we can plainly see the flames from burning — which has been burning these last three days.'

Several letters have been received written about Whit-Sunday, some of them tell of services attended and visits from the Chaplains. Two write about the poisonous gas. PTE GORDON HUNT says, 'the gas they use is awful, we were ten miles or more away from it, but it made our eyes smart and when you get to the large Hospitals and see the sufferers gasping for breath, it makes you forget you are living in the 20th Century. But what beats us is that we are not allowed to use it back.'

We much regret to hear that W. TOY has been wounded, but is much better, and that P. HUDSON is also amongst the wounded. Miss Iliffe had a letter from him only two or three days ago.

---

[1] Compare this rate of fire with the fifteen rounds per minute claimed by the Royal Fusiliers (Lyn Macdonald, *1914: The Days of Hope*, Penguin, 1989, pp. 95–6).

JULY 1915

8 June: Allied forces take Neuville.
15 June: Battle of Givenchy.

Extracts from Letters

1. From SAPPER C. FLETCHER, in France. June 10th: 'I received the badge, thanks, which recalled many pleasant memories of a few years ago ... Yes, I heard the Bishop of London[1] at Easter. The address was most interesting. He described this war as a "Holy War", a war which we should consider ourselves specially chosen to continue until "Right" had conquered "Might" and the cause of Democracy and Liberty throughout the world completely established. I am in a small town in France quite close to the Belgian frontier. I attended an evening service a few Sundays ago, held in a schoolroom. A terrific cannonade was proceeding during the service. One is quite accustomed to these heavy bombardments. But the noise of the guns, the rattle of the windows, and the vibration caused by this bombardment made the service, to my mind, most impressive. At times one could hardly hear the Chaplain's voice. We concluded the service by singing the hymn appropriate for relations and friends at home—"Holy Father in Thy mercy" (595). The following morning, walking across the Market Square, I observe several motor lorries preceded by a Chaplain slowly and solemnly walking towards the cemetery. The lorries contain the remains of fallen comrades. And coming in the opposite direction, towards the hospital, one sees a long line of motor field ambulances, some of the occupants being the victims of these horrible gases which the enemy, or rather savages, are employing. It is a most horrible means of waging warfare, anything the Germans can use to kill or mutilate will be utilised in their extreme desperation to destroy life. Well, such are some of the almost daily sights here. Also groups of refugees, women and innocent children homeless ... Perhaps you will be able to understand my thoughts the first time I viewed all this terrible life of suffering. I could not help wondering whether there could possibly be a God to allow such things to occur. And then one

---

[1] Arthur Foley Winnington-Ingram (1858–1946), Bishop of London 1901–39. He visited servicemen in France, Flanders and Salonika as chairman of the Central Council of the National Mission.

remembered that this is a "holy war" and the words which surely are applicable "God moves in a mysterious way, His wonders to perform". So far I have not encountered these poisonous gases, we should be quite six miles away from the firing line ... We have a very nice and considerate Chaplain. A friend of mine was confirmed a few weeks ago by the Bishop of Pretoria.'[1]

2. From PRIVATE J. WHITAKER, Grenadier Guards, June 8th: 'A short time ago we were in a three days charge and we had a very rough time of it. We were very successful, capturing about four thousand prisoners and various pieces of artillery and machine guns. After we came out of that attack we had a few days rest and we had earned it. A few days later we went in another attack but were not quite so successful ... The Germans started shelling us last Thursday night about 8 o'clock and kept it up all night. One shell dropped about two yards behind my dug-out blowing the parapet down and also knocking the roof of my dug out in. Luckily I was not hurt so I moved as quickly as possible. It was a good job I did, as the next shell that came along blew my dug out in the air. I am pleased to tell you I was able to receive Holy Communion at Whitsun—I have the Church Magazine sent out to me every month, so it keeps me in touch with the people and the good work that is going on at St Michael's.'

3. From PRIVATE W. SARSFIELD of the Grenadier Guards, an old Scholar whom the Vicar had lost sight of, June 21st: 'Being one of your old scholars I thought a line from me would let you have an idea about the lads of St Michael's Sunday School. There are a lot of lads who I have dropped across and we very often have a chat in the trenches about our school days. They are doing the best of work on the battlefield. I have seen some very brave deeds done with some of the old scholars and no doubt you will be very proud to know about them. They have asked me to drop you a line before, but we have had some very hard fighting, and I am writing only about 50 yards from the German trenches. We have had to keep very low and out of sight. They are just firing at us now for all they are worth. Shells are dropping just in front and on the top of our trench. They are very frightened, in fear we are going to give them a taste of the bayonet, and if you could only see them getting ready to run away, they put up their hands and ask for mercy ... We are just going to have a well earned rest and share up our parcels of cigs we have had sent us, and have a nice cool smoke behind the guns.'

---

[1] Michael Bolton Furse, Bishop of Pretoria (1909–20) and of St Albans (1920–44). In 1915 his brother was GSO1, II Corps in Flanders.

No letters were published in August 1915

SEPTEMBER 1915

*9 July: German forces in South-West Africa
surrender to General Louis Botha.
6 August: New Allied landings at Suvla Bay, Gallipoli.
8 August: Hostilities commence against German East Africa
with the shelling from the sea of Dar-es-Salaam.
Allied casualties in east Africa were to be one battle
casualty to 35 lost to illness and disease.*

Letters from some of our Soldiers

Letters have been received from many of our lads at the front. We make some extracts from some of the more generally interesting epistles. PTE HARRY COULSON who is in the 10th Sherwood Foresters writes, Aug. 13th, from Belgium, to which country the Battalion went about the middle of July: 'Last Friday night I went in the trenches for 24 hours in order to get some idea of what trench life is like. After taking an exciting short cut and dropping suddenly down time after time to escape observation when the "flares" went up, and also hearing a few bullets whiz past my face, we arrived safely in the line. It was rather quiet here and we got on very well. The Germans sent a few shrapnel shells over in the afternoon, but beyond a bit of damage to the entanglements and sandbag parapet no harm was done and our artillery dropped a few over their trenches by way of exchange. We came out again all right and reached camp about 6.30 on the Sunday morning.' And again on Aug. 23rd: 'I am sitting to write this letter on the platform of our sandbag parapet. Apart from the sentries and several on fatigues, our fellows are resting quietly, reading, writing, or gaining some sleep lost during the night. Our artillery is exchanging greetings with the German artillery and shrapnel and other shells are flying about over head and bursting a distance away. The German lines are about 130 yards away. We have been here since a week last Sunday, in the trenches all the time, and are beginning to get used to things a bit. A pal had a narrow escape, a "wiz bang"[1] burst close to him and a piece smashed the handle of his entrenching tool and ripped a piece out of his bayonet scabbard, it frightened him somewhat but he is quite unhurt. We take our turns to do an hour's sentry duty and look out. I do not at all dislike the duty during the night only sometimes it is a terrible job to keep my eyes open. The back of my hands are covered with little lumps caused by mosquito bites during the night. My face is free from them because I happen to wear a sleeping helmet which keeps me warm and as only my eyes and mouth are visible I suppose that is why I have escaped. We are living very well, the food being both sufficient and good.'

The Vicar has also received another letter dated Aug. 29th, in which Private Coulson writes of the very unsatisfactory arrangements made by the Chaplain of his Regiment as regards services for Church of England men.

PTE H. ASHBY of the Grenadier Guards wrote on August 13th. In the course of his letter he says 'prospects seem very bright out here at present, but of course we only know of what is going on on our immediate front, but we do occasionally hear of the glorious deeds that different regiments are doing on our right and left, and from what I can gather all things are working very bright indeed, which all points the way to a speedy and lasting finish ... The crops are now at their best. It forms a striking picture to see the women harvesting in the absence of their menfolk, as early as 4 a.m. until dark. A striking and welcome contrast to the terrible conflict raging but a few hundred yards away.'

It is also worth while giving the views of another lad about slackers: 'I shall not be sorry when this war is over, I don't suppose you will either, Sir. War is war, but this is simply murder. When I was home on sick furlough I noticed plenty of the lads in Derby who are able to enlist but won't. If they were only out here and saw the sights and think to themselves a bit, they would enlist at once. If you see any of them just have a few words with them.'

SERGEANT DISPENSER F.L. BEWLEY, who has been home on four days special leave, has sent some interesting letters since his return to the front. On arriving in Belgium he found that the corps had moved from where he left them and writes as follows:

'I think I told you we had moved into a warm spot, in fact rather too hot to be pleasant. I came here last Saturday night to relieve the other dispenser for a rest, and it was a bit of a contrast from the previous Saturday. We are well in front of our Artillery, and about a mile behind

---

[1] For a definition see footnote under October 1915.

our trenches, so you can imagine what a terrible noisy place it is, and what a lot of shells we have over us. We are in very cosy dug-outs, but it is just as though we were all rabbits. We are fairly safe as regards shrapnel, but if a shell were to drop plump on the roof, things would be in rather a mess. That's the only danger, we never know when we might be blown up. There are some very big guns here, especially one in the field behind us, and every time it fires the concussion is so great that it puts all the lights out in the dug-out. We have been very busy at times, and have had as many as 150 to 200 cases through a night. It is day and night work here and so we get asleep when we can. The battalion fellows absolutely worship our stretcher bearers when they fetch them in, for they have to go about two miles over fields and exposed to shell fire all the time ... they have done some splendid work, and the poor chaps get back in the early morning about exhausted.'

(Col. Wraith[1], who is the Officer commanding the Corps in which Sergeant Bewley serves, is at home on short leave, and speaks highly of his Dispensers, including Sergeant Bewley. *Ed.*)[2]

A few extracts from letters received from PETTY-OFFICER J. BEWLEY, Armoured Car Division, R.N.A.S., may prove of general interest. This force has been operating with General Botha's[3] men in South-West Africa, and has now been ordered East, the action as far as South-West is concerned being over. One of the letters is dated July 30th, in which the writer states: 'our boat comes in and we expect going aboard to-morrow. It is a fine big boat (the *British Prince*) and we are busy getting the cars on. On Sunday, July 18th, we had Church Parade at 11 a.m. and a service in one of the rooms on the boat in the evening. On July 21st we could see the Table Mountains, and by 10 a.m. we were in the dock at Cape Town, afterwards entraining to a place called Rosebank 5 miles the other side of Cape Town. On Thursday, July 22nd, General Botha landed in Cape Town, and the armoured car men acted as a Guard of Honour. It was an extremely wet day. On the 23rd we moved to some very large barracks at Wynberg, consisting of about 100 large corrugated iron sheds. The barracks are situated in beautiful towns and we are quite at home here.'

After describing the Table Mountain the writer mentions that they are now employed taking the engines of the cars down and overhauling them

---

[1] E. Arnold Wraith. As a major was O.C. the depot of the 1st North Midland Field Ambulance depot at 91 Siddals Road, Derby.

[2] i.e. Harry Rolfe.

[3] Gen. Louis Botha (1862–1919). Respected Afrikaner general in the Boer War. He offered the British military assistance in August 1914.

in preparation of action in the East. Petty-Officer Bewley has sent home some interesting photos taken while the cars were operating in South-West Africa, also some of the everlasting silver leaves from the Table Mountain, and Princess Mary's Christmas Gift, which only arrived some weeks back. The cars seem to have been used with great success in the recent actions, the capturing of the capital Windhok being reported in the *Derby Express* some time back. It is rather amusing to note that a German aerial observer in reporting the force of the division to his officers mentioned that 'they appeared to have few guns, but a quantity of "water-carts"'. In the action which followed however, they discovered that the 'water-carts' were capable of doing a considerably larger amount of damage than they had anticipated ... Part of the squadron are returning home, but the writer and others are by this time probably engaged 'doing a bit more' for the Empire, in East Africa.

We have just heard as we go to press that one of our communicants, GUNNER ARTHUR ROE, has been seriously wounded on Sunday, Aug. 29th. He was hit on the shoulder by a German shell. The Corporal of his battery wrote to his mother, 'No one regrets losing him more than myself, for he was above [all] a brave fellow and a son to be proud of. His duties took him in all directions, he came back from his journeys through shell swept roads and never turned a hair. We shall all miss him.'

OCTOBER 1915

25 September–6 November: Allied forces launch Champagne and Artois-Loos offensives.
25 September–8 October: Battle of Loos.

Our Soldier Lads

GUNNER ARTHUR ROE, who was wounded on August 29th, is now in hospital at Brighton and is doing as well as can be expected, but it will be some time before he is able to get about. The Vicar received a letter from him shortly before he was struck by the fuse of a German shell, in it he says: 'I must tell you that we are all quite happy though every now and again we have to dodge shells, but we haven't had a casualty yet, but we are the luckiest battery out, I think, all the other batteries have had casualties. The present position is the third one, and we have been bombarded three times, on one occasion the roof of the farmhouse we were stopping at was blown in, but we all happened to be in our dug-outs and were bombarded three hours, sixty pounders too. I have been in several nasty corners myself, being the orderly, if there is any message to go to another battery I take it, but I never bother. The worst time of all was when I stood and saw a fellow belonging to the H.A.C. killed instantly, as I had made a proper chum of him. He had just come out of the moat after bathing ... We see some fine sport with aeroplanes, what pleases us most is when we see our air gun bring a German down, like we did the other day.'

We shall all wish Gunner Roe a speedy recovery. Another of our lads has been wounded in the head somewhere in France, his name is PETER HUDSON, whose mother lives at 30, Rivett Street. The last we heard of him was that he was in a hospital in France. We have also to record another death. HERBERT LOWE, of the Derbyshire Yeomanry, was killed in the landing of troops at the Dardanelles, but we have not heard particulars. Private Lowe was a fine young fellow of 20, and was confirmed at St Michael's 5 or 6 years ago. 'May he rest in peace'. We need hardly say how deeply we sympathise with his relatives.

The following extract is from a letter received last month from PRIVATE H. COULSON: 'We are still in reserve to our other two companies who are in the trenches. We are in a pine wood in huts (lean-to) made of pine logs covered with branches and soil. At times during the day a whistle will sound when we all have either to seek cover or to stand still in order to escape observation, as an aeroplane is passing overhead. It may get shelled with shrapnel and bits will fall to the ground all around. Stray bullets too pass with a whistle overhead from all directions, owing to the peculiar shape of our line hereabouts. It is getting dark now and we have been very busy to-day digging a new communications trench. I had a hot experience the other night, a party of us were returning from a fatigue and as we were just entering a trench which led back to our huts, our artillery suddenly opened fire on the Germans. The sky was lit up by the flare from the guns and shells whistled overhead, the Germans getting a bit suspicious opened rapid fire and bullets began to pass over, then all calmed down again and became quiet, but it was a hot short time. You ask me the difference between a shell and a whiz-bang. Well, a shell might be a high explosive like a Jack Johnson or a coal-box, or it might be a shrapnel which bursts in the air. A Whiz-bang is a small shell which is fired at short range and has a low trajectory and it bursts in the air. It comes at a terrific rate and can only be heard when it arrives. You have no sooner heard it whistle past than you hear the bang of the explosion, hence the name.[1] Every day seems the same here, but we can tell when Sunday has passed; because that night an issue of tobacco and cigarettes come over with the rations on transport and we get them given out to us on Monday morning.'

NOVEMBER 1915

5 October: Allied troops land in Salonika.

Our Soldiers

The number of those connected with St Michael's who are serving King and Country continues to grow. The following have joined the army quite recently, Scoutmaster A. Bewley, W. Burrows, W. Goodchild, W. Greenlay, C. Willatt and R. Thompson. Altogether 104 are serving, 6 have been killed, and 2 are in hospital badly wounded. We much regret to record the loss of CORPORAL ARCHIBALD ELVIDGE of the R.F.A. He was confirmed at St Michael's a few years ago. He joined the army very soon after war broke out and after training on Salisbury Plain proceeded to the front, he was promoted corporal while in France. It is said that a German shell dropped amongst a party of eleven men and two officers, and all of them were instantaneously killed. R.I.P.

The Vicar has been able to visit two of those who are wounded during the past month. ARTHUR ROE at Brighton is doing well and is now able to get about a little. PETER HUDSON in King George's Hospital, Stamford Street, London, is still confined to bed but is making progress towards recovery.

Extracts from letters sent home by CAPTAIN EDWARD PARRY-JONES, 5th Batt. S. Wales Borderers (Pioneers), Sept. 30th: 'It's an awful time since I wrote I'm afraid, but there have been big things doing and I have had very little time. Your letters arrived just before the attack and I read them in the trenches, and very glad I was to get them. Of the attack itself I cannot say more than you may read in the papers, partly

---

[1] 'Jack Johnsons' (after the then world heavy-weight boxing champion) and 'coal-boxes' were names given by British servicemen to shells fired by German 15 cm artillery. They emitted black smoke on detonation. 'Whizz-bangs' were shells fired by 77 mm German artillery.

because I am not allowed to, and partly because I know very little, though the air is full of rumours. It was a good effort and our part was to create a diversion and help our own Army and the French further down south; this we did as you have read, though our causalities were heavy. For our own particular job we were in reserve and had to keep in touch with the Batt. in front of us. I went into the trenches the night before, and got about an hour's sleep that night. I saw the attack start the next morning at about 6.30 a.m. and had to sit in the support trenches, and watch the wounded come down, whilst the shells were literally raining over us. It wasn't at all pleasant watching the poor beggars who had been hit coming back. Our company had to remain in the support trenches in case we were wanted (our job was to line a communication trench from our front line to the German line) but as the attack was not pushed home, in fact we never got near their trenches, we did not come into action, and about 8 o'clock that night we were told we could go home. It poured all day in torrents, and, when we reached our billets we were wet through and pretty well "beat". There were some awfully plucky things done that day. The Welsh and R.W.F.[1] who led the attack got rather badly hit and were caught in a fearful storm of bullets from 40 machine guns on their right flank. A Welsh Officer and Sergeant dug themselves in about 40 yards in front of our lines and established a sort of dressing station, and from there went out in that awful fire, collected wounded, treated them roughly with iodine and bandages, and then at dusk, brought them into our front lines. Neither of them were doctors or even R.A.M.C., but they undoubtedly saved many lives and have both been recommended for the V.C.

There is very little doing on our front just now, though I expect there will be another big attack shortly, at all events we shall be a few miles nearer the Rhine before November I'm sure.'

Oct. 24th

'I've been kept pretty hard at it but hope to get a rest for a day or two. I am very well, though I can't get rid of my cold, and am getting rather tired of this old war. If we could get a move on I shouldn't mind it so much, but it is rather deadly working in the same section week after week. However I think the wily Bosche is getting to the end of his tether. He is not half so uppish as he used to be, in fact one can do one's work at night in the open in much more safety than formerly, also a lot of shells have been picked up marked August and even September 1915,

---

[1] Royal Welch Fusiliers.

which seems to show that they are using their shell as fast as they can make them. Anyhow, though I'm getting a bit sick of it, the Hun has got to be "strafed" and the longer it goes on the surer is his defeat.'

List of our Lads somewhere at the front

Harry Ashby
Lt. Robert Barker
George Bewley
Joseph Bewley
Cecil Bewley
Oscar Bewley
Sergt Theodore Bewley
Frank Browne
Arthur Collard
Harry Coulson
William Cross
Karl V. Duncan
L-Corp. Henry Eyre, *wounded*
Caleb Fletcher
Laurence Hallsworth
Bert Harrison
Eric Hardy
Sergt James Hill
Peter Hudson, *wounded*
Arthur Garton
George Lambton
Norman Powell

Reginald Plant
Arthur Roe, *wounded*
Percy Robinson
William Sarsfield
John Whitaker
Sam Whitaker
Tom Woolley
John Baker
Arthur Baker
Joseph Cocker
Harry Butler
William Foy
George Hutley
Henry Lowe
John Lowe
Harry White
Sidney White
Albert Thornton
Gordon Hunt
Henry Lambton
Leslie Norton
William Plant

FALLEN IN BATTLE

Sergt Sam Fetterplace
Tom Weston
George King

Arthur Smith
Herbert Lowe
Archibald Elvidge

'May they rest in Peace'

DECEMBER 1915

22 November: Battle of Ctesiphon, Mesopotamia.
Western Front relatively static during the winter months.

Our Soldiers

The following letter is exceptionally interesting because the writer, PRIVATE S. WOOD, a member of Mr Hudson's Bible Class, was one of those rescued from the Hospital Ship *Anglia*, which was mined and sunk in the English Channel on Nov. 17th.[1] He writes from the Hospital at Leicester. 'I was on the Hospital Ship *Anglia* coming home to England. We left Boulogne at 11 o'clock, had an hour's nice run, then came to a choppy sea for about half-an-hour, then all of a sudden came a crash—we had struck a mine. There was a bit of a rush for life-belts and the boxes of life-jackets. I and another chap stopped the rush by starting to give them out as men came up. I had one left for myself. Then up to the boats they rushed but only managed to get one out. I went along the deck to see if there was anything I could do, I saw one poor fellow with his head bandaged and his arm in a sling, I gave him my jacket, he said "Look after yourself, it's going down", but I prayed to God (only a small prayer) for the safety of us all and tied him up well, he was useless to himself, and told him to get to the side of the boat, then I turned back and saw that a Torpedo boat, No. 4, had arrived to our rescue. I helped about 20 to get over the rails, then I saw another ship had arrived, but a man on the Torpedo boat told me to get over myself, and I got over just in time to make a big jump for it, I just managed to get hold of the side, my legs in the water, but I hurt my side in the fall. When they got me up on board I felt a bit queer. Then the other ship struck a mine and went down in quick time. We also struck something and started to take in water so we picked up as many as we could get at, then we had orders to go to Dover, and we had nine inches of water in the bottom of our boat. We simply flew through the water to Dover. We had lost nearly everything, but I am sorry we could not do anything for the brave chaps in their beds below, their cries were awful.'

[1] 139 crew and wounded servicemen were drowned.

JANUARY 1916

19 December: Sir John French replaced by
Sir Douglas Haig as C-in-C, B.E.F.
Allies evacuate Suvla and Anzac Cove, Gallipoli.

Letters from the Front

We print some recent letters received by the Vicar from our lads in France, they help us to realise something of what it means to be out there. It is quite wonderful to note the spirit which inspires them all and their cheerfulness under such terrible conditions. PTE HARRY COULSON writes on Dec. 20th: 'We have been up in the line for such a time. We came out on Saturday night for a few days rest. When I got to camp I found your second letter and the cigarettes awaiting me. I offer you my warmest thanks because a cigarette is often a boon and a comfort on this job when nothing else would answer ... One afternoon up in the firing line the Germans bombarded us for two and a half hours. They sent every kind of shell they had and there was not a break of a minute. It was "hell" absolutely. They must have sent thousands over altogether. I sat in a dug-out which was continually on the rock, a waterproof sheet which was fastened across the front was blown away by the concussion of one shell, several times I was deafened by the noise and stifled by the smoke of shells bursting close at hand, there was also a continuous rain of mud, earth and timber, and all one could do was to try and calmly resign oneself to one's fate. It was awful, the ground round about was like a ploughed field when it was over. I lost my pal, Corporal F. Tyler, he was killed by a shell, I shall miss him, he was such a good friend, may God have mercy on his soul and comfort his parents. We came down on Saturday night, on Sunday morning we were rushed up again in reserve under shell fire. The Germans had made a gas attack and we went up in case we were wanted. However it was not our part of the line, but we got shelled pretty well and gas also. May we never come under gas again. Our artillery has given them some stick for it since.'

DRUMMER H. LOWE also wrote on Dec. 20th: 'It was indeed a great pleasure to me when I received your letter of good wishes and card the other day and especially right away out here to know the good people of St Michael's have not forgotten me. I am now anxiously looking forward to the time when we shall all be safely back again with those we love. I am firmly convinced that the time is not far distant, please God it may be so. We are now having a week or two of rest, we are expecting to be moved to Egypt, on any date now, at any rate it will be a warmer climate and the fighting cannot be more severe than here, because with the terrible weather we have had lately it is awful. My best wishes for a blessed Christmas to all my friends at St Michael's'.

PRIVATE G. BISHOP also wrote on the same day: 'I received your welcome letter and card and am pleased to know you remember me at this Christmastide, hoping we shall all meet together for the next. We are having some nasty weather here, but we are all as happy as can be and shall be still happier when we get the final victory, as I am sure we shall. We had a nice service at where we are this morning and I am sure we are all earnest in our attendance.'

PRIVATE FRED BROOKS wrote on Dec. 18th: 'Well, Vicar, we are at last doing a bit of something useful. We have been in two parts of the line since we came out. Our first line was in the trenches where Michael O'Leary won the V.C.,[1] the conditions there were very good and I was very much interested although that is where we had casualties. In the second part however from which we have just returned for a rest, the conditions were very bad. It was simply all mud and water. We are at present billeted in barns, etc., some way behind the firing line. We are staying here till after Christmas and hoping, when we return, that it will be part of the line where it is a little less of bath-all-day-long kind of stunt, even if more dangerous.'

FEBRUARY 1916

8 January: Allied evacuation of Helles, Gallipoli, begins.

Extracts from Letters from some of our Soldiers

From DRUMMER J.W. BAKER, France: 'Just a few lines to thank you and the good friends at St Michael's for that very nice parcel. I have often thought about the old Church when I have seen one out here what the Germans have destroyed, they never leave one standing. There is a village we have left that they have smashed up, the graves and tombs in

---

[1] L-Cpl Michael O'Leary, 1st Batt., Irish Guards, won his VC for an action at Cuinchy on 1 Feb. 1915.

the churchyard are torn up, you can see the coffins all smashed. We must thank God that such a vile enemy has not been allowed to land in our dear Country. They will never reach England now, they are beat, it is only a matter of time, when our leaders think it time to strike them they will get it in the neck, it will be a death blow for Germany.'

From PTE J. HENRY MAWSON: 'I received the parcel, thank you all, it is a most splendid parcel. The words of the hymn on your card are in my mind every day, I shall never forget them. We often sing the hymn out here.'

From PTE J. HENRY LAMBTON: 'I think we all had a good Christmas, but rather quiet, and we never managed to get to the Church Service and Communion, for it was cancelled owing to the bad weather ... This is rather a rough life, but I have mostly found that fellows' thoughts are with One above when there is any danger. The 2nd Sherwoods, in the charge at Hooge,[1] sang three hymns before they went over the parapet. I must tell you we have never seen the trench for four weeks, so we have had a good rest, and I am ready to take my turn again to give others a chance.'

From LANCE-CORPORAL TOM LONGDON, Jan. 16th: 'The life here is very much the same, we go into the firing line for a time and then back for a rest, which is really no rest at all. We are in the firing line now and we get shelled, but so far I have not stopped one. The aeroplanes have been very active in this district, I notice we have lost 10 in a fortnight the reason is that our pilots are too daring. If a German in a plane sees one of ours he immediately turns round and makes for home. The villages all round here are smashed to bits and the churches are full of shell holes ... I saw Fred Brookes to-day and he had just returned from the trenches, he had had a very narrow shave, a sniper just missed him, the bullet grazed his temple and made a flesh wound, but he remained on duty. The sniper just previously had got a man in the same way, right through the head ...'

In a previous letter Longdon wrote: 'We got shelled at Headquarters very bad, we all got into the cellar and expected every minute the house would topple on the top of us, but it did not. Also there was a cart loaded with bombs outside and shells fell all round it, but didn't touch them. The wounded and dying were fetched into the cellar and it was awful. Men lying dead by the road, horses and vehicles all smashed to bits, one man had both his legs blown off and another was fearfully cut up'.

[1] Assault on 'Sanctuary Wood', near Hooge, Ypres, 9 August 1915, 1.45 a.m.

From PETTY OFFICER JOE BEWLEY to his friends, British East Africa, Base Hospital, Dec. 11, 1915: 'You will be anxious to know why I have not written, but I am down with Malaria. I had to go into hospital at Nairobi. We came in a hospital train beautifully fitted up, each compartment has four beds, then there is a big kitchen coach, and nurses and doctors travel with the train. We passed through a large game preserve and the wild animals came close up to the line, but as the train got up to them they rushed away. It was quite an interesting journey, but I did not feel well enough to enjoy it. I expect by the time you receive this I shall be quite well again and amongst the fighting forces again. I only hope I shall not miss any fighting whilst in hospital.'

Dec. 17, 1915.

'I am now feeling much better and the doctor has allowed me to get up for the first time to-day, and am taking a little food. By the time this reaches you I hope to be back again at duty. I see there is some good news in this morning's paper, General Sir H.S. Smith-Dorrien[1] is coming to take command out here. So look out for some big things happening. I hear our cars were in action the other day. It is very much cooler here—more like an English summer and quite a pleasant change from sweating all day. I shall never forget the day we landed, the sandy ground was just like walking on a red-hot oven—to say nothing about the sun over head. With Cecil now in Greece you will have sons nearly all over the world, and when we all get home again and write our experiences it should make a very big and interesting book.'

Since these letters were written, Official notice from the Admiralty has been received dated Jan. 4th, to say 'Petty Officer Joe Bewley is dangerously ill with Enteric Fever.'

Jan. 27th. On enquiry at Whitehall we have been thankful to hear that he is now on the 'out of danger' list.

From PTE OSCAR BEWLEY, Cairo, Jan. 18th: 'I am now quite well again and with my Regiment once more, and ready for the next move, which by the orders will be on Tuesday next week. The Officers have given all those who have come back from hospital a very good wel-

---

[1] Sir Horace Smith-Dorrien (1858–1930). Commander, British Second Army. During the second battle of Ypres in May 1915 he proposed a limited withdrawal of the forces under his command as he regarded further assault as fruitless. He was dismissed on spurious grounds of ill-health. However, he could not take up his posting to East Africa due to illness. He never held a further major command. He was Colonel of The Sherwood Foresters.

come—not many of the old ones being left. We had a splendid little service here on Christmas Day. Our Chaplain said that he did not recognise our Regiment again, but he hoped that the new men would follow the example of the old ones, as they have such a good name—not only in Egypt, but on the battlefield as well. You will be interested to know that Karl Duncan is here, he came out with one of the drafts. I've met several other Derby boys, and at Christmas and New Year we had rare good times together. I received a letter and Christmas card from the Vicar—for which I thank him but the parcel has not yet arrived. The one you sent me from home I received about a week after Christmas, it was very good, especially the plum pudding. Everyone in our tent tasted it and wished the senders as well as the makers the best of luck. Well, cheer up! Everything will be all right in a very short time now, and remember "every cloud has a silver lining".'

Pte Oscar Bewley had been ill with Dysentery and Jaundice contracted in the Dardanelles.

MARCH 1916

21 February–18 December: German Verdun offensive.
9 February: Military Service Act comes
into force in Great Britain.

Death

We regret to record the death of Petty Officer Joseph Bewley, one of our communicants, whose illness was mentioned in our last number. He died at Nairobi, in East Africa, on Jan. 5th, of pneumonia, following upon enteric fever. He was driver of an Armoured Car, and his officer wrote of him to his mother: 'An excellent driver, always steady and willing to do any thing, I regarded him as one of my very best men, and one whom I cannot replace. He was extremely popular in the squadron, and officers and men, one and all, join with me in offering you our deepest sympathy in your sad bereavement.' We are sure that all our readers, as they pray for our departed friend, will join in the sympathy expressed in the above letter. Mrs Bewley has still six sons wearing His Majesty's uniform.

Our Recreation Rooms for Soldiers

Our Schoolroom was opened as a Club for the 3/5th South Staffs. Regiment on Tuesday, Feb. 8th. There was a good attendance of soldiers and a sing-song was arranged by Mr Hudson, who, with the Vicar, welcomed the men. Lieut.-Colonel Crump was also present. Many ladies of the congregation and other helpers had provided refreshments free, which proved very acceptable. Every night for three weeks the rooms were used, at first there were not many who attended, but gradually more and more found them out and frequently they were quite crowded. Games of all kinds were provided and one part of the schoolroom was curtained off as a reading and writing room, writing paper and envelopes being supplied gratis. Refreshments were ready from 5.30 to 9 p.m. at extremely low prices, e.g., halfpenny for a cup of tea, in fact everything except cigarettes was sold at halfpenny. Ladies of the congregation took it in turn to be responsible for the managing of the buffet each night. The soldiers, who were our guests, were a fine set of men and we were gradually getting to know each other, when much to the regret of both hosts and guests the order was given for closing the Rooms as they were required by the authorities for quartering more troops. Many of the men asked if we could not find another place to accommodate them, for they had enjoyed so much our hospitality. We fear, although search has been made, that it will not be possible to secure another suitable room.

Extracts from some Letters

From TROOPER KARL DUNCAN, Salonika, Feb. 12th: 'My address, as you see, has altered for we have left Alexandria and are now in Salonika, Egypt being no longer my place of abode. We arrived on Sunday, February 6th, after being on board ship three days, and the disembarking was one long fatigue. All one night we were busy unloading kits, etc. The climate here is much different from that of Egypt, and at present we are up to the ankles in sludge. Everything is different there being no natives going about bare-footed, instead, the Greeks go about with sacks as their footwear. The country is very hilly here, more like the Peak of Derbyshire, but of course the hills are much higher, being snow covered. I am going on fine though very muddy. I cannot say much in this letter as it has to be censored. Please remember me to the choirmen. The other night a hostile aeroplane came over our way, it being shelled once, made it go off. The scarf and mittens which Miss Hope sent me, through you, have come in very useful here.'

CORPORAL COTTON writes from the same neighbourhood, February 10th: 'I was very much pleased when I was sorting a mail out to-day and saw a parcel addressed to myself. I was astounded to see it was from you and the kind friends of St Michael's. It was a grand parcel and I don't know how I can thank you all for being so kind and thoughtful. It is things like this that bind us closer together. I am quite well out in this historic country, I often pass the road that leads to Mars Hill (Acts xvii) I expect you would like to travel here and see some of the haunts of the great St Paul. You will be pleased to hear that our Chaplain is coming to talk with me and get me ready for Confirmation, he tells me that the Bishop is coming here shortly. We have very hot weather here during the day and very cold at night, I don't mind that, but when it rains here it is awful.'

PRIVATE FRED BROOKS, in France, on Feb. 3rd, after thanks for New Year's parcel which included muffler, helmet, etc., he writes: 'The same evening I received your parcel we were in reserve billets and were sent up to the trenches at midnight, how useful those woollen things have been to me. It was very cold indeed when we went in, although I was only in for two nights. The reason I was only in for such a short time and also why I have not been able to write you, is because on the second night I was on sentry duty and you understand one has to look over the top of the parapet after dark, well, I was looking over and they, the Germans, were busy as usual sending up their flares and one of their snipers spotted me, so of course he had a few shots at me and missed, but after I had returned the compliment and done likewise—missed, he waited for the next flare going up and then he managed to get me. Luckily it was not very serious, the bullet just grazed my right temple, not sufficiently serious for me to come to England with. I have had a good rest with it however at the dressing Station. I am quite better now, with the exception of a rather bad head-ache which troubles me occasionally and am waiting to join my battalion, which has returned to the trenches again since ...'.

We regret to learn that two more of our lads are on the wounded list, LANCE-CORPORAL NORMAN POWELL, who was hurt in action at Persian Gulf in January, and PRIVATE GEORGE WHEATCROFT who is now in Hospital at Liverpool and tells of his experiences in a letter to Miss Iliffe, his Sunday School Teacher, dated Feb. 24th: 'The accident happened on my birthday. I had three horses and was riding the middle one and my horse dropped down suddenly, I do not know whether it was shot or just an accident, well, anyway it dropped right across my leg and the sword hilt cut underneath my knee. The wound has now healed up but has left my leg very stiff. I have had about enough of hospital life,

I had six weeks in Alexandria and a fortnight's voyage in a hospital ship, then a ten hours' train ride, now I am in this hospital, which is the best of the lot.'

APRIL 1916

French forces hold Verdun.
8 March: Battle of Dujaila, Mesopotamia.

Extracts from Soldiers' Letters

From PRIVATE C. WILLATT of the 6th Seaforth Highlanders, who, although enlisted only a short time, has recently gone to France, writes on March 9th: 'Just a few lines to let you know I am still alive and kicking and am in the best of health. We are stationed just outside a small town "somewhere in France" not far from the coast. The country round here is sandy and rather well wooded and we are under canvas, 12 in a tent, there being three other Derby fellows in my tent, who enlisted with me. We are having a lot of snow and rain and it is cold, so you see it is not ideal weather for tents. We have been here about a week now and are finishing our training, the chief items being bayonet fighting, bomb throwing and firing rapidly at a short range. Of course everything is much stricter and the training I had in England was very weak in comparison with what we do over here. The French soldiers look quite out of place in their blue and grey costumes against the English khaki. We have our services in large huts on a Sundays and I enjoy them very much, although they are rather short, because of the large number of men, they have to have many services. We might be here a week or two, or we may move to-morrow, it depends on the casualties of the battalion in the trenches. Kindly remember me to my friends at St Michael's, as I have not time to write to them all, so good-night Vicar.'

PRIVATE GORDON HUNT writes to Miss Perrin, on March 17th: 'We are in the trenches and have been for some time and have been having a warm time of it most days. Yesterday morning the Germans blew a mine up not far from us, and of course our men had to turn out and stand fast. We got 'strafed' a bit by shells but managed all right. We are looking forward to the finish now, for the French are going strong at Verdun, and although they have lost a little ground they have put plenty of Germans "out of mess". We are in an old German trench and in one of their dug-outs, it is a very good one too, for we are well underground and it is fitted up with beds and seats ... It is a long time since we met any more Derby lads but we hear we have some behind us, and if so we shall have a good time when we meet, for we have sports and often a bit of supper together when we meet a local Regiment ... '.

Letters have been received by the Vicar from L. CORPORAL T. LONGDON, PRIVATE H. COULSON and others in France; also from SERGEANT H. COX and PRIVATE KARL DUNCAN, these write very cheerfully from Salonika.

Tidings of our Wounded Lads

PRIVATE PETER HUDSON, who was wounded badly in the head, has now returned home, discharged from the Army, with a pension. He seems fairly well except at times. PRIVATE G. WHEATCROFT is going on well at Liverpool. GUNNER A. ROE writes on March 15th, from a Convalescent Home: 'I am getting along splendidly now. My arm is just about healed, except for one little piece that small pieces of bone keep working out of. I have more movement in my arm than ever I expected, knowing that the top part was shattered. I expect to be home in a month's time ... Please remember me to my friends in the Church.

L. CORPORAL NORMAN POWELL is in Mesopotamia and the Vicar has had two letters from him, one dated Feb. 7th, in which he says: 'I am wounded in both hands and head. I got hit whilst I was fighting against the Turks. I am in hospital at Amarah.' In his second letter, dated Feb. 20th, which only reached England a few days ago, he appears to have been moved to another Hospital and writes: 'Well, I am a lot better now, my head wound is healing up and my hands are also healing. I went to a grand concert last night, which was held in the Y.M.C.A. place, I quite enjoyed it. This hospital is a good one, we have good beds, good clothes, and plenty of good food ... Plenty of ships come in here each day ... I suppose that it is cold in England. It is very hot here ... '.

We have heard that TROOPER JOE COCKER has been wounded but cannot learn particulars. We have also heard that L. CORPORAL JACK REDFERN had been wounded, but in a letter received last week from a mate of his it was stated that he had been killed by a sniper. RIP.

MAY 1916

9 April: German offensive at Verdun renewed.
29 April: Kut-el-Amara falls to Turkish forces.

Extracts from letters to the Vicar

PTE K.V. DUNCAN, Salonika, April 7th: 'We have now moved right on to the frontier and are doing patrol work on the dividing line. We find it a big change from Egypt, but as regards climate now it is the Spring here and the days are very warm. I am pleased to say I do not feel sorry I am where I am, as I feel quite content ... After three days' sailing we arrived at Salonika and one's spirits were not bucked up by the state of the ground. Every step taken mud came up to your ankles, ugh! The first fatigue was unloading the mules and horses and it was a very ticklish job. Mules are so trying, if they think they will not move they won't. We did have a job with one, after a quarter of an hour's coaxing to go through the door, all he would do was to shove his head through and "Hee-Haw". The rest of the day was spent in fatigues and three-quarters of us all night as well. At six in the morning the order was given to pack our saddles and then saddle-up. This done, we moved off though not mounted. We walked through the town, causing no little excitement among the peculiar looking Greeks. (He tells of the various places he went to) ... We had Church every Sunday morning and the Chaplain's name is Revd Edward J. Powell, from Nottingham.[1] From — we used to go up to a place — from there three patrols went out daily. A patrol consists of an Officer or N.C.O. and three men, and their duty is to visit places and see that there has been no preparations for helping the enemy. In most of the villages the people were friendly, but in some we had black looks. The nationalities are mixed, Bulgarians, Turks, Greeks and Serbians. We have some fine times on these patrols for we have to cook our own meals, which I like, as one can fry cheese and eggs and make tea. On one patrol we had to visit a white house which stands on a hill

---

[1] Edward John Powell, Univ. of Cambridge, B.A. 1904; Cl. Tr. Sch., Camb. 1904; deacon 1904, priest 1905; assistant curate, St Mary's, Nottingham 1904–10; chaplain of Cinder Hill, Nottingham 1910–20; TCF 1914–19; Bathurst, Gambia 1920–4; chaplain of All Saints, Marseilles, dio. Gibraltar 1924–5; Archdeacon of Morocco and the Isles 1926–7; chaplain at Frankfurt w. Stuttgart, Wilbad and Baden Baden, dio. London (N. and C. Eur.) 1928–33.

similar to Bunker's Hill.[1] From this house you can see right into Bulgaria and in the Balkan war it was often the cause of many a severe engagement, I was told by our interpreter. We used to stop at this house for three hours to cook our food. We never saw anything unusual round that way, but we might do where we are now, as only hills separate us from where the Bulgars are massed together. We have numerous Air raids here, but as soon as a hostile craft shows he is shelled from all directions. It is as exciting as watching a football match, to see shells bursting round an aeroplane, wondering if it will get hit.'

PTE C. WILLATT, in France, April 9th: 'I am now billeted in a small French village a few miles behind the firing line but still within range of the guns ... I have had my first dose of fire and was in the trenches for six days, four in the firing line and two in the supports. We had very fine weather and the trenches were dry, but the dug-outs damp ... My worst experience was building up a part of our parapet which the Boches had blown down with a trench mortar. We were working like niggers from 9 till 11 p.m. with pick and shovel, and I wasn't at all sorry when we had finished, as the Germans were only a few yards away and they were constantly putting up flare-lights. I have been to Church service which was held in a French Chateau which seemed to have been shelled. It seemed very strange to go to Church with rifle and bayonet and 150 rounds of ammunition in your pouches. We had a short sermon and three or four hymns which we all knew, including "Onward, Christian Soldiers" and I leave it to you to guess how it was sung.'

CORPORAL E.O. THOMAS, in France, April 13th: 'We are billeted in a barn in a small village. The life is very monotonous and strange to say we would far rather be at it in the trenches, providing the weather would keep fine. We have been in the trenches three times and have seen some heavy bombardments. Our Battalion has been very fortunate, as our casualties were very small, and has won for itself a very good name while in the trenches, i.e., as being one of the smartest Regiments of the New Army at the front ... It is almost incredible what a man can stand and if folks at home only knew what the men out here go through, and that cheerfully, they would count it a miracle and they would not be wide of the mark ... In the trenches my worst enemies have been rats and rain. The shot and shell we get accustomed to, but loss of sleep we cannot ... I have had several narrow escapes, but up to now I'm pleased to say I've not had a scratch ... the rats upset me more than the enemy.'

---

[1] Bunker's Hill lies between the villages of Quarndon and Duffield. The Easter Monday walk for the Sunday School children 'and others', and often preceded by the St Michael's band, was to Bunker's Hill starting from Five Lamps, Duffield Road.

PTE W. BURROWS, in France, April 19th: 'I have been at the base now for a fortnight, but we are under orders to move up the line at any moment ... I liked Rouen, but the town where this camp is situated is awfully dirty ... I went to Holy Communion last Sunday in the Chapel of the Church of England hut, it was a very nice service indeed.'

L-CORP. T. LONGDON, in France, April 19th: 'We are not so near the line this time, the Head-quarters we should have gone into have been shelled so frequently and we have moved a little further back. This is a typical French village with its Church and mud square, it boasts of one pump in the middle of the square and it's a treat to see some of the fellows trying to get clean again after a spell in the trenches. I should love to be able to attend St Michael's on Easter Day, I have not had a single opportunity of going to Church whilst I have been out here. If there is an English Service on Easter Day I shall attend, but I do not suppose there will, for we are expecting things just now. All leave has been stopped and so I shall have to wait a little longer for mine.'

PTE J.H. LAMBTON, in France, April 26th: 'I shall never forget one sight I saw. We were coming out of the trenches on Good Friday morning and sat down on the road side for a rest. The sun was just breaking through and at the side was a piece of ground covered with crosses. All our fellows made remarks about it. We are having some lovely weather.'

JUNE 1916

Letters from the front

The number of our men from St Michael's who are now somewhere at the front increases month by month, from many of them letters come and all of these are wonderfully cheerful, considering the conditions under which they are written. We are so glad to know that many, if not all, who are communicants were able to make their Easter Communion. Here are some extracts: the 1st is from PTE ERIC HARDY, written to his parents, he is in Salonika, and the letter is dated April 24th: 'We have moved up to within a few miles of Doiran Lake, of course having

Taubes[1] overhead, about four a day on the average, we have a fine
arrangement for fixing out our Maxim gun[2] and we hit one the other
day, made him fly on one side to his lines again. We had a ripping little
stream running through our camp and fished for chub with line and bent
pins and used to have them for breakfast. You will be pleased to hear I
took my Easter Communion on Good Friday, in the open of course, all
the time a Taube was flying overhead dropping bombs, but not one on
our camp.[3] I also received the Vicar's Easter Card on Easter Day, which
was good and reminded me of many past blessings at the dear little
Church, it was good timing too, was it not? The other day I spent
observing on a hill all day with our gun and could see Uhlans[4] patrolling with their lances, through the glasses, but they never came within
range, worse luck! Of course we are always being called out at night on
alarms and often have to stand till daybreak, sometimes from midnight
till 6 a.m. ... The Greek women run away from you when they see an
English soldier, so we don't see much of them, but they are a dirty
ragged lot, like gypsies. We have slouch hats now (like Australians) and
all look topping on horse back, like a lot of cowboys.'

The Vicar also had a letter from PTE HARDY at the same time.
SERGEANT E. H. COX, who is also with the Salonika Force, writing
to the Vicar, says: 'I must tell you about our grand surprise on Easter
Sunday. Being a long way from Salonika, and only a small party, it is
almost out of the question for us to have a Church Service every Sunday,
but special arrangements were made for us on Easter Day, and not only
did we have a short service, but a Communion Service afterwards. I shall
never forget it, I cannot possibly describe how lovely it was. Many

---

[1] The Taube ('Dove') was an early monoplane designed by Igo Etrich in 1910. There
were many variations of the basic design. Its reputation led to almost any German aircraft
being called a 'Taube' by Allied soldiers, particularly in the early months of the war.

[2] The Maxim gun was the first automatic machine-gun, invented by Hiram Maxim
in the USA in 1884 and serving as the basic design for subsequent heavy machine-gun
manufacture.

[3] This incident is described in G.A. Strutt, *The Derbyshire Yeomanry War History
1914–1918* (Derby, Bemrose, n.d., *c.* 1920–5), 126: 'April 21st [1916] was Good Friday,
and as the Padre could not come to us on Easter Day, it was decided to hold our Easter
Day service on the 21st instead. Whilst communion service was in progress, a Boche 'plane
chose the opportunity to visit us. Flying at a low altitude, he dropped three bombs whilst
we were kneeling to receive the Sacrament, but these, I am glad to say, all fell in the
Manchesters' camp. Gillett [Lt H.E. Gillett] promptly got on to the Boche with his
machine-guns a few yards away from the extemporised communion table, and though the
service continued without interruption I am afraid that our minds were not filled with the
thoughts with which they should have been'. The aircraft was hit and came down behind
enemy lines. Lt Gillett died in hospital from malaria in November 1918.

[4] German lancers.

thanks for the Easter Card you sent me, I shall keep it with me always and bring it back with me, when (if it is God's will) I once more return to England and St Michael's'.

From PTE WILFRED BURROWS, somewhere in France, May 21st: 'Since my last note to you I have travelled about the north of France quite a lot, having been attached to two different divisions since leaving the base, until a little over a fortnight ago I joined our own Battalion. We came out of the trenches last Wednesday, after a ten days spell, and, as you can guess, not very sorry to do so. We had a fairly quiet time excepting the last night, when we gave the enemy a pretty hot Artillery bombardment and afterwards a bombing raid, which was in last Thursday's paper. I was very sorry about Herbert Fletcher, he was blown up by one of the mines, he is buried in the cemetery in the village in which we are billeted. The weather now is lovely, very hot, but whilst we were in the trenches some days were very miserable owing to the rain, which makes the trenches miniature streams, your boots stick in the sludge and often refuse to budge. I am glad to say I am keeping very fit and well. Charlie Willatt is transferred to the Royal Engineers. Pleased to say we have a fine Chaplain to our Battalion, who thinks a lot of "his boys", and of course takes the services when we are in billet. With best wishes for all my friends at St Michael's, etc., etc.'

From 2ND LIEUT R. BARKER, France, May 24th: 'I often think of you all at St Michael's, especially on Sundays. Thanks very much for your Easter card, it arrived while I was in the trenches. I am pleased to say that we were out on Easter Day, and I was able to attend the Holy Communion Service, at 8.30. It seemed very different from the usual Easter Day. We also had the ordinary Church Parades and in the afternoon I was on parade teaching some men bombing. A week last Saturday night we left the part of the line that we have been in for the last two months and we are now about 50 miles behind the firing line in a very pretty village. We marched all the way here, we did about 10 miles a day. I don't think anyone was sorry when we arrived here. It is very nice to be able to walk about without hearing guns all the time. The two months that I have spent in the trenches have not been so bad. I had an exciting time once or twice, and I had a bullet through a long trench coat I had on just above the knees'. (PTE H. COULSON is in the same village as that from which Lieut. Barker writes).

From CORPORAL E.O. THOMAS, in France, May 10th: 'We arrived at this billet yesterday from the trenches, after having broken our journey for three days at a "stand to" billet. This is the so called "Rest billet", but I can assure you it is wrongly labelled, as there is more humbug than rest to be found here.[1] We arrived in this very billet on Good Friday afternoon and left for the trenches early on Easter morning. In the meantime we have been in the trenches undergoing a varied and rough experience, isolated from the outer world in the day time owing to its dangerous position, the only means of communication being at night, when rations and letters, etc., were brought us by parties told off from the reserve trenches at the rear. Should a man be wounded he could not be removed until night, the stretcher bearers attending to him in the meantime. One night I had taken out a wiring party in front of the trenches, the bombardment was so terrific that I was ordered to bring them in again until things had cooled down a bit, we finished the job after being out four hours. We were fortunate in having dry weather while in, what we suffered from most was want of sleep. Everywhere the men stuck it well and seeing that our rations had gone astray and the water supply ran short the last day, everyone took the situation with a good heart. We arrived in billet about midnight and found the floor a soft place to lie down our weary limbs.'

We regret to learn, from a letter received May 31st, that Corporal Thomas is unwell and in hospital. The other wounded and sick belonging to us seem to be doing well. A letter from CORPORAL CECIL BEWLEY, written in hospital, at Salonika, tells the Vicar that he 'is getting back his strength very nicely and hopes before long to be in England'. PTE NORMAN POWELL, who was wounded in Mesopotamia and was sent to Bombay, is now in a Military Hospital at Cairo, and appears to be doing well. PTE G. WHEATCROFT is now nearly convalescent, and GUNNER ARTHUR ROE is getting on fairly well, but is not yet able to come home from the Hospital in Sussex, to which he has recently been sent. We all hope and pray that these and all our brave soldier lads will be with us safe and sound by next Whitsuntide.

JULY 1916

13 June: Wilhelmsthal, German East Africa, captured by Jan Smuts.
Western Front in June: Preparations for the battle of the Somme
indicated in the letters.

---

[1] Probably a reference to an insistence on drill and route marches while in rest camps.

Our Soldiers

We are glad to know that the sick and wounded amongst our soldiers are progressing favourably. Since our last issue PTE WILFRED BURROWS has been seriously wounded in France, he is now in a Hospital in London. He writes, June 13th: 'I have three wounds in the shoulder, one in the stomach and a large one on the loin, all on the right side, but am glad to say they are not dangerous, and that I am getting on very well, but of course practically helpless for a bit.' CORPORAL E.O. THOMAS is now in Hospital at Bristol. He says, in a letter dated June 17th: 'Our Hospitals at the Base appear to be evacuating. In our convoy there were over 800 patients, which to my mind points to some forward movement about to he made very shortly,[1] if so they will require all available beds. Before going to Hospital at the Base I suffered a good deal for three days in "the Reinforcements Camp" and here, for the first time, I came in contact with the compulsionists,[2] and as one came straight from the trenches I could not help but notice the vast difference in character between him and the man who had volunteered to do his bit. Man is naturally selfish and it was very much in evidence here, but you go into the trenches and see the difference, it is a brotherhood there, having tasted, having seen the awfulness of this horrible war, Tommy has mellowed down and possesses one beautiful spirit in a bond of union, a brotherhood which will, I hope, have an effect on the life of our country for generations to come. I am very happy here and improving slowly.'

The Vicar has visited PTE GEORGE WHEATCROFT in a Convalescent Camp at Blackpool, he was pleased to find him much better from the wound he received in Egypt. CORPORAL CECIL BEWLEY is on his way home and when last we heard of him was at Malta going on well. We were very pleased to see his brother Oscar home on leave from Salonika, he looked, as he said he felt, 'in the pink'. He has now rejoined his regiment.

CORPORAL TOM LONGDON wrote from France early in June: 'I found every thing here much the same when I returned, but since then we have been expecting things. The Bosches were fairly active with their artillery for a time, and one night whilst in the line they sent over a tremendous number of shells which make you weep, and I did cry, I could not see for a long time. I had one or two narrow shaves from Air-plane shells, one fell within ten yards of me, but fortunately it was

---

[1] A reference to the Somme offensive which began on 1 July 1916.

[2] Conscripts, following the coming into force of the Military Service Acts, 1916.

a dead one. They seemed to chase me with them one day as I went to dinner, they dropped them in a ditch by the road side, talk about sprinting, I reckon I beat all records that day. We have been out of the line a few days now, we were fetched out rather hurriedly, and ever since we came out we have been standing to, ready to shift at two hours' notice. The reason for that is, we have been expecting something to happen, but up to now it has not come off, but we are still looking forward to the beginning of the end.'

Death of Norman Powell

It will be remembered that Private Norman Powell was wounded in Mesopotamia last January and has been in Hospitals in Bombay and Cairo, we quite hoped he was convalescent and on his way home. The Vicar heard from his father of his death and the following letter from the Chaplain at the Hospital at Cairo gives details. He was one of our Scout Patrol Leaders and a favourite with us all, he enlisted the very day before his Confirmation and we have not seen him since, except once when he made his communion at St Michael's. We believe that he has passed to his rest having fought a good fight, and in God's good time he will receive the Victor's crown. Meanwhile we pray, 'Grant him, Lord, Eternal rest, and let light perpetual shine upon him.'

No. 27, General Hospital,
Abbassieh, Cairo, May 26th, 1916.

Dear Sir,

A poor lad has just died in this Hospital from the effects of an old gun wound in the head, apparently a bit of the bullet was left in and gradually worked its way into a dangerous region. He was brought into this Hospital in an unconscious condition a day or two ago, and though they operated at once and did all they could to save his life, he passed away yesterday and I have just laid him to rest in the Cemetery at Old Cairo, where so many of his comrades lie, who have given their lives for their country. The boy's name is Norman Powell, a Private in the 3rd Leicesters. Apparently they cannot quite learn who his next of kin are, so I am writing to you as it seems he was well known to you.

I am Chaplain to this Hospital and saw the lad frequently while he was here and though he could not speak to me I feel sure he understood when I prayed with him almost to the end. He grasped my hand for an hour or more before he passed away, and I am thankful to say he did not suffer much at the end.

The Nurse told me he was praying all the while his last dressings were done, and during the night was asking to be taken to Church. I feel sure he was a good lad and most assuredly he met his death like a brave soldier, and has entered into the reward of those who have shown the Greater Love and died for their Country and those they loved. I gave him a small Crucifix to look at when he could not speak and the Sister placed it round his neck before he was laid to rest. I may add he was buried with military honours, and all in the Hospital and both nurses and doctors did all that could be done for the boy. It seemed so sad for so young a lad to die out here and so far away from home and friends. I am venturing to write to you, because I know what a relief it is to those at home to have a few details in addition to the bare facts announced by the War Office, and am sure you will kindly communicate with his friends and assure them of my sympathy and prayers. Please excuse a hurried letter as I am writing in haste to catch the outgoing mail.

> Sincerely yours,
> J. Baghot de la Bere, C.F.[1]

Khaki Prisoners of War Fund

16th June, 1916

Canon H.R. Rolfe,
St Michael's Vicarage, Derby

Dear Sir,

I enclose formal receipt for the amount of £3 14*s*. 0*d*., being a collection from the children of St Michael's Sunday School, who have so generously given up their prizes for our poor men who are imprisoned in Germany.

I am very grateful indeed to you, and the children for their kind help.

[1] John Baghot de la Bere, Worc. Coll. Oxford, B.A. 1891, M.A. 1898; Cudd. Coll. 1891; deacon 1893, priest 1894; assistant curate St Luke, Maidenhead 1893–6; Leamington 1896–9; St Mary Redcliffe, Bristol 1899–1902; vicar of Bedminster, 1902–19; TCF, 1915–16; vicar of Prestbury, Gloucester, 1919–43; Miss. of Help to India, 1922–3; hon. Canon of Gloucester, 1937.

Yours truly,
G.E. Raine,
Hon. Secretary

[A similar contribution was made to the British Red Cross]

AUGUST 1916

1 July (to 18 November): The Somme offensive begins with 27 Allied divisions advancing across No-Man's-Land, seven-eighths of them British. On that day, of the horror of which Robert Barker, Laurence Hallsworth, Harry Coulson, Owen Parry Jones and William Good- child write so graphically, British forces suffered 58,000 casualties, of which 21,000 were killed including, among the dead, William Foy, J. Henry Lambton and Harry Lowe from St Michael's and, among the wounded, Harry Coulson, Laurence Abell, Frank Browne, John Baker and George Greensmith. Two St Michael's men, Theodore Downman and John Baker, were taken prisoner. The losses were greater than on any other single day in the history of the British Army.

Our Soldiers at the Front

The British offensive to the north of the River Somme began on July 1st. For a whole month our troops have been fighting with splendid courage. We have paid a heavy price for the results achieved. Some of our own lads are in the lists of killed, wounded and missing. 2nd Lieut. Theodore Downman, Privates Henry Lambton and John Baker are amongst the missing. L-Corporal Henry Lowe is killed and L-Corp. F. Browne, Privates L. Abell, H. Coulson, George Greensmith are wounded but going on satisfactorily. The Vicar has also just received a letter from Sergt H. E. Cox dated July 21st, he has been in a Hospital at Malta, ill with malaria, but he is getting better.

There are so many interesting letters from those who have been in the recent 'push' in France, that it is difficult to make extracts. Here are a few. From PTE H. COULSON, wounded before Fricourt: '... It was with strange feelings that I advanced with the others through the gaps in our barbed wire across "no man's land" into what was left of the German wire and their trenches, to the remnants of some buildings to the north side of the village. The havoc wrought by our artillery is indescribable. Dugouts were bombed and prisoners rounded up. We continued the advance and cleared a small wood. We dug ourselves in and spent the night. In the morning we had to charge another trench under a small fire of shrapnel. We found the trench full of German equipment scattered everywhere. Many prisoners were taken that morning. I got hold of a very nice German helmet, but in helping to carry one of our wounded to a safer place I lost it. Our haul included several machine guns and field guns.'

From 2ND LIEUT ROBERT BARKER, July 15th: 'I have been through the first battle of the "push", the taking of Fricourt, etc. You can guess we had a very exciting and rather rough time, but I would not have missed it for the world. This Battalion has done its share of the work, and we have captured several very important positions. We took nearly a whole Battalion of Huns prisoners, just in one move, we were on the top of them before they knew where they were. The taking of one trench stands out in my mind more than anything else, and I don't think I shall ever forget it, perhaps because I saw two of my best friends killed almost by my side. We failed to take the trench the first time and were in "no man's land" unable to move either way. During that time I was buried by a shell and hit by a piece of shrapnel in the finger, it was not much, I managed to get in four wounded men after a great struggle. I was left 2nd in command of the company, and for a part of time commanded it. The next time we went for that trench we took it with flying colours. The Huns simply ran for their lives and I am afraid neither officers nor men had any mercy for any one ... Soon after we were relieved by another Battalion. Now we are some miles behind the line resting and are quite enjoying ourselves, after more than a fortnight with the same clothes on all the time. There is a lot more I could say but I cannot remember everything just now, it still seems almost like a dream.'

From PTE L. HALLSWORTH, July 4th: 'I have been through the worst battle that this Battalion has ever been in, God alone knows how I have escaped death. The bombardment lasted 5 days and the last two days was terrible, the night before the attack the bombardment grew in intensity until it was impossible for one to speak and we had to yell at the top of our voices to make ourselves heard, the men kept getting knocked out one by one up to the time of making the charge. At a specified time it was "up boys and at 'em", we had let loose the cloud of smoke under cover of which we slowly advanced. Good heavens! I shall never forget it, it simply rained shells and shrapnel and bullets were whistling through the air in hundreds. As soon as I got over the parapet

I commenced to walk over that terrible "no man's land", it was at least
500 yards to the enemy's trenches, they blazed away at us and our men
were falling in scores and I really do not know, only that God was with
me, how I escaped. On and on I went never knowing at what second I
should be hit. Cries of help from wounded and dying comrades rose all
around me. I got nearly up to their wire or what was left of it. The
smoke was beginning to get thin, I could see the enemy's trenches and
knew they could see me. I lay down behind my two boxes of ammunition, they saved my life, for I should have had a bullet through me but
for them, we had to retire and at last I reached our advance trench and
had to stay there till it was dark, about 14 hours. The trench was packed
with wounded I did what I could for those around me, I dressed their
wounds and stopped the bleeding and gave them a drink of water and a
smoke, and any moment I expected being knocked out by a whiz-bang
for they were dropping all round ... Out of my section there are 5 who
got back out of 27 and out of the Battalion only 130 men answered the
roll call ... Always pray for my safety for God is my only helper and
defender.'

   In a letter written July 21st, he wrote home: 'I am quite well, I expect
you have heard of the death of Harry Lowe, he was L-Corporal of the
stretcher bearers, I suppose he was shot while attending to wounded
officers. A week last Sunday I managed to go to Holy Communion. It
was held at 7.30 in the morning in a small room which the Chaplain
managed to get. We stood up during most of the service, except during
the Consecration Prayer when we knelt down in fours and so received
the Blessed Sacrament. It is no easy matter to go to Holy Communion
at that time without your mates wanting to know "what's up", of course
I tell them I am going to Holy Communion and when they see that I am
not afraid of them knowing, I hear no more about it. I went to two other
services that day, that was our first gathering together after our ordeal of
a week ago, so you may be sure there was none of us but what had a
purpose for going to the service and that was to thank God for His
goodness in bringing us out of that terrible battle.'

   From a letter written by CAPT. OWEN PARRY-JONES to his
relatives: 'Our Guns were busy bombarding the German lines for 5 days
and you should have heard the row for the hour or so before the attack.
Well, our infantry went over the parapet at 7.30 a.m. on Saturday, July
1st, and did awfully well as you have seen. They went right over the
three lines of German trenches on into the village of Montauban behind.
The Germans fought scrappily, some surrendered practically at once,
others fought pretty hard. Our division did awfully well and attained all
their objectives in less than the time allowed them. The casualties were

small, though one or two regiments lost very heavily ... My men had the job of clearing the wounded down from the front line, where they were gathered together and dressed, to the advanced dressing station which was in the village behind us, by means of wheeled stretchers. We made the Boche prisoners help in carrying stretchers and they did quite well. They were glad to be out of it, but for the most part were a most brutal and degenerate looking lot. They were all Bavarians opposite us, and said they were fed up with the war and that the Prussians were the only ones who had got any fight in them now. I did not get any sleep for 48 hours and was pretty tired by that time.'

The Vicar has received other letters, including one from CORP. TOM LONGDON dated July 27th, giving a graphic account of his experiences, but unhappily want of space prevents us from giving extracts.

The Boy Scouts

... The following letter has been received by Mr and Mrs Powell from the Chief Scout conveying his sympathy with them in the death of their son Norman Powell.

'I hope you will accept this brief word of sympathy in the loss of your son. I did not know him myself but from what I have heard I know that he was a true Scout. I am sure that the thought of his splendid patriotism and self sacrifice will be some consolation to you in your great sorrow, and can assure you of the sympathy and admiration of his brother Scouts.'

> With very sincere sympathy,
> Believe me, yours truly,
> Robert Baden-Powell

SEPTEMBER 1916

20 August: Allied offensive in Mesopotamia begins.
Western Front: Stalemate.

Letters from the Front

From PTE H. ASHBY, of the Grenadier Guards, written August 3rd: '... Considering the adverse circumstances and conditions things seem to be progressing wonderfully well, and every individual man seems of the opinion that the war will come to a swift close, at least that's how it appears to me. You asked me some considerable time ago, if ever I had seen a man named John Whitaker, who belonged to St Michael's, and as you said, a Guardsman. Since you last wrote, I never saw him until yesterday, but it was some time before I could fully recognise him even then, until he asked me if I had heard from St Michael's lately. He asked me to inform you that he is feeling wonderfully well, but like the remainder, anxious to get home again. He is with the Stretcher Bearers in my Battalion and, needless to say, doing splendid work amongst the wounded, which one must admit is a thankless job, because the bringing in and the immediate dressing of the wounded fall to their lot, as also does the burying of the dead, which of course is an absolute necessity. I have often noticed them during the heat of a violent action walking about in the open unprotected, and absolutely unconscious of the dangers to which they are exposed, giving consolation to some, bandaging others, in fact doing everything to the best of their abilities for the well-being and comfort of the wounded, without the slightest thought for their own welfare. One hears too little of the silent but wonderful work that this particular branch of service is doing, and no one can speak too highly of them, or ever pay them too many compliments.'

From a letter received from PTE FRED FLETCHER of the Argyle and Sutherland Highlanders, dated August 13th: 'I am obliged for your letter received last night. It is nice to receive letters from Derby. We were in the fighting line last week, 6 days, am now resting, but expect to be off shortly for the trenches again. We had a very hot time, shells bursting round us, the explosions were terrific, the holes made by them would bury a horse and cart, but our platoon escaped without injury, except for one or two who had shrapnel wounds. We sleep in barns, very comfortable after a long march and after a long railway journey. The village we are now in is fine, one would think there was no war in progress, but I have seen villages absolutely shattered by the Huns, nothing left but the walls, or part of them standing. We have had very hot weather ever since we left England, I am proper brown and feel A1. I saw Archie Duncan the first place we were at and went to the Church Army Hut with him for Service, which we enjoyed immensely. Have not seen him since, it will be over a month ago. Have never seen a Church of England minister since I came over, should like to meet one, although have made full enquiry, but, no doubt, shall come across one before long. Am glad I shall not be forgotten at St Michael's.'

CORP. T. LONGDON wrote early in August of his experiences in the line, he is usually at Headquarters. 'We went into the line about a fortnight ago, and to begin with stayed at the Depot for a couple of days. During that period I had to go up into the thick of it three times in one day, and the last trip I went up a valley which is a terrible valley of death, I did nothing but dive and run all the way because they had a barrage of shell fire on it and I had to get through so I chanced it, and I can assure you it was jolly warm work dodging into holes and out again and then sprint till another scream came warning of another shell and a dive again. They sent for me to go to the advance Headquarters, I got there and found them in deep dug outs (German). The luck seemed against us for the next three days Fritz did nothing but shell us and it was impossible to get out of the dug outs at all. I did not get a wash, shave, or my boots off for over a week and I was a perfect picture when I did get out. I had a very near touch when we shifted from the dug outs to an open spot in the middle of the night. We found some trenches and I was looking for a decent spot to sleep in when "whiz", a shell nearly took my head off and burst at my feet. The explosion knocked me over and dazed me for a bit and when I pulled myself together to see if any parts were missing, I found I was all right, but a fellow ten yards away got a piece through the neck, I considered myself jolly lucky and I thanked God for my escape. We shifted again next morning and we had no sooner dug ourselves in than they found us out and gave us a very trying time, and we have to work all the time this kind of thing is going on and one has to run the gauntlet time after time to get things signed ... You cannot imagine what a present day battle field is like, dead bodies, horses and men lying all over the place. Our fellows buried them whilst they were on supports to occupy their minds, as the strain is terrific, and what with shells coming and shells going the whole earth vibrates.'

Another letter was received from Corp. Longdon on August 31st, he still writes cheerfully.

The Wounded, Sick and Missing

Since our last issue we have had news of some of those of whom we then made mention. 2nd Lieut. Theodore Downman is now known to be a prisoner, as also is Pte John Baker, who is said to be seriously wounded. No news has been received of Ptes H. Lambton and W. Foy who are reported missing. To the list of wounded must be added the names of Captain Edward Parry Jones, 2nd Lieut. R. Barker wounded in the arm, at home and doing well, also Pte Arthur Foster seriously wounded in the thigh and now in a Manchester Hospital. Pte Karl Duncan writes from a Hospital at Malta, where he has been sent suffering from malaria. Most of the others mentioned in the August Magazine are doing well.

OCTOBER 1916

3 September: British forces occupy Dar-es-Salaam, East Africa.
13 September–15 December: Allied offensive from Salonika.
15 September: British forces first use tanks on the
Western Front, at Fler-Courcelette, the Somme.

Our Soldiers

We are sure that all our readers will desire to express their deep sympathy with Mr and Mrs Downman in the loss they have sustained in the death of their Son, 2nd Lieut. Bernard Downman, who was killed in an attack on the enemy on Friday, Sept. 22nd, he was only 20 years of age, and had intended to take Holy Orders, and was at Cambridge when he joined the forces. He has died a noble death and we pray that God will give him more and more light and peace. Our sick and wounded soldiers are doing well, including Pte Fred Brookes, in hospital at Stockport, with trench fever. We regret to learn that Pte Archie Buck is seriously wounded in France. No news has come respecting H. Lambton and W. Foy, reported missing. We congratulate Corp. T. Longdon on his promotion to be Sergeant, and Pte G. J. Gleeson to be Corporal. The Vicar has had several letters from lads at the front, but few of general interest.

SERGEANT A. COTTON writes from Salonika: 'It is awful out here with the terrible heat and the flies. Most of us are affected with sun blisters on the hands and when they break the flies get at them and they turn into terrible sores. I have 4 now, 2 on each hand. Mr Ram,[1] our Chaplain, is still with us, he held a service last Sunday night in our camp, he has, like the rest of us, gone very thin.' PRIVATE W. GOODCHILD says, in a letter from the front in France, dated Sept. 15th: 'Harry White is here, I often see him. We have been paraded to-day to see one of our chaps presented with a Military Medal for carrying a man in from the German wire, who was wounded whilst patrolling. I have been on patrol in front several times but my nerves are not very good, they have not been right since July 1st, we had a terrible time then. Whilst a Rugby football match was in progress last night, at the back of the lines, one of our planes fetched an enemy observation balloon down, it burst all in flames. Our airmen are a lot superior to the enemy's, they go about in dozens and very often we see from twenty-five to thirty all together going over their lines, but I have not seen one hit. When Fritz's solitary plane comes over it is like a speck in the sky. Ours often loop the loop above their lines, Fritz does not like it, he doesn't half rattle away with his machine guns. We seldom have a Chaplain long, but they all seem nice fellows. Hoping you are "in the pink" as I am at present, &c.'

PTE K. DUNCAN writes from Malta, where he has been in a convalescent camp, recovering from malaria, on Sept. 11th: 'Walter Ray and Arthur Smith are here with me. Walter and I go for a bathe every morning at 5, the sea is very calm. I do not expect to stay here much longer, as a draft is being prepared for the active service camp. Fellows are still coming away from Salonika in large quantities, through sickness. Another disease has broken out there, according to rumours in camp, but I can quite believe it, as disease is written in all the inhabitants' faces. Every one puts it down to the late Balkan War, as bodies were buried no distance in the ground. Also the Greek method of doing away with dead cattle is very dirty, as whenever an animal died they would skin it and leave it ... Went to Holy Communion and night service yesterday, very nice indeed.'

---

[1] Humphrey Scott Ram, St John's College, Manitoba; deacon 1910, priest 1911 Rupertsland; assistant curate of Melita, Manitoba 1910–11; rector 1911–13; TCF 1914–19; perm. offic. St Pancras, London 1913–14 and 1919–21; rector, St Michael's and All Angels, Winnipeg 1921–6; chaplain S. Afr. Ch. Rwy Miss., dio. S. Rhod. 1926–30; vicar of St Pietersburg 1930–1; rector of Lydenburg 1931–3; St Boniface, Germiston 1933–41; Parkview 1941–5; vicar of Wookey 1946–8; L. to Offic., dio. St Jo. Kaffr, 1948; curate of Hermanus, dio. Capetown 1949–50; p. in c. Hout Bay 1950–4; L. to offic., dio. Capetown 1954–8, dio. Natal 1958–68.

NOVEMBER 1916

1–20 October: Renewed Allied offensive; British forces attack Ancre Heights and Transloy Ridges, Somme.

Our Soldiers

To the list of wounded we must add the name of 2ND LIEUT. GORDON HARDY, whose arm was injured by shrapnel during the 'push' on the Somme. He is in hospital in London, and doing well. There is still no news of the missing lads, W. Foy and H. Lambton. The others who have been sick or wounded are doing well. We regret to learn that LIEUT. A.H. BEWLEY is now sick in a London hospital [Royal Free]—we wish him a speedy recovery. Writing to his friends from France on Oct. 11th, he says:

'Well, I have just endured six days of what has been described as "hell on earth".' I have got through safe and sound, and without a scratch, but it is only by God's protection, and I am very grateful. I think I told you that we were occupying trenches taken from the Germans a week or two back, and my Company started in the reserve line. After two days my platoon was ordered to reinforce the front line, and we were in until the day before we came out to billets (about sixty hours). We don't talk about days or nights here, they are all one. During that time I went through more war than you see in other parts of the front in a month or months. When we went in there were German dead lying about some half buried in the trenches and the dug-outs: well, when passing some I had to hold my nose and smoke furiously. I don't know if you have heard of a "barrage" but it is a heavy shelling (a regular hail of shells) on the line, generally followed by an attack and in those sixty hours I think we endured four. I am glad to say my platoon didn't suffer so badly as some (1 killed and 3 wounded). The poor fellow who was killed got a burst of shrapnel in front of him, several pieces entering his face and chest. He died in three minutes. Another was blown off the fire step, wounded in both legs. I replaced him with another man who shortly afterwards was blown down the dug-out behind him, but escaped without a scratch. Another of my men had a shell burst in front of him which exploded a bomb practically under his nose. It smashed his rifle to smithereens, and blew him to the bottom of the trench, but didn't injure him beyond a shaking. I could tell of other things but won't harrow your feelings too much ...

'I stood all the terrible sights without a shudder. There seems to be a special strength given to us in these awful scenes ... Owing to difficulties in getting supplies up we have been living on bully beef and biscuits. Water was at a premium, and we had to do without any for several hours at a time because it couldn't be got up, and the poor chaps were offering each other 5 francs for a sip from the bottle ...

'Our people did a bombing push on the left and gave the Boches "gippo", and a half-an-hour after we had the pleasure of seeing one of our officers leading a string of eleven prisoners down to Battalion Head Quarters ... Our chaps were marvels, and to see lads (mere boys) and older men stand up to a regular hail of all the shell the Huns could think of was a sight to see—joking all the time. Then stretcher bearers and runners with messages getting buried by shells and getting up again and "carrying on". Fritz is absolutely whacked, he can't beat the British spirit ... I don't know how long we are out for, but despite all the horrors I shall be ready again when the time comes ... Some people say that going over the top is the worst event in fighting, but our chaps who went over some weeks back say that the last four days beat it hollow.

'I wish you could see us now. Everyone as happy as school lads just out of school. We are in a hut. Two tables set with good things. Candles stuck in jam pots, gramophone going, singing, shouting, dancing—it takes me all my time to write this for the noise ... I would not have missed my chance to do my "bit" for anything, and am looking forward to the next "strafe".'

CAPTAIN OWEN PARRY-JONES was killed by shell explosion early last month in France. He was admired by his brother officers and all who knew him, and we but express the feeling of our readers when we say how deeply we sympathise with his relatives and friends. RIP.

Of 2ND LIEUT. BERNARD V.R. DOWNMAN who was killed on Sept. 21st, his Captain writes that 'he had retired to the dug-out to read in the front trenches in the evening, when a shell burst amongst a party of men, and Downman was found lying dead, his Bible by his side, his face quite peaceful, showing that death was instantaneous. He was always willing for the most dangerous work, and quite happy through it all too.'

A Memorial Service for these officers and other soldiers connected with St Michael's was held on Oct. 16th, at 3.15 p.m., Mr Hackforth and Canon Massey conducting the service.

> 'When our day of work is ended,
> When by death we leave this life,
> May we meet with arms extended

> Him for Whom we fought in strife,
> Sacrificing earthly joy and earthly life.'

B.V.R.D., Dec. 1912

An interesting Photograph

In the *Daily Graphic* for Nov. 2nd, there is to be seen a picture in the centre of the paper of a group of 10 brothers and sisters on War Service at home and abroad. They are the 7 sons and 3 daughters of Mrs Bewley. Truly a splendid family record.

DECEMBER 1916

12–18 November: Last Allied offensive in Battle of the Somme begins. The key objective of the 51st Highland Division is Beaumont Hamel.

Our Soldiers

With deep regret we have to record the death of one of our Choirmen in France on Nov. 13th, PTE A.W. DUNCAN. He was in the 6th Seaforth Highlanders and enlisted in 1915. In the last letter the Vicar received from him, early in Nov., he wrote: 'During our last spell in the line conditions, owing to bad weather, were most trying. Gum boots were issued as the water was up to our knees in one part—that was when the kilt had to be held out of the water. I did not "kid myself" I was wading at the seaside, as the mud had a tendency to hold my trench waders. Over many such incidents at night time we had some great laughs. ... Pleased to say we are now resting in a village some distance from the line. This morning a celebration of the Holy Communion was held in a barn near our billet: this was the first opportunity we have had during eight weeks to attend Holy Communion. The padre in charge had erected quite a nice altar, and the service was much appreciated by those present.' The captain commanding 'A' Company wrote to Archie's parents saying: 'It is with the deepest regret that I write to inform you that your son was killed in action on 13th Nov. He took part in the advance of which you must have heard in all the papers, and though it will be a source of pride to you to know that he fell in "a successful action", I know only too well the sorrow that will fall on your home by his loss. He was a most excellent soldier and proved invaluable to the officers of the company by his capabilities as a draughtsman. Will you please accept my warmest sympathy, and that of the other officers and men of his company.' R.I.P.

LIEUT. A. H. BEWLEY is, we are sorry to know, still sick and remains in England. PTE LAWRENCE ABELL, wounded on July 1st, has been discharged, but he is feeling better, though his arm is almost useless at present. LIEUT. GORDON HARDY is at home for a time and going on satisfactorily. SERGT WILL WHITEHEAD, a former Choir boy, is reported missing, but from present information his friends fear that he was killed in a recent attack on the Somme. It is also believed that the two missing privates, W. Foy and H. Lambton have been killed in France. PTE E. LLOYD has been badly wounded, and PTE ARTHUR FOSTER who, was wounded some weeks ago and is in hospital at Manchester, after a very trying time, is now making progress towards recovery—he writes cheerfully. One of our Sunday School teachers, PTE W.H. WALKERDINE, has been seriously wounded recently in one of the advances on the Somme; when last we heard he was at the base in France, but probably he is now in England. PTE FRED BROOKS is better and has returned to his regiment. PTE H. COULSON returned to France six weeks ago, but is in another regiment (6th Northumberland Fusiliers). In a letter dated Nov. 18th, he says: 'the weather is getting beastly cold now, and the rain and mud in the trenches make matters anything but pleasant. I was buried twice in one day, having a narrow escape from a shell.'

In a letter from SERGT TOM LONGDON received early in Nov., he wrote: 'I started back on Oct. 19th, and chased my Brigade all round the country in a cattle truck until the 22nd. The next day we went into action for the third time in the "great push". Things are much worse this time; we are up to the eyes in mud and water, on ground that is all shell holes. It rains every day, and the dug-out that I have got leaks somewhat. I had a shower bath in bed last night after a heavy downpour. I have never been in such a state in all my life—I am one mass of mud—all my things are wet more or less, and hot food is out of the question. The rain puts everything out. I cannot help but laugh at times when a dug-out collapses on a fellow, it's a very funny picture I can assure you. I have seen several of these wonderful new war machines, and I have been inside one, they are proper "knock outs" ... We have done well to-day, the weather is a bit better, and I should be able to get warm for a few hours, with luck.'

We give these extracts to help our readers to realise something of what our boys have to suffer, not only from the danger from shells, etc., but also from the many discomforts and miseries of the trenches, and yet, in spite of all, they are so splendidly cheerful. They are truly wonderful. God bless them!

JANUARY 1917

13 December 1916–27 February 1917: British offensive, Kut, Mesopotamia.
21 December: British forces occupy El Arish, Palestine.

Our Soldiers

There is not much to report of our sick and wounded soldiers except that all are going on well. PTE WILFRED BURROWS who was wounded some time ago has now been discharged, and has returned to his former employment.

PTE W. H. WALKERDINE is now in hospital at Edmonton, and on Dec. 10th wrote as follows: 'I was exceedingly lucky during the advance on Nov. 13th, having been shot through the left thigh, the bullet went in just ½ in. from the artery. Had it penetrated the artery, the doctors say they could not have done anything for me ... Well, Vicar, I will just give you a brief description of my experience in "going over the top". We marched on the Sunday evening (Nov. 12th) a distance of seven miles to the lines. We were put into shell holes in the rear of the first two lines, being the fourth wave over, and having to take the fourth line and stand the counter attacks. The first shell hole was a Jack Johnson and the bombers were put into that, six of us and a corporal. There we stayed all night, Fritz putting them over occasionally just to let us know they were still there; needless to say our guns, hundreds of them, sent a few over telling Fritz the boys would pay them a visit in the morning. But as the night before an attack it was unusually quiet. We made the best of things and anxiously waiting for 5.45 a.m., wondering to ourselves who would come out of it all right.

'Many a prayer went up from the shell holes that night. Fellows who had hitherto been careless now realised what Christ meant to them. At last 5.45 a.m. came; over we went, guns roaring, lights going up, machine guns all about us—still you went on like one dazed. The noise was terrible. After we had gone some two hundred yards we had to stop about 30 minutes till they had taken the second and third lines. It was then one felt so helpless—bullets flying about and you lying flat not being able to fire. The mist was heavy, and it made the whole thing very trying. After the 30 minutes were up, we again pushed on for we must take Beaumont Hamel. Well, just as we were among the Huns' barbed wire, or what remained of it, I got hit by a bullet through my left thigh, so I tumbled into a shell hole, just to pull myself together to enable me to get back—no easy job what with shrapnel and large shells still flying. I was lucky, but the sights I saw—men horribly smashed, dying and dead. I hope, Vicar, never to see another sight like it. At last I reached the field dressing station and had to lie in the open all day Monday until Tuesday morning, when the German prisoners came and took us down to the ambulance, and from there to the hospital. What a relief to be out of danger! Now the whole thing seems like a dream. I hear ARCHIE DUNCAN lost his life in that push.'

We have heard nothing further of Archie, excepting that he is buried in the cemetery near the place where he fell. Lieut. Wragg, our Choir-master, writes of him in a recent letter: 'My thoughts go back to some splendid services we have had at old St Michael's, which reminds me of Archie Duncan, the best boy I ever trained. I shall never forget the tone of his voice, and can hear it now. His singing of the "Sanctus" in Gounod's Messe Solemnelle was a great feast to me. I believe he lived a clean life, and am sure he died a noble death.'

FEBRUARY 1917

January: The Western Front—stalemate.

Our Soldiers

We regret to record that two of our lads have fallen recently, one, PTE WILLIAM SARSFIELD, who was killed in December and PTE WILLIAM GOODCHILD, who died a few days ago. We have not heard any definite particulars yet. 'May they rest in peace.'

For the second time TROOPER KARL DUNCAN has been sent into Hospital at Malta from Salonika, suffering from malaria. In a letter dated Jan. 10th, he says: 'the Maltese ladies are very kind, as every Tommy coming off the Hospital boat, receives cigarettes, matches and a drink of cocoa. I am exceedingly well at present.'

We fear that the parcels sent out to the lads in Salonika, to reach them in the New Year, have been lost in transit, as, though the Vicar has had letters dated the middle of January, no mention is made of the receipt of parcels. Those which were sent to France and Ireland reached their destination in many instances.

SERGEANT T. BEWLEY, who had been on leave, writes from France on Jan. 10th: 'I was surprised when I arrived back to find your Christmas parcel waiting for me. I thank you very much indeed, as it is a fine parcel and the contents are very acceptable, the card I shall put with the rest of my souvenirs ... I enjoyed the services at St Michael's very much on Sunday, especially as it was the first Church I had been in for the past seventeen months.'

PRIVATE W. GOODCHILD, recently reported dead, wrote on Jan. 7th: 'I received the parcel safely and I thank you and all who helped to provide it. Well, I am getting along very nicely just now, but we are having such a wet time, it is up to the knees in mud and water in the trenches, and it is *mud*, I can tell you. If you stop for a second you get fast, and several times chaps have had to be pulled out, therefore leave their gum boots behind and then there *is* a mess. But still we keep trudging on merry and bright paddling about in it as if we were at the sea-side.'

PTE FRED FLETCHER, in a letter dated Dec. 31st, says: 'Thanks very much indeed for the lovely parcel. It was such a nice useful one. It is very cold out here now and the warm scarf will be very useful.'

SERGEANT TOM LONGDON wrote on Jan. 7th: 'Thanks very much indeed for the nice parcel which I received yesterday. The contents were intact, and at the present minute I am enjoying the toffee ... We kept up Xmas and the New Year and had a real good time. It reminded me very much of the old choir treat, only it was a little more rough and ready. Every man attending either waited, carved or collected the dirty plates and washed them for the next course, you see, we only had one plate each and we usually carry on, but being a special feast we had them washed. We had a nice little sing song till 10.30 p.m. We have to keep strict hours in the Army.'

We are glad to know all the sick and wounded are progressing satisfactorily.

A/B J. MIDGLEY wrote from France on Jan. 8th: 'Just a line to thank you very much for the welcome parcel, I am very pleased with the socks and scarf ... I was pleased to see your photo on the card and the verse about packing up our troubles in the old kit-bag. We do pack up a lot of them. But never mind, I can stand it and wait for peace.'

DRIVER JAMES AULT also wrote from Salonika in the New Year: 'I am now to be discharged from this Hospital Camp, where I have been

undergoing treatment for a disease contracted on board ship coming over here ... The Chaplain of this camp arranged two very nice services for us last Sunday, Holy Communion at half-past six and there was another little service at eleven o'clock. He is Chaplain to two Hospital Camps near here and he seems to be very hard worked. I should like to have been at home for the Christmas service in the old Church. Every day will be the same now. It has been a very dreary time in this camp for being isolated we were not allowed in the Y.M.C.A. Hut or any other place where men are, and we could get no books to read. We do not see much of the Greeks, but by what we do see they seem to have some very funny ways. We see a great deal of the Russian and French troops, and very nice fellows they are too ... Though very hilly and rough this is a nice country out here and we are having some very hot weather now.'
SAPPER L. HALLSWORTH has been home on leave for a few days and was on January 20th married to Miss Daisy Hughes at St Michael's. We wish them every happiness.

MARCH 1917

21 February–31 March: German tactical withdrawal to Hindenburg Line between Arras and Soissons: Operation Alberich. Mesopotamia: Turkish forces retreat.

Our Soldiers

We stated in our last month's issue that we feared that the New Year's parcels sent to the lads in Salonika had not reached their destination, but happily this is not the case, for the Vicar has received many letters thanking St Michael's for them, and often quoting with approval the lines on the card enclosed in each parcel:

DON'T WORRY

'What's the use of worrying?
It never was worth while!
Pack up your troubles in your old kit-bag
And Smile, Smile, Smile!'

The Vicar has a few copies of the New Year's card left and will be pleased to give them to applicants.

SAPPER S. WHITAKER writes from Salonika, Feb. 2nd: 'Just a few lines to thank you very, very much indeed for the lovely parcel which you so kindly sent, and which reached me on Jan. 29th. It is such a long time since I wrote that you must begin to think I had forgotten you, but I assure you such is not the case. I very often think about you all, especially on Sundays when we are in Church. It is surprising the many various places which have been converted into places of worship. Of course one cannot get to Church every Sunday, as our work often takes us where it is impossible to attend the Services, and we have to take what opportunities are offered us, which you may depend we do as often as possible. The weather here is very changeable—at Christmas quite warm and sunny, while a few days afterwards it was very cold—and this last day or two it has been awfully wet and cold, and up to the boot tops in mud and water, in places knee deep. In spite of all this the boys manage to keep fit and well and a smiling face. Although very often wet through to the skin we are happy enough, and always have a song to keep our spirits up.'

SERGT C.A. COTTON writes from Salonika, Jan. 30th: 'I wish to thank you for the parcel and greetings you and your friends sent to me. I received the parcel quite safe and sound on Jan. 28th, and everything was in perfect condition. We are having some terrible weather; last night it was blowing a hurricane, raining hard, and freezing at the same time, and to make matters worse our guide ropes of the tent broke down and the tent collapsed at two in the morning, so you can imagine what a jolly time we had. But we got up next morning not much worse for our adventure. It was hard at the time "to put our troubles in our kit bag and smile" I can assure you. I hope to see you some time this year.'

TROOPER ERIC HARDY, who has been on leave in England in the New Year, also writes from Salonika: 'I have arrived back at my regiment quite safe and sound about a week ago. Today I have received the St Michael's parcel, so I conclude I arrived before it and so have got it after all—for which many thanks. The candle was specially welcome, as we are generally short of them. I have arrived amid snow and ice so it is rather damp underfoot, but as you say "Pack up your troubles in your old kit-bag", it does not worry us much.'

PTE H. COULSON sent a letter early in February from France. He says: 'Your parcel has never reached me, I am very sorry to say. I am writing this in a Church Army Hut that has just been erected, and where our Chaplain is always present in the evening. All the lads speak well of him and say what a grand man he is, and I believe it too. I went to

Communion on Christmas Day. We were in billets then. It was held in a barn of two compartments, in build and style very similar, I should say, to the one where the Christ Child was born. We were so packed that there was no room to kneel down. We stayed in the one part of the barn for the first part of the service amongst the forms and tables, etc., then approached the Presence in the inner room. A board across two trestles for an altar, covered with a clean white cloth, two ordinary candles burning, the priest, wearing his cassock and clean surplice over his uniform, and in a semi-circle round officers and men received once more the precious Body and Blood of our dear Lord. It was a Celebration I shall never forget.' He writes again on Feb. 20th: 'We have recently done a fairly long march, and we have spent a few days in some old trenches some distance behind the present front line. I lived with several chums in a German dug-out about 30 feet below ground. We were quite warm and comfortable. I am at present away from the Battalion for a short time on another signalling course. There are twenty of us living very "comfy" in a decent sized dug-out in a village that has been shelled pretty well at one time. In fact now, at night time, a shell or two will whistle over the top. They just whistle as they pass our door to let us know they are there.'

We congratulate SERGEANT J.C. HILL on his promotion to be Company Sergeant Major Instructor since he returned from England after being on leave. He is in France.

The wounded are making progress.

Our Roll of Honour

As we have not published a Roll for many months, and there have been several changes, we now give a list of the names which is as accurate as we can make it.

Names of Men from this Church on Active Service

IN FRANCE

Henry Ashby	Gordon Hunt
George Bewley	George Hutley
Sergt Theodore Bewley	Sergt Tom Longdon
George Bishop	James Mawson
Frank Browne	James Midgeley

Archie Buck
Joseph Cocker
Arthur Collard
Harry Coulson
Tom Duffy
Ben Edwards
Thomas Everington
Fred Fletcher
Caleb Fletcher
Laurence Hallsworth
Sergt-Major James Hill
Bert Harrison

Leslie Norton
John Patrick
Arthur Rose
Albert Smith
2nd Lt Kenneth Stiven
Ben Robshaw
Cyril Robinson
Harold Sharp
John Whitaker
George Wheatcroft
Walter Lloyd
Harry White

IN SALONIKA

James Ault
Oscar Bewley
Sergt Henry E. Cox
Sergt E. Cotton
William Cross
Karl V. Duncan

Arthur Garton
Eric Hardy
Harry Jackson
Walter Ray
Arthur Smith
Sam Whitaker

EGPYPT

Fred Leeson

INDIA

Harold Innocent
Corpl Evan Thomas

Benjamin Fox
Ralph Cholerton

SAILORS

George Lambton
John Hughes

Reginald Plant
Reginald Thompson

IN GREAT BRITAIN

Frederick Allsopp
Sergt Arthur Baker
2nd Lieut. Robert Barker
Sergt Frank Bewley
Corpl Cecil Bewley
Fred Brookes
Sergt F. Bates
L-Cpl Wm R. Burrows
Harry Butler
Ferdinand Butler
Arthur Clark
Harry Cocker
Sergt H. Curzon
2nd Lieut. A. Dean
Frank Fox
Corpl G.J. Gleeson
Corpl Greenlay
Frederick Hallsworth
Arthur Jones
John T. Lander

Sergt George Merry
Frank Leighton
William Plant
Sergt A. Powell
Harold Smith
Tom Walker
Richard Whitehurst
Lieut. T.A. Wragg
Fred Wright
Herbert Jessop
Capt. Harry Warburton
Frank Norton
Frank Stone
Joseph Lowe
George Bridgett
Fred Dowler
Robert Walker
Arthur G. Timson
Fred Cox
Cuthbert Frith

Fred Mart

PRISONER OF WAR

2nd Lieut. Theodore Downman

WOUNDED OR SICK

John Baker
2nd Lieut. A.W.H. Bewley
2nd Lieut. Gordon Hardy

Arthur Foster
W.H. Walkerdine
Capt. E. Parry-Jones

DISCHARGED WOUNDED

Laurence Abell
Wilfred Burrows

William Brown
Peter Hudson

Alfred Hewitt   Harry Jackson
Arthur Roe   Sergt Henry Eyre
Tom Woolley

DEPARTED THIS LIFE

Sergt William Fetterplace   2nd Lt. B. Downman
Tom Weston   Capt. O. Parry-Jones
George King   William Foy
Arthur Smith   Archie Duncan
Joseph Bewley   Henry Lambton
Herbert Lowe   William Whitehead
Harry Lowe   William Sarsfield
Archibald Elvidge   William Goodchild
Norman Powell

It is possible there may be some omissions and inaccuracies—the Vicar will be pleased to put these right.

APRIL 1917

March: British successes in Mesopotamia; set-backs in Palestine; Allied Lake Prespa offensive from Salonika. 17–18 March: Western Front: British forces take Bapaume and Péronne, Western Front.

Our Soldiers

We have, with much regret, to record the death of another of our soldiers, PRIVATE W. HORTON who was badly wounded in the 'big push' now going on and, after a few days, died at the clearing station. He was a devoted father and leaves a wife and two young children to mourn his loss. We deeply sympathise with them and for him pray that eternal rest and perfect joy may be his. We have also heard that 2nd LIEUT. KENNETH STIVEN has been seriously wounded, apparently by accident. He still lies at a clearing station in a French town, and is, we are glad to know, going on satisfactorily. CORPORAL W. GREENLAY

has just been removed from France, after a very short stay, to Birkenhead. He gives the reason in a letter written from Etaples,[1] France, on
March 19th: 'You will no doubt be surprised to see that I am in Hospital
so soon, and I am "crocked" for walking for a time. I have had my knee
put out again and I am afraid I have played my last game of football
unless I get operated upon and something removed, and then it will be
weak for some time. All the boys that I came out with are up the line
now looking for Fritz and his little party, perhaps making him break
sprint records, for it's just about time they were running.'

SERGEANT TOM LONGDON writes a very cheerful letter dated
March 18th: 'I am afraid it would be too long a letter if I included all
the events since I wrote to you last, so I will summarise them. First of
all, we have been in the line for 7 weeks in the same old district, and
have just come out for a rest. We had one or two exciting times up the
line and Fritz nearly sniped me with a 59[2] one day. We were living in
dug-outs during the very cold spell. You ask why I have changed my
number. I have also changed my Regiment. I have been transferred to the
A.S.C.[3] as Chief Clerk to the Brigade and I am looking forward to a
change of rank. The Staff put me in command of the Office. I have five
clerks under me and I am responsible for the work and discipline of the
Office. Considering that I was only 20 on the 15th of this month, not so
bad.'

MAY 1917

9 April: Allied Nivelle offensive begins.
British forces attack at Arras (to 17 May).
16 April: Second battle of the Aisne (to 20 April)
18–19 April: British forces repulsed by Turkish and
German forces in the Second Battle of Gaza.

---

[1] Étaples was to become the largest base camp in France. The hospital was possibly
No. 24 General Hospital where Vera Brittain served as a nurse.

[2] This refers to a 5.9 cm shell; see *The 5th Battalion, The Sherwood Foresters. War
History 1914–1918* (Derby, Bemrose, 1930), p. 74, which refers to a bombardment of '5.9'.

[3] Army Service Corps.

Our Soldiers

Another of our lads have been killed, on April 4th, in France—CORPL HARRY COCKER, only 22 years of age. R.I.P. We are thankful to know that those recently wounded are making good progress towards convalescence. Since our last issue we have to add the names of Ptes Richard Sharp, John H. Turton, William J. Nix, and Reginald Marshall to our Roll.

SERGT A. POWELL, R.A.M.C. has recently gone to France, and writes on Easter Day:[1] 'We've had a rough time, but have been very fortunate and pulled through the worst kind of danger. We have been out about 2 months now, and were in action a week before the Division came up. We were moved up to the firing line straight away as soon as we landed. We followed the advance right up all the way. You can practically guess where we are by the newspapers. Our Division has suffered pretty well. The Notts. and Derbys. have caught it very hot this last week. We have had the worst kind of weather all along—very discouraging and depressing for advancing. But to-day (Easter Sunday) it has been a lovely day with a brilliant hot sun. It seemed like providence, although it is no different from any other day, except to those who have been good Churchmen in civilian life. We get no services up the line. We are coming out of the trenches in a day or two. As a matter of fact we left our last line of trenches weeks ago. What we've got now are what we have hastily dug up, but it is mostly open fighting now, we use anything for shelter ... We have been highly praised for our valuable work in the field.'

PTE H. COULSON writes from France early in April: 'I visited a village Church this weekend, one of the finest I have ever seen. The oldest part of it, the tower, must have been built about the transition period of our Church architecture from Norman to early English (about 13th century). The walls were covered with framed coloured prints ... What was most interesting to us was a framed picture, hanging on one of the pillars of the "Great Sacrifice" and round the picture the names and numbers of British Soldiers buried in the cemetery near by. A shelf under the picture carried two vases of flowers, which are kept filled with fresh flowers, and over all is a British flag. A fine tribute surely to our fallen heroes.'

---

[1] 8 April 1917.

JUNE 1917

3–5 May: British forces attack Hindenberg Line at Arras.

Our Soldiers

We much regret to have to add another name to our list of departed heroes, viz., PTE GEORGE WHEATCROFT, who was killed early in May,[1] in the great battle then going on in France. He was one of our Sunday Scholars and a member of the Football Team. So far as we can learn the wounded are going on satisfactorily. During last month the Vicar received several letters from our lads at the front. There is not much of public interest in them—the Censor is very strict—but we give a few extracts. PTE KARL V. DUNCAN, who is at present in St Andrew's Hospital, Malta, wrote: 'Yesterday was my outing with Dr Helen Greene (who is at St Paul's Hospital, Malta), an outing which I shall always remember as one of the most pleasant in the island. Calling for me at 3 o'clock, with a pony and trap, we commenced our excursion. There was another fellow with us, a Manchester boy who was wounded in Salonika. The conversation was chiefly about Derby, and St Paul's Bay appeared a very short distance, though it must be six or seven miles. We went to the British Red Cross Tea Rooms for tea, and were joined by another lady Doctor who was very jolly. After resting we started again, Dr Helen driving, and I arrived back at 7.45 p.m., seeing more of Malta during the afternoon than in the rest of my long stay here.'

From PTE JACK WHITAKER, a stretcher bearer, writing from France, says: 'The Germans have been keeping us very busy just lately, but sometimes we do not have a shot fired at us ... It is a great consolation to know that the friends at St Michael's are always remembering us in their prayers, for our task is very severe. We have got one of the finest Chaplains out here, and he has been very kind to me, and also a great help. But he is not like the dear old Vicar who taught us. I know no one will ever take your place in the boys' hearts ... We are all looking forward to peace this summer.'

Jack's brother, SAPPER SAM WHITAKER, writes from Salonika: 'While we are in this country we have two Easters. I dare say that sounds odd to you, but it happens like this—the English Easter this year

---

[1] In fact on 23 April 1917.

came on April 8th, or the 98th day of the year, which, on the Greek Almanac is only March 27th or the 86th day of the year, which brings them 13 days behind us, so their Easter came on April 22nd. Of course Good Friday happens the same. I may say, it is a sight well worth seeing to see the processions going to and from the various Churches, especially at night when all of them in the processions carry lighted candles.'

PTE FRED MART writes on May 20th from France: 'We are having grand weather. It is a shame this war is on at such a time; it is a treat to hear the birds singing; the firing, and shells don't bother them, they carry on just the same as usual.'

JULY 1917

7–14 June: Battle of Messines, Flanders.

Our Soldiers

We are glad to know that the wounded are going on satisfactorily. Several have been in Derby lately, including LIEUT K. STIVEN, LIEUT A.E. DEAN, and PTE W.H. WALKERDINE, SERGT T. LONGDON has also been on leave, and GUNNER JOS. COCKER from France. We regret to record the news that SERGT OLLERENSHAW, whose children attend our Sunday School, has been wounded early in June. The Chaplain writes on June 18th, B.E.F., France: 'He is doing quite satisfactorily, his wounds are clearing up very nicely, and are now dressed entirely once a day instead of twice, and although he has a good deal of pain he is very patient. He eats well. I am very glad to send this reassuring report. He is a fine type of man and we know each other well.'

The letters from the front become, one thinks, less interesting, because the Censor is just now very strict. CYRIL ROBINSON, who is now a wireless operator attached to the Royal Flying Corps in France, has written recently: 'I am pleased to tell you that we have a very good Chaplain at the Head-quarters. I believe he is well liked by everyone. I go every Sunday morning to the Holy Eucharist at 7.30 a.m., but unfortunately I'm generally the only one present. I cannot understand it. There is, I believe, always a good attendance at the evening service, although I am not able to go myself ... I am sorry the Sunday School Children had to miss their treat this year, but I suppose it was stopped by the Food Controller's Order ... I'll be very glad for you to publish in the Magazine any news contained in my letters. I think the question will be as to whether I've anything interesting to give you, for it seems that the only excitement and interest I have got is sitting in my little wooden hut, taking messages by wireless. I expect to have heaps to do soon, as I shall be continually at it from 4 a.m. to 9.30 p.m. Of course you will understand the difficulties, with a rigorous censorship, of relating all we would like. I hope everything goes well in the Sunday School, and that a good attendance of Scholars is the rule now-a-days. I often wish for a peaceful and happy Sunday afternoon at St Michael's.'

Sherwood Foresters, Prisoners of War

The Vicar sent 6 guineas to the Committee for providing parcels for soldiers who are prisoners of war in Germany. The money represents the amount which would have been expended in [Sunday School] prizes for 1916. The prize winners gladly gave them up for the sake of our men who are in captivity. The following is the letter from the Hon. Secretary to the Committee acknowledging the receipt of the cheque.

Office: PARK STREET, DERBY
9/6/17

'We are very grateful to the children, and think it is very good indeed of them to give up their prizes to help the Prisoners of War. We are using the money for the benefit of Pte Elsmore. We shall send him three food parcels each month at 7/- each during the next six months. The enclosed lists are of the contents of some of our parcels, and they are varied each time. The address of Pte Elsmore is as follows: 10124, Pte E. Elsmore, 2nd Batt., Sherwood Foresters, Soltau, 3009, Hanover, Germany, and if any of the children are able to write to him we feel sure he would appreciate a letter. His mother is Mrs Glover, 71, Yates Street, Derby.

Yours faithfully,
Florence Bourne Wheeler,
Hon. Sec.

SPECIMEN LISTS

This Box contains:-   This Box contains:-

Meat Rations   Rabbit
Sausage   Beef Stew
Jam   Vegetables
Biscuits   Tea
Fish   Milk
Vegetables   Biscuits
Tea   Margarine
Milk   Pudding
Margarine   Cigarettes
Cigarettes

AUGUST 1917

31 July–6 November: Third Battle of Ypres
(known as Passchendaele).

Our Soldiers

LIEUT. T.A. WRAGG has, after long delay, at last set sail for some-where in the East.

PRIVATE ARTHUR FOSTER, who was wounded some months ago, has received his discharge. Our other wounded soldiers are making good progress. We have received many letters during the past month and here are some extracts.

PRIVATE KARL V. DUNCAN, who has been in Malta for some months after repeated attacks of malaria, wrote on June 22nd: 'Perhaps by the time this reaches you I may be on my way, to, or landed in the country where I spent my Christmas in 1915,[1] as I expect to go shortly. Though there is nothing official, I think we shall finish where Norman

---

[1] Salonika. Note Karl Duncan's circumlocutions to avoid censorship.

Powell was wounded.[1] I have travelled some miles since leaving Derby, and, if not under pleasant circumstances, I am seeing plenty of life. I am quite well at present and having a jolly time, especially as regards swimming, it reminds me of Margate, for the sea was calm there. The sun is terribly hot and the sea is the only place where one feels comfortable. Every day the other occupants of the tent and myself are to be found larking in the sea. I cannot say, Vicar, how much I appreciate your teaching me how to swim, when I was in the choir. It is a common sight to see big fellows lying on the rocks, unable to go in as they cannot swim.' Sunday, 10.30 a.m: 'Have just come back from Church Parade. The Service was lovely, bringing back happy recollections of St Michael's The singing is very hearty.'

PRIVATE FRED ALLSOP is on his way somewhere out East and wrote from Durban, S. Africa, on June 17th: 'We are in camp here for a few days before going on further. It is a grand place to spend a holiday. I am writing later when I know my address. It is now midwinter and 110 in the sun.'

PRIVATE F.W. BROOKS wrote from Hospital in France, on July 7th: 'I am in Hospital again having been wounded, but not very badly. We were in a trench "somewhere" waiting for a smack at Fritz, when one of his shells hit right on the parapet, wounding three of us. I had only said a minute before that "he would go and hurt someone". Mine is very little however and nothing to worry over, one little bit in the arm and two bits in the head. I am getting on finely and do not suppose I shall be here so very much longer. They soon repair one now. I am in a nice hospital on the coast facing England. No luck for "Blighty" this time ... Our Chaplain is a very nice man indeed, Vicar, he has won the Military Cross once.'

Mr Hudson has recently received two interesting letters from France, the first from SAPPER L. HALLSWORTH, dated July 1st: 'You see by the date that it is just twelve months ago since I spent the most awful day of my life and which I verily believe changed the whole of my future aspect of life. Yes, just 365 days exactly to this minute, now 8.30 p.m., I was wondering still, and had been wondering for the past 20 hours if I should live to see the remaining hours of that day. The past 14 hours or there about I had spent in "No Man's Land" in a small ditch-like trench, most of the occupants of which were dead or wounded and those who were not, including myself, were in imminent risk of

---

[1] Persian Gulf (see March 1916). In fact Duncan remained in Salonika for the remainder of the war.

becoming one or the other. I had waited since 8.0 that morning for dark, so that I could get out of the trench and so get to our men, for to show your head was certain death. Well, it is on occasions like these, when one's thoughts naturally wander to our Maker. I may say that I spent more time in prayer, in fervent and heart-felt prayer, than ever I had done before. Now I believe that I was spared, because I have some special duty to fulfil, but what that duty may be, I have not as yet any idea. Well, I will now "carry on" as the Sergeant says. I am pleased to say I am quite well and keep on smiling. We find it very hard at times, I'll assure you, and there are times when I long to be in dear old "Blighty" again. What a fine country England is. With all due respect for France and the people who inhabit it, from what I have seen of it, and I have been the whole length of the country, from Flanders to the Mediterranean, it is not a patch on England.

Thank you, Mr Hudson, for that very nice parcel ... How are things looking at the dear old class, and how are all the members, very few left now, I expect ... You will be pleased to hear that I managed to go to the Holy Communion this morning, on the first day of July, and my thoughts could not help but go back to that terrible time I was having at that minute 12 months ago. Even as I knelt in that humble Church Army Hut, the guns were booming in one continuous roar their awful message of death. There were nine of us, all told, at the Service and you have no idea how the quietness of the early morning service with the continuous boom of the guns impresses one and fills one with a feeling which I have experienced but yet cannot describe.'

The other letter is from O/S CYRIL ROBINSON, dated July 19th: 'At the time I received your kind letter I was taking my little part in a big "strafe". This meant that I had only 3 or 4 hours each day for sleeping, so that you will realise that it became impossible for me to answer in a proper manner those people who were kind enough to write me ... Unfortunately in writing to my friends I'm placed at a disadvantage, because if I wanted to give any idea as to what part our work plays in an advance, I should be obliged to go into details and this, of course, I'm not allowed to. I wish I were able tell you something about it, as you would then be able to understand what an important part wireless telegraphy is playing in this great conflict. You understand how very overworked I was in my recent position, as, apart from the mental activity involved, my ears were all broken out, and were so very sore that the process of getting the telephones off my ears at the end of the day was an extremely painful experience. I moved to another part of the line on the 8th, and on the 10th I was removed to a Field Ambulance Hospital and two days later I was sent down here in an Ambulance

Train. I am still feeling very ill, although I am a little improved since admission ... of course I am very glad to have come out here as it has proved a very grand experience to have been attached to the Army, and to have been able to get an insight into the very remarkable way in which the war is being conducted on land, but I long for the sea, to which I properly belong. I am now at the Hospital in Boulogne.'

SEPTEMBER 1917

20 August (to 15 December): French offensive regains territory in the Second battle of Verdun. Third Battle of Ypres continues.

Our Soldiers

The Vicar continues to receive many letters from the front, but only extracts from a few can be printed as having interest for others. A letter from TROOPER KARL V. DUNCAN came on August 22nd from Salonika, it took a month to come, in it he says: 'This is my first letter to you since I arrived back in Salonika and it is now well over a month since I had your last letter, my address now is Trooper K.V. Duncan 75677, 1st Derbyshire Yeomanry (Corps of Dragoons), Salonika Forces, Greece ... Our trip from Malta was very exciting and some day I will relate the incidents of the voyage. I am at present at the base, but cannot give you any idea when I shall rejoin the Regiment. All the fellows who were with me at Malta are here in the same tent, so we are jolly company ... The weather here is at present extremely hot, making things uncomfortable during the day and night. There is a big difference between Malta and this place, both in character and customs. I am at present quite well and hope I can remain so, as I am fed up with going in Hospital.'

O/S CYRIL ROBINSON wrote on August 4th: 'I have been in Hospital but am now at No. 12 Convalescent Camp, Boulogne Base. I have had trench fever and neurasthenia. I have now got quite free of the former, but am still very weak and shaky. I'm afraid I shall require a good long rest before I shall have got rid of the neurasthenia. I am fortunate in being at a very nice camp, where I can get a quiet restful time and so perhaps after a few weeks I may get all right again. Prior to going to Hospital I had made a move to another part of the line, where there have been some very big artillery duels, but I had only been there two days, when I was removed to a Field Hospital ... My brother Joe has been very lucky so far in the army. He is in the Royal Garrison Artillery. He was made a Bombr and a Corporal one day and 10 days after was made a Sergeant. He is now in Italy.

PRIVATE F. DOWLER wrote on August 10th, 'In rest billets': 'Though I know your time is pretty well occupied with correspondence from the boys at the Front, I thought perhaps you would be interested to know that I have been in France for the past month and done one turn in the trenches, coming out last Monday night. During my time up the line things were said to be fairly quiet, but the shelling on both sides was pretty consistent, but I think there is no doubt whatsoever that we have a great superiority both in guns and munitions. It is certainly a very trying experience to be under fire for the first time, but one gets more or less used to it in time I suppose. As a member of a Machine Gun Team, I with my team, have to go out night firing, which means that we have to take out the gun after dark into "No man's Land" and strafe Fritz in his trenches, or perhaps fire on a cross road down which he brings his transport, or ration parties. It is interesting, but somewhat dangerous work, as the German is very sharp at picking out the direction of our fire. However in spite of all the dangers and unpleasant experiences generally, I am glad to say that I am in good health and spirits, and like all the fellows out here, simply longing for the day to come when we shall all be travelling homewards again.'

The following extract is from a letter written by the HON. & REV. E. R. LINDSAY,[1] he enlisted as a Private in the R.G.A.[2] and is now a Bombardier, who, when stationed at Derby, attended St Michael's and made friends with the Vicar: Aug. 16/17. 'We are just on our way up the line. Though we all hope the war may be speedily finished, we are going ahead and into it with, I firmly believe, a good conscience. Many of the men grumble a good deal, because they don't like it (as though anyone did!) and because they view the issues of the war only from the point of view of their own back garden instead of it being a matter of the Christian faith and principles. But their grumble is never too deep to prevent their going farthest in the world's work. The Englishman is a remarkable contradiction. He depreciates himself too severely!!'

PRIVATE FRED WRIGHT, R.A.M.C., has been slightly wounded in France and wrote on Aug. 5th: 'With reference to my wound, if it can

---

[1] For details see p. 127.

[2] Royal Garrison Artillery.

be so termed, I can assure you that I am, as the saying goes, "fit as a fiddle". You would like to know how it happened. Well, in brief, two of us had to bring a wounded Tommy down from the line and to our misfortune the road was being shelled, but after a roughish journey, we had well nigh reached our destination, when there was a terrific "Bang"!! and the whole three of us were carried into the air, at the same time I felt a burning sensation in my hip, I can tell you we did not stop to look for souvenirs, but finished our journey all badly shaken up, but nothing serious ... No, I have not seen Sergt. Powell.'

PRIVATE H. ASHBY of the Grenadier Guards is now in Hospital at Leeds. Writing on Aug. 15th, he says: 'I am extremely sorry that I have not written to you for such a long time, but truthfully, I and all have been so fearfully busy preparing for the "big push" that we have had very little sleep during the last 2 months. I am very pleased to say that the work allotted to us was done so thoroughly and well that we were enabled to add another victory to our laurels. You will be grieved to hear that I am now lying in Hospital at Leeds, as the result of a wound received at Ypres. We (I and 19 more men) were on our way up to the trenches to build some bridges across the river[1] over which the troops were to advance. The Germans must certainly have seen us because a shell dropped unfortunately plumb in the centre of our party, and a most fearful explosion followed and as a result every individual was hit, 15 or 16 wounded and the remainder killed. I was badly wounded in the thigh and arm, but am very pleased to say I am going on extremely well and expect to be sent to a Convalescent Home shortly, thence home to Derby for a few days.'

OCTOBER 1917

20 September: Second phase of the British offensive near Ypres begins.

Our Soldiers

During the past month one of our Sunday Scholars, DRIVER JOE COCKER, R.F.A.,[2] has received information that he is to be the

---

[1] Probably the Steenbeek.

[2] Royal Field Artillery.

recipient of a Military Medal. We heartily congratulate him on this reward of merit. The following gives the reason for this award: 'At Bully Grenay[1] on the 13th July, 1917, an enemy high velocity gun started to shell the village close to the wagon lines of B/230 Battery. An esta-minet[2] was hit and four Canadians who were inside at the time were wounded. One of them rushed into the cellar before the house was hit and was consequently buried by the debris. Four drivers of B/230 Battery, assisted by a Bombardier of D/230 Battery, proceeded to extricate the wounded men, the shelling continuing during the operation. An ambulance was fetched, and two of the worst cases were put inside. Just as the ambulance was leaving, another shell burst in the road, hitting the ambulance, and again wounding the wounded men, also injuring the driver and attendant. The ambulance was too badly damaged to be moved, so the drivers proceeded to get the wounded men out of the ambulance and carry them to a place of safety. These men also removed several horses to a place of safety, and had it not been for their prompt action, some horses would have been hit. Driver Cocker was one of the four drivers above named.'

We regret to say that during the past month, several of our men have been injured and are now in Hospitals in England. PTE JIM STEVENS has been gassed, and is now suffering from bronchitis. He writes cheerfully, and says: 'I was in the third battle of Ypres. My word, it was a sight to see our big guns, how they rattled away, I thought the gunners had gone absolutely mad. We had not been bombarding long before we got some prisoners—they said they would not face it. We fire about 5 shells to Fritz's [1]. I am getting on all right.'

PTE HARRY WHITE, wounded in the arm and leg, writes from the War Hospital at Bradford: 'I can assure you I am going on fine—never felt better in all my life—my leg is quite better, and my arm is healed up, but I cannot use it, and I am sadly afraid I never shall. I am expecting to get discharged soon. I got wounded at Lens. I got a bullet through my thigh, and shrapnel through my arm just below the elbow.'

SERGT THEO. BEWLEY, R.A.M.C., has been gassed, but is going on satisfactorily. GUNNER F.R. LEIGHTON was wounded in the arm in one of the recent attacks in Flanders, and is now in Hospital at Leicester and is going on well. TEL. CYRIL ROBINSON is now in a Convalescent Camp on the sea coast. In a letter received about a fortnight ago, he says: 'I was taking a stroll in a neighbouring seaside

---

[1] Approximately eight miles south of Givenchy.

[2] A Belgian cafe.

town one evening last week when I met Mr Staley,[1] who is an Army Chaplain, and is doing duty down in this district. He looks remarkably well. He made numerous enquiries about his old friends at St Michael's.'

GUNNER FRED ALLSOP has reached Mesopotamia and writes, on Aug. 10th: 'It has taken us almost 4 months to reach here. We stayed in India a week, so you will see we have had a good journey ... It is too warm for me here; every breath you take scorches your throat and lungs, and it is necessary for us to wear blue goggles to protect our eyes, and spine pads to keep the heat of the sun from our backs. There is not a brick nor stone here—absolutely nothing but sand and tents.' THE REV. W.R. JOHNSON[2] has reached the Balkans. In a short letter dated Sept. 7th, he says: 'I have arrived here in the Balkan Mountains. At this moment I am sitting in the shade of a rock, in perfect weather, and am writing in a little time off from my work as Mess orderly ... I often think of you all now that I'm in this strange land.' The Vicar has had many other letters, but there is no more space for extracts.

NOVEMBER 1917

12 October: First British assault at Passchendaele, Ypres.
15 October: German forces renew offensive in East Africa.
23 October: French force Germans back to Oise-Aisne canal.

Our Soldiers

We regret to have again to report several casualties amongst the men connected with St Michael's. Mrs Oakley of 3, St Michael's Lane, has received from the officer commanding the R.A.M.C. that her son Charles, aged 19, was killed instantaneously by a bomb on Sept. 25th. R.I.P. One of our communicants, formerly a choir boy, PRIVATE JOHN WHITAKER of the Grenadier Guards was killed when he was on duty as a stretcher bearer, there has been no official communication and there is a bare possibility that he may have escaped, but the Chaplain has written to the Vicar in a letter dated Oct. 27th: 'I fear it is very true about John, though in these battles mysterious things do happen. He was

---

[1] For details see p. 134.
[2] For details see p. 126.

as fearless as ever doing ten men's work, cool and brave as he ever was, a gallant man, a keen Christian, a regular communicant. He was tending cases where sniping and shell fire was very severe. The place where he was working received a direct hit and those inside were killed or wounded I fear. I have no first hand information and those who were with him are not here to tell, and there were many bodies lost in the terrible mud. All I can say is that I feel no doubt as to his death, but I do not know of his body being identified by anyone after being hit ... He is a great loss to me. He helped me in anything I was doing and I had unbounded respect for him and feel I have lost a true friend, those who love him may well reverence his memory and be proud of the way he met his death.' R.I.P.

SECOND LIEUT. PERCY C. NORTON, one of our communicants, has been missing for more than a fortnight. He was in the R.F.C. and with others went out on an offensive patrol over the German lines. He and his comrades fought a gallant fight against heavy odds and that is the last known about him. He was seen to fall, and there is hope that he may prove to be a prisoner in German hands.

LIEUT. HARRY WARBURTON, of the Canadian Forces, a communicant and formerly in the choir, is now in hospital, having been sent from France suffering from shell shock and trench fever. In a letter to the Vicar written on Oct. 17th, he says: 'You will be glad to know I am making good progress although I still have a high temperature, but not quite so high as it was the night I got laid out. My time in France no doubt was very short, but during the time I was over the top three times, in two raids and was only out of trenches three days. The night I had a premature with one of my guns I got blown fifteen feet away and there I lay for one and a half hours in the pouring rain. I certainly was very fortunate in getting off the way I did as the men of the gun crew (four) got their legs blown off. May God bless them. I will never forget them as long as I live. Only ten minutes before the premature, it was on Sunday evening, we were singing that dear old hymn "Fight the good fight".'

L/CORPORAL FRED MART, another of our communicants, is also in hospital at Rochdale. He was wounded in hand and back during the recent severe fighting near Ypres. In a long letter to the Vicar dated Oct. 20th, he tells something of his experiences and we quote some of it because it helps us to realise a little of what our soldiers are undergoing for our sakes. 'I think myself lucky to be alive and can hardly realise that I am in England again. We relieved the Lancs. and Yorks.; the night after we were just ready to advance when the enemy sent some gas shells over. We soon had our helmets on. Then our artillery sent the

Germans a good dose and we set off over ground which was full of shell-holes. We got into some of these while our artillery put a barrage over and as soon as it was dawn we attacked and took all our objects. The Germans made a counter attack in the afternoon, but we were too good for them, very few got back. Their aeroplanes kept on bombing us but we fetched two down. I was busy sniping some Boches when a lump of shrapnel hit me on the hand as I was just loading again. I was just getting in another shell-hole when something like a hundred-weight hit me on the back and some more hit my helmet and knocked me down. I had to stay in the shell-hole all night, shells were coming like rain. I crawled about till I was beat, then I went to sleep. When I woke up it was daylight so I got out and I could see some of our Division and made for them, they took me for a Boche and fired at me, so I crawled a bit farther and shouted then they stopped. Soon after I saw some stretcher bearers taking a man across so I followed them for 2 miles then they just put a ticket on me and told me to go straight on. I went another 2 miles before I got to a casualty clearing station, there they gave me some bully beef and a drink of tea, that was after being without anything for two days. I was glad when they put me in a Red Cross Motor Van and took me to another C.E.S[1] and gave me some dinner and I went under an operation and in due course I arrived in England. I am thankful to say I can get about a little now.'

On Oct. 28th, a letter came from PTE. F.W. BROOKS saying that he was in a Hospital in Cheshire suffering from some dislocation of the right knee, caused by a bad fall in the trenches. We are glad to know that Privates J. Stevens, H. White, and F. Leighton are going on nicely. We have had many interesting letters during the past month, but cannot give more extracts from want of space. We may, however, mention that our Choirmaster, LIEUT. T.A. WRAGG, has written from Salonika on Oct. 6th, where he has come across his late Choir boy, Karl Duncan, who had grown almost beyond recognition, and also Oscar Bewley, who was very well, and happy as usual.

DECEMBER 1917

6 November: British and Canadian forces take Passchendaele Ridge.
7 November: British forces take Gaza.

---

[1] This should probably read C.C.S, i.e. Casualty Clearing Station.

17 November: British take Jaffa.
20–30 November: First major British tank attack, Cambrai.
30 November–7 December: German counter-offensive at Cambrai.

Our Soldiers

We learn, with deep regret, that another of our Choirmen, SERGT ALBERT POWELL, R.A.M.C., has been killed in France. He was the only brother of Norman Powell, who died in Hospital at Cairo, having been wounded in Mesopotamia—'may they rest in peace.'

Sergt Powell was killed on Oct. 22nd. His uncle sent us the news, for his parents died within a few days of each other the last time he was on leave. The following is a copy of the official letter:

'Your nephew was attached for "water duties" to this Battalion, and it was necessary for him and his men to be with the Companies in the line. He was killed instantaneously by a shell while passing along a trench. He made an effort to get under cover, but only reached the entrance to the dug-out. The shell hit the dug-out entrance and killed him, burying him under the debris. His body was taken out that evening and taken down to the Cemetery where he was buried. Sergt Powell was a good soldier and always did his duty well.'

Since our last issue news has reached his friends that 2nd LIEUT. PERCY C. NORTON, who was in the R.F.C., has been made prisoner by the Germans. He had gone out on an offensive patrol and fell in the enemy's lines. We are glad to know that our sick and wounded are going on satisfactorily. LIEUT. GORDON HARDY has returned to duty in Derby. 2ND LIEUT K. STIVEN and PTE H. WHITE have been discharged owing to wounds received in France.

JANUARY 1918

1 December: German forces cleared from German East Africa.

Our Soldiers

Though the Vicar has had very many letters from our lads at home and abroad this Christmas there are none which would be of interest to our readers, except that they will be glad to know how deeply those in

Hospital in England (10/-) and those in training (5/-) appreciate the gifts which were sent them at Christmas. There has not been time to receive letters from those who are in France or elsewhere abroad in response to the gifts sent to reach them early in the New Year. The following letter accompanied the 10/- note, which was sent to each in a registered envelope: 'My dear — , We send you a little present to let you know that you are much in our thoughts at this Season. We think it better than a parcel, which may never reach you. We hope that you may be able to get something which you need. We are longing for the day when you will be back again in the old Town and with old friends. We constantly pray that you may be kept safe in body and soul through all dangers and difficulties, and in God's good time be restored to your home. With best wishes from myself and St Michael's people. I remain your sincere friend, H.R. Rolfe.'

Seventy-three letters and presents have been sent at a cost of £32 10*s*. There are two or three whose addresses are not yet known, and these will be sent to as soon as possible. We reckon that the total amount will reach £34 or £35. Towards this the Vicar has received £30 14*s*. 3*d*.—nearly double the amount raised last year.

We believe that all the sick and wounded in Hospitals are doing well, but WILLIAM GREENLAY has been discharged unfit for active service. We have just heard that GUNNER FRED ALLSOP is in hospital at Baghdad suffering from dysentery, but he is going on well.

FEBRUARY 1918

21 January: German high command issues orders for the 'Kaiserschlacht', the opening of the spring offensive on the Western Front. German forces are massed for the assault.

Our Soldiers

We have to record with deep regret the death of another of our communicants, CORPORAL E.O. THOMAS, which occurred at Forest Hall, Newcastle-upon-Tyne, on Jan. 19th. The cause was gas poisoning in the hut wherein he was sleeping. An inquest was held and the verdict was death from misadventure. The Corporal joined the Army in 1915, and had served in France and India and was expecting his discharge, for he had been invalided home some weeks ago, and spent his Christmas in an

English Hospital. The funeral was on Jan. 28th, at St Michael's. We extend our sincere sympathy to his wife and children. R.I.P.

Those of our lads in Hospitals in England are doing well. Several have been home on leave in the New Year. We have had no further news of GUNNER F. ALLSOP who is still, we believe, in Baghdad. GUNNER F. HALLSWORTH is now in India. The Vicar has received letters from all but one of those in England and France to whom New Year's Gifts were sent. We give a few extracts to show how much they appreciated the present provided by the congregation: 'It is as you say, the money is a great deal better than a parcel.' 'Thanks very much for the cash, I think it was very good of you and the people to send your old boys a gift like that, it came in very handy indeed.' 'I often think of you and now I have your photograph it brings you much closer to me, at present I am hanging it on the wall in my dug-out, but I shall take jolly good care not to leave it there when we move.' 'I thank you, and through you, the people of St Michael's for the present which I received today. I am sure it was a very good choice of yours in sending the note, as many things, which are not included in parcels from "Blighty", are easily obtainable out here—your 10/- is really a parcel of just the things I want.' 'I was very pleased with the 10/- enclosed and as you say, it is far better than sending a parcel, as some of mine have gone astray, which should have arrived before Christmas. We had a merry time this year and far better than I expected. Every thing was A1.' 'I received your kind Registered letter quite safe and I have had one of the finest Christmases in my life and the note was very handy, we clubbed together and bought a few extras and we made a jolly crowd.' 'I am sure it is very kind of you and all to send such an acceptable present, for as you remark a parcel is not sure to reach its destination, and with money we can get a few luxuries.' 'I send many thanks for the present which I shall find very useful when I go down the line, where I can get something which I need, such as soap and other little things. It is a lot better that way than sending parcels which are very likely to get lost or damaged on the way.'

The following extract is from a letter written by the HON. AND REV. E.R. LINDSAY, a private in the R.G.A. now in France: 'Your idea of sending a 10/- note with that nice letter instead of a parcel is excellent. I can quite understand the lads' delight, for 10/- will buy, I should think, more things than you could buy with the same money in Blighty, and you have left it to the lad himself to get just what he fancies. 10/- equals 13 francs 60 cents., and a good plum pudding, as much as two persons can reasonably tackle, costs only two francs at our Canteens, so you doubly benefit them.'

MARCH 1918

21 February: British take Jericho.

Our Soldiers

The Vicar has now received letters from all the lads at home and abroad to whom New Year's gifts were sent, except the two or three in India and Mesopotamia, and he hopes to hear from them before next month's Magazine is due. He is glad to say that all of them received their registered letter safely except one. In France enquiries are being made about it and of course that one will receive it shortly. The men in Macedonia were all much pleased with St Michael's presents—we give two extracts from letters received: SERGEANT E.H. COX: 'Please accept my thanks for the present and I should like the same to be conveyed to all at St Michael's. Sorry I've not written before, but a day or so after it came I met with an accident whilst having a friendly game at football and I'm now in Hospital recovering from a broken collar-bone—makes things rather awkward when one has a "wing up".' SERGEANT C. COTTON: 'I was glad to know that people in dear old England still give a thought to the soldiers away from home. I am pleased to think how sensible you and your co-workers are in sending a "Bradbury" out to me instead of a parcel. I know (having been the postman for our battalion for three years and more) of the unavoidable waste of food stuffs sent out here ... I shall treasure your Photo and always carry it about with me ... I hope to be with you some time this year, I am longing for a service in your dear old Church.'

We are still without news of GUNNER F. ALLSOP who, when last heard of, was in Hospital in Mesopotamia. PRIVATE W.G. SANDER-SON writes from somewhere in Palestine, 'I am pleased to say I am very well and, as you will know from the newspapers, in the region of very important operations. I never thought a few months ago that I should be able to see something of The Holy Land. I cannot say very much, but I will say this, that the people at home don't realise half enough what we owe to our Navy for the safe escorting of Transports.'

DRIVER JOE COCKER is expected home on leave shortly when he will receive the Military Medal which has been awarded him.

In a letter written in December, GUNNER F. HALLSWORTH tells of his experiences in India: 'I have arrived in India quite safe. We left Durban on the 8th, and very sorry to leave it too, and after dropping some troops in German East Africa arrived in Bombay, we entrained at once and started on a 5 days' journey to Nowshera. The accommodation on the train was very good, but the food was worse than it was on the boats and that was bad enough. So, against advice, we bought eatables from the native "Wallahs" on the various stations to relieve our hunger. We passed through Agra, Delhi and Lahore. On arrival at Nowshera we were sent on to Peshawar, a city on the N.W. Frontier. Troops are there to quell any rising of hostile tribes ... We came out here at a lucky time, as winter is just starting and at present during the day it is just like a hot summer's day in "Blighty", but at night and early morning it is very cold. Pleased to say I was able to communicate last Sunday at our Garrison Church here, I enjoyed a nice Choral Celebration, being the first opportunity I had since I left dear old England. I have joined the choir and we have a pleasant morning and evening service in the day. The Chaplain, who holds a Bible Class every Wednesday night, and a very nice class too, has been in India several years ... By the time I get a letter from Derby it will be 4 months since I heard from the dear old home and it seems a lot longer than it is really ... Give my kindest regards to all my friends at St Michael's.'

We have also received a letter from the REV. W.R. JOHNSON, who was in the Balkans then: 'I'm far from Salonique and I never meet any old friends, though I keep an open eye. Our convoy was on the mountain, but is now near a town on the plain. By the way that newspaper paragraph was dreadfully wrong—I'd never tried to enlist in the British Army and now what I'm in is the Red Cross work of a Voluntary Ambulance convoy. My period of service will be up next month.'

APRIL 1918

21 March: German offensive begins the Second Battle of the Somme, the 'Kaiserschlacht' offensive (to 5 April).

Our Soldiers

Ever since the great German attack began, a fortnight ago, we have been fearing to have news of casualties to our own men. So far, one has given his life, PTE W. E. LLOYD, a member of Mr Hudson's Bible Class. He was badly wounded and sent across to a Hospital at Southampton, where he succumbed to his injuries. He is to be buried in Derby and the first part of the funeral service will be at St Michael's. R.I.P. Another soldier, A/B J. MIDGELEY was badly gassed and sent to a Hospital in Kent. In a letter received on Easter Day he says: 'I have been helpless four days. Lost the sight of my eyes, but they are quite all right now. It was caused by gas used by Fritz. I was one of the last to give up hopes of stopping. I am not out of bed yet. But cheero! I say, I am out of it, and just missed being taken prisoner to make roads in Germany. I know very well you will be thinking of us all and I daresay you have written to my old address, "somewhere in France".'

Several of our men are now in England to be trained as officers, including SERGT G. MERRY, SERGT T. LONGDON and CADET F. BROWNE.

On making up the account we find that 77 gifts were sent out to our men for the New Year, all have been received that were sent to France and Salonika, we have not yet heard from the others. The total cost was £34 5s. and the subscriptions amounted to £30 14s. 3d. Mr Hudson has, with his usual generosity, made up the adverse balance of £3 10s. 9d.

MAY 1918

1 April: RAF formed to replace the Royal Flying Corps.
9—29 April: Battle of the Lys.
12 April: Germans take Armentières.
24 April: British victory at Villers Bretonneux.
29 April: Main German offensive on the Western Front ends.
30 April–4 May: British forces attack in Transjordan.

Our Soldiers

We heartily congratulate LIEUT. R. BARKER on his promotion to be Captain and also for having won the M.C. We have had a letter from GUNNER F. ALLSOP who is in Mesopotamia, giving the welcome news that he is now in a Convalescent Camp. Also letters from SERGT H. BAKER and GUNNER F. HALLSWORTH acknowledging with many thanks the gift sent in the New Year from St Michael's. LIEUT. T.A. WRAGG writes cheerfully from Salonika, and is anxious to know how the Choir acquitted itself at Easter. Many letters have also been received during April from our lads in France, RFN REG MARSHALL, BOMBR A. PALMER, SERGT J. BEWLEY, SERGT EVERINGTON,

PTE A.E. BISHOP, DRIVER W. PLANT, SAPPER H. SMITH, etc. We hear that PTE F. DOWLER is recovering from the effects of gas. But we regret to know that nothing has been heard of SERGT G.J. GLEESON for some weeks—his friends are naturally very anxious. TEL. CYRIL ROBINSON has been discharged, suffering from shell shock.

With much sorrow and deep sympathy for his wife and parents we have heard of the death of SIGNALLER HARRY B. COULSON on April 12th. His Officer wrote to his father to tell him that his lad had been struck by a shell and instantly killed. He expressed his deep appreciation of the worth of H.B.C. as a man and a soldier. We shall greatly miss his frequent letters and so will many of his lads to whom he often wrote. We trust they will copy his good example. He was planning all sorts of ways in which to help in the Scout Troop, of which he was Assistant Scout Master, and in the Sunday School where he was a regular and successful teacher. On Sunday, April 28th, at the Choral Eucharist (a service which our friend loved) mention was made by the Vicar in his sermon of the loss we had sustained and he pointed out how we should still continue to remember the departed in our prayers. He also referred to the many we had already lost in the war and that the Holy Sacrifice then being offered would be especially on their behalf. R.I.P.

The following letter, dated March 12th, has been received by the friends of PTE W.G. SANDERSON, who is in Palestine: 'I got up 5.20 and had a walk into St George's English Cathedral in modern Jerusalem and attended Holy Communion there. It was a lovely morning with brilliant sunshine and at that time, not too hot. I did enjoy it as it was the first Communion since I was aboard the Troopship. Later in the day, accompanied by our own Head-qrs Officer we went to the Holy City, armed with special passes to admit us into the old part of the City. Our Officer then dismissed us after kindly paying for a Guide to show us round. I will try and give you an idea at least of some of the principal things I saw. First let me tell you that the Old City is surrounded by a very old thick wall with Gates—Jaffa Gate, Damascus Gate, St Stephen's Gate, etc. (which are now guarded by British Troops). Well, we walked right round the City on the outside first. The 'Jaffa Gate' is the principal and the one through which General Allenby passed *on foot*.[1] Then comes the Damascus Gate. Passing round we saw the valley of Jehosha-

---

[1] Gen. Sir Edmund Allenby, having taken command of Third Army south of Arras in Oct. 1915, was transferred to command Allied forces in Palestine in June 1917. He took Jerusalem in Dec. 1917 and walked into the city (as not to emulate the Kaiser's triumphal entry on horseback in 1898) on 11 Dec.

phat and the Pool of Siloam coming to St Stephen's Gate, outside of which the martyr was stoned. Then passing King David's Tower and Absolom's grave we came to the Jews' Wailing Place—a portion of the old wall where the Jews go to wail over the loss of their City. This they have done for hundreds of years, and there were some there as we passed, crying and beating their breasts. The streets are very narrow, and well, not as clean as they might be. We then walked on and passed each of the fourteen Stations of the Cross: places where incidents in that last journey of our Lord actually took place, and over some of these stations were built Chapels, which we visited. These stations terminated at the Church of the Holy Sepulchre, which is on Calvary, and is the identical place where the last tragedy of all took place—the Crucifixion of our Lord. Here, heavy with the smell of incense and surrounded by lights is the Stone on which Christ lay in the Sepulchre. We then saw Herod's Palace. The Hall of judgement where Christ was scourged and condemned by Pontius Pilate. These places are of course in ruins now. We passed on to the Garden of Gethsemane where we spent some little time looking round, and then came to a Church hewn out of solid rock underground and had to go down many steps. Here it is said that the Blessed Virgin died and Her tomb is just beneath the High Altar. Then each of us were handed lighted tapers by the priest in charge and we explored the hidden Catacombs. Coming once more into daylight we each had a drink of water from the BVM's Well in the centre of the Church; after that we journeyed to the Mosque of Omah, an imposing Mohammedan Temple in Eastern style with a huge, rich Oriental Carpet covering the entire floor. We were not allowed to enter this place, but could see inside. The people all remove their boots or shoes and leave them outside before entering, and even the Military Governor of Jerusalem had to do the same when he went inside to inspect the building. Of course most of the natives wear no boots or shoes. We then saw a number of Mohammedan at prayer in the open. We then went into a most gorgeous R.C. Church built by the Kaiser some years ago for the German Colony. This Church took eight years to build and is a fine place. After a few minutes rest inside we ascended to the top of the tower where a most wonderful view could be obtained of the Holy City and surrounding country. We could see Bethany, and even, in the distance, Jericho. Arriving back for dinner tired out but thoroughly satisfied with our experiences. These are of course only a few of the principal sights we saw, and we hope to go to Bethlehem[1] in a few days.'

JUNE 1918

*27 May–6 June: Third phase of the German offensive
on the Western Front, beginning on the Aisne.
29 May: German forces take Soissons and Rheims.*

Our Soldiers

We much regret that we have to record the death at the front of another of our workers, SERGT G. JAMES GLEESON of the North Staffords. We mentioned last month that his friends were very anxious at not having heard of him for several weeks. About the middle of May they received information that he had been killed in action, and subsequent enquiries show that the Sergeant was killed by an exploding shell on April 17th, less than a fortnight after his landing in France. It appears that he must have been in the thick of the fighting very soon after he joined his battalion. The Officer Commanding his company wrote: 'At the moment of his death I was within a few yards of him. He died instantaneously, and owing to the situation, which was extremely critical, it was necessary to bury him at once. The position of the grave is on the southern slope of Kemmel Hill, territory now in enemy hands. Although he was with me but a short time, I found him a skilful and gallant N.C.O.: his good work at Messines, four days previously, will always be remembered by the Officers and men of his company.' In telling this story no wonder the *Derby Daily Telegraph* headed it 'A hero of Kemmel Hill.' We, of St Michael's, feel that we have lost a zealous worker and it is a great grief that we should have lost almost at the same time two such men as Signaller Harry Coulson and Sergeant J. Gleeson. 'May they rest in peace.'

We are glad to know from a letter received from Mrs Downman that her son, LIEUT. THEODORE DOWNMAN has been released from his German prison, and is now in Holland. LIEUT. A. DEAN, who was

---

[1] W.G. Sanderson, then demobilised, wrote about his visit to Bethlehem in the Magazine for January 1920.

wounded some time ago, is now out of Hospital and convalescent, he has gone to stay with our old friend the REV. W.R. JOHNSON, who has returned from the Balkans to his living in Cornwall. Letters have been received during May from several of our friends in Salonika, including LIEUT. T.A. WRAGG, PTES KARL DUNCAN, A. GARTON, JAS. AULT, and SERGT COTTON. We have had news from many of those in France, including PTE JOHN TURTON, who has recently gone to the front.

PTE A.G. TIMSON, PTE A.E. BISHOP and L-CPL C. WILLATT, all write cheerfully but are evidently longing to be back in 'Blighty'. PTE W. G. SANDERSON writes from Palestine on April 24th: 'I received your Easter Card which I shall keep to remind me of the many happy Easters I have spent at dear little St Michael's, fortunately I had the opportunity of attending the Holy Sacrifice at 6 a.m. on Easter Day in the Holy City and later, another service, for this I was very thankful. I am in the best of health and happy ... The sights I have seen will never be forgotten and I shall have much to tell you all whenever we are privileged to meet again.' LIEUT. LESLIE NORTON is now at home suffering from shell shock and his brother is a prisoner in Germany but seems to be in fairly decent quarters.

CAPTAIN ROBERT BARKER in a letter received by the Vicar on May 29th refers to the M.C. which he has gained, but does not give details, he only says, with becoming modesty, 'I only did my duty, as any officer would have done had he been placed in the same position that I was ... I've been commanding a Company for some time now, and I have one of the old choir boys in it, Robert Walker, he is my runner and he is a very stout fellow in the line too.'

JULY 1918

3–12 June: German Aisne offensive halted at
Château-Thierry and Belleau Wood.
9–13 June: German offensive near Compiègne;
Battle of the Matz.

Our Soldiers

The following letter has been received from Mrs H.B. Coulson from Sir Robert Baden-Powell, the Chief Scout: 'Dear Madam, It is with deepest regret that I have just heard of the death in action of your husband. Although your loss is very great yet I hope that the manner of your husband's death is of some consolation to you. The thought that he died upholding the ideals which he had taught to his Troop will be an inspiration to the Scouts of Derby to follow his example and to carry out their duty, as he did, at no matter what personal cost. With deep sympathy in your loss which is shared by the Scout Brotherhood. Believe me, etc., etc.'

The Vicar was very pleased to receive a letter on June 6th from GUNNER FRED ALLSOP, of whom little had been heard for some time. It was written on April 11th from Mesopotamia. He had only just received our New Year's parcel, for he says, 'I am writing to thank you and all the good people of St Michael's for your good wishes and present to me for Christmas and the New Year. It is awfully kind of you to think so much of the lads who are away, and news from people at home is appreciated so much out here, although it is getting rather old by the time it reaches us. Since I came out of Hospital I have not received a letter from anyone until yesterday, and it has been a most trying time looking forward from day to day. Now it has come all at once. Besides yours I received several letters from home, the Church Magazine for December, and sixteen papers; besides these there are a great many more for me, and have yet to receive those which have been sent to me this year. I am pleased to say that I am quite well now ... During Holy Week Services were held every evening. I thought many times of St Michael's on Palm Sunday as we sang "Ride on! Ride on!" under the palm trees. On Easter Day there were three Celebrations. I am hoping that I shall be at St Michael's Church next Easter Day.'

TROOPER KARL DUNCAN wrote from Salonika on May 28th: 'Everything here is O.K. bar the weather and that is too hot for one to feel comfortable, though we are now served with spine pads, sun helmets and shorts. For myself I am quite well, though Walter Ray is down with malaria—just another relapse—which one looks upon quite undisturbed[1] ... Things out here are very quiet, our regiment still doing the usual patrol. Some of the boys are in bivouacs, though Walter, myself and two others are in a tent. We have a fine display of photographs, the prominent one being the St Michael's Football Team,[2] taken in the garden in

---

[1] Karl Duncan's CO, Lieut.-Col. G.A. Strutt, wrote in the Derbyshire Yeomanry's *War History* (p. xv) that 'hardly a single man escaped being down with malaria—most of them got frequent relapses'. Martin Gilbert writes of 'the scourge of the Salonica Front, the malarial mosquito' in *The First World War* (1995), p. 356.

[2] See p. xxiii. Karl Duncan had been secretary of the football team, 1913–14.

our last season.'

PTE FRED DOWLER sent a letter from France, dated June 7th: 'I am pleased to be able to say that I am feeling much better, but my chest is still somewhat troublesome. This gas the Germans are now using is terrible stuff. I have no doubt that in a little while I shall pull round again, but the awful sights and experiences of the last 2 or 3 months have left their mark on me and together with the sad news which I have received about some of our boys have affected me more than I thought possible. Harry Coulson, gone! Jim Glesson, gone! Well do I know where the latter fell and the churchyard where he is buried. At one time a most beautiful spot, and even now (in spite of the terrible strafing given to Kemmel Hill) part of the old Church remains.'

Letters have also been received from LIEUT. WRAGG, L-CPL. C. WILLATT, DRIVER JAMES AULT, PTES J. TURTON, A. COLLARD, REG MARSHALL, BOMBR A PALMER and others.

AUGUST 1918

15 July–4 August: Second Battle of the Marne.
18 July: Allied counter-attack begins.
20 July: German retreat on the Marne.
22 July: Allied forces cross the Marne.

Our Soldiers

We announced in the May number that LIEUT. R.A. BARKER, Notts. and Derbys. Regiment, had won the Military Cross, but it was not till Monday, July 29th, that the *London Gazette* published the fact, and adds: 'He took charge of a company when the company commander was killed, and successfully repelled three attacks, handling his men with great courage and determination. His work at all times was particularly praiseworthy.' All our readers would wish us to renew our congratulations to this gallant officer, who was one of our Church workers. We regret to learn that for the second time LIEUT. BARKER has been wounded, but fortunately the injury is not serious. We wish him a speedy recovery and we hope to see him on leave shortly.

Our readers will be interested in the information that our men are scattered over the world, besides those in Great Britain, most of them are in France, some in Salonika and India, one each in Mesopotamia and

Palestine and we are not sure of Italy, but there is one grave belonging to us in East Africa.

We hear that CADET G. MERRY is qualifying for the Air Service and CADET T. LONGDON for the Tanks, whilst F. ALBERT SMITH, a former choir boy, has now just volunteered for service as a telegraphist on a submarine in the Mediterranean. Wherever our brave lads may be we pray continually for their welfare.

During the past month letters have been received from PTES A.E. BISHOP, R. MARSHALL, F. HALLSWORTH, K. DUNCAN, W. PLANT, and others. GUNNER F. HALLSWORTH wrote from India: 'I have been sent back to Peshawar to rejoin my battery as a signaller, having recently passed a very stiff six days' examination at Nowshera after a 6 months course there. I passed 1st Class and attained the best sending average (on all instruments) in the School. Sorry to say the weather is still increasing in heat, and it is hot, the average temperature these last few days has been 115 in the shade. I have joined the Church Choir here. It is quite a nice Church. It is queer to see the punkahs[1] in action during service ... Sorry to say we are not allowed in the city (which looks so interesting) as it is very dangerous for British Troops, especially in the Pathan quarters. They possess a very bitter feeling towards us. I send some post cards of Peshawar and a group of Pathans is shown.'

TROOPER KARL DUNCAN makes one's mouth water in these fruitless times when he says: 'The trees round about our camp are laden with fruit and we have many visits to lighten their branches, apricots being our favourites, though mulberries are very plentiful, grapes, plums and apples require a week or two more before they are ready for eating ... Lieut. Wragg has formed a concert party, though up to the present it has only given one performance. The singing was gorgeous, it was like old times, Vicar, to sit listening to Mr Wragg. He is the pianist and the mainstay of the party, though the rest are very good.'

F.A. SMITH, ORD. TELEGRAPHIST, wrote on July 20th: 'I am now at Portsmouth, waiting to have a course in Wireless Instruments, prior to leaving England for the Mediterranean (Malta to be exact) for work as a wireless operator on a submarine, for which I, along with 9 others volunteered when in Chatham. No doubt you know that I have had 4 months on a mine sweeper, working from Dover, the greater part of the time spent at French ports. Now of course I am going in for a different class of seafaring altogether. It will be much more dangerous and more

---

[1] A punkah was a Palmyra leaf fan or large cloth fan worked by a cord.

exciting. We expect being out there 18 months at least. A long time to be separated from home, but, Vicar, I volunteered with a good heart and shall go out with a good heart and do my duty to the very best of my ability.'

Our Roll of Honour

Our last Roll of men connected with St Michael's Church was published in March, 1917. We hope this is up-to-date and accurate, any omissions or mistakes should be reported to the Vicar. Many of the men now on home service have been abroad and returned wounded or sick. Some are in training for special duty.

IN GREAT BRITAIN

Reginald Allen
Lieut. Alec W.H. Bewley
Sergt Cecil Bewley
Sergt Frank Bewley
George Bewley
Fred Brookes
L-Cpl W.R. Burrows
Sergt Harry Curzon
Lieut. Gordon Hardy
George Brian Froggatt
L-Cpl Harold Innocent
Arthur Jones
Capt. E. Parry-Jones

Frank Leighton
Cadet Thos. Longdon
John Marshall
L-Cpl Fred Mart
J. William Marshall
Cadet George Merry
James Midgely
William T. Nix
Percy Smith
James Stevens
Frank Stone
William H. Walkerdine
F. Wainwright

IN FRANCE

Sergt Theo. Bewley
George Bishop
Albert E. Bishop
Sergt James Bladon
George Bridgett
Archie Buck
Harry Butler
Ferdinald Butler

Herbert Jessop
John Johnson
John T. Lander
Joseph Lowe
Reginald Marshall
James Mawson
Alex. Oakley
Arthur Palmer

Arthur Clarke
Joseph Cocker
Arthur Collard
Fred Cox
Fred Dowler
Tom Duffy
Ben Edwards
Sergt Thos. Everington
Caleb Fletcher
Fred Fletcher
Frank Fox
Cuthbert Frith
2nd Lieut. Eric Hardy
Laurence Hallsworth
Sergt-Major James Hill
Gordon Hunt

William Plant
John Patrick
Ben Robshaw
Arthur Rose
Albert Smith
Harold Smith
Harold Sharpe
Richard Sharpe
William Arthur Smith
John Turton
Robert Walker
Charles Willatt
Richard Whitehurst
Tom Walker
Henry Weston
Fred Wright

George Hutley

IN GREECE

James Ault
Oscar Bewley
Sergt Henry E. Cox
Sergt H.C. Cotton
William Cross

Karl V. Duncan
Arthur Garton
Walter Ray
Lieut. Thos. A. Wragg
Sam Whitaker

IN EGYPT OR PALESTINE

Fred Leeson

William Sanderson

IN MESOPOTAMIA OR INDIA

Frederick Allsopp
Sergt Arthur Baker

Benjamin Fox
Frederick Hallsworth

Ralph Cholerton

SAILORS

John Hughes	Reginald Plant
William Foster	F. Albert Smith

George Lambton

PRISONERS OF WAR

Lieut. Theodore Downman	Lieut. Percy F. Norton

Reginald Thompson

DISCHARGED
(Discharged or Sick)

Laurence Abell	Harry Jackson
John Baker	Lieut. Leslie Norton
William Brown	Arthur Roe
Wilfred Burrows	Cyril Robinson
Sergt Henry Eyre	2nd Lieut. K. Stiven
Arthur Foster	Tom Woolley
William Greenlay	Harry White
Alfred Hewitt	Capt. Harry Warburton
Peter Hudson	(in Canada)

DEPARTED THIS LIFE[1]

Joseph Bewley	Herbert Lowe
Henry B. Coulson	Harry Lowe
Harry Crocker	Walter E. Lloyd

---

[1] To these 27 names would later be added Capt. Robert Arnold Barker and 2nd Lieut. Charles Eric Hardy who were killed in Oct. 1918, together with 2nd Lieut. Kenneth Cummin Stiven who died as a result of war wounds in Jan. 1920 and who was added to the list by Harry Rolfe (see Magazine for Feb. 1920). Thus there would have been 30 names on the marble memorial to the Fallen in St Michael's. Rolfe records in the magazines the names of two further servicemen who were killed: L/Cpl Jack Redfern and Pte Herbert Augustine Fletcher, but a photograph of the interior of the church which shows the memorial appears to record only 30 names, though these are illegible. The memorial is no longer in the church and its whereabouts are at present unknown.

Lieut. Bernard Downman
Archie Duncan
Archibald Elvidge
Sergt Sam Fetterplace
William Foy
Sergt G. James Gleeson
William Goodchild
William Horton
Capt. Owen Parry-Jones
George King

Charles Oakley
Norman Powell
Sergt Albert Powell
William Sarsfield
Arthur Smith
Evan O. Thomas
John Whitaker
William Whitehead
George Wheatcroft
Tom Weston

Henry Lambton

SEPTEMBER 1918

*8–15 August: Allied Amiens offensive
commences on the Western Front.
20–29 August: Allied Albert offensive opens.
26–29 August: Allied Scarpe offensive opens.*

Our Roll of Honour

In addition to the names published last month (those were of men connected with the Church), we give a list of men who belong to H.M. Forces and whose homes are in the parish.

Joseph Brown
John Bestridge
Samuel Bestridge
William Geary
Alfred Hewitt
William Hickton
Tom Harrison
Joseph Huntley
George Knight
Stephen Leahy
William Martin
Benjamin Martin

Robert Mason
Thomas Morley
James Mullen
Tom Mullen
Austin Murphy
John Swords
John Timson
Arthur Waterfield
H.J. Wheeler
Ernest Woodward
John Wooley

Our Soldiers

Several of our lads have been home on leave recently and we were pleased to see most of them looking, as they would say, 'in the pink.' One of these was DRIVER JOSEPH COCKER, R.F.A., who was presented at the Normanton Barracks with the Military Medal he won on July 13th, 1917. An account of his exploit was given in the October Magazine last year, He and four others rescued some wounded men from a house at Bully Grenay under severe shelling. We understand that the men who have been so long in Salonika are being granted leave. One of them, DRIVER JAMES AULT is now at home, but we regret that he still suffers from malaria contracted when on service.

Amongst the letters received in August was one from LIEUT. T.A. WRAGG, in which he writes of the possibility of leave for the lads at Salonika. He also mentions meeting one of his choir-men, Sergt Harry E. Cox: 'Your letter had not been here more than a couple of hours when who should come to my tent but Harry Cox. I had not seen him since we were in England. You can guess it was a surprise to me. He tells me he has a splendid berth. He is R.Q.M.S. at G.H.Q. Except for looking a little older he is about the same ... We had a long enjoyable chat, and revived many old memories. I told him of the remarkable coincidence of your enquiry.'

We were also pleased to have a letter from PTE FRED ALLSOP, who is still in Mesopotamia, and to know that now he is keeping quite well. A third letter to be noted is from Palestine written on July 29th, by L/CPL W.G. SANDERSON: 'Since my first visit to the Holy City of which I told you in a previous letter, I have paid a number of visits, but being in a different district I cannot get there now. We are now just outside a very old town, which is also very dirty, but it is most noticeable that after British occupation (especially in the larger towns) they begin to get much cleaner and the people also seem to "buck up". There is a Church in the town and I attended Holy Communion and then Evening Service, which was quite like home, We sang hymn 595—it was very fine and made us think a bit. I thought of St Michael's and how this hymn is sung so frequently on Sunday Evenings. A few of us, along with the Chaplain, are trying to form a little C.E.M.S. branch, open to all Churchmen, but owing to the movements of Troops this will be very difficult ... It is very hot indeed here and we do not expect it any cooler until November, when rain may come. I have seen many wonderful sights since leaving dear old England.'

As we are going to press we hear that PTE R.A. MARSHALL has been wounded in the recent fighting and is now in Hospital at Newcastle-on-Tyne. As he wrote a long letter to his mother on Aug. 18th it must have been within the last few days that he was wounded. We hope to hear that he is going on satisfactorily and wish him speedy recovery.

OCTOBER 1918

2 September: British forces breach first Hindenburg Line positions.
15 September: Allied breakthrough in Bulgaria.
22 September: Turkish resistance in Palestine collapses.
27 September–1 October: Allied forces assault on Canal du Nord, Hindenberg Line.

Our Soldiers

Many of the men have been home on leave during September, including CAPTAIN ROBERT BARKER M.C., PRIVATES CROSS, JAS. STEVENS, A. BUCK, F. BUCK, H. SMITH, H. WESTON, F. LEESON and B. FROGGATT, all looking well. The names of EDWARD SKINNER, WILLIAM PERCIVAL and TOM SHIPLEY are added to our Roll. We regret that last month we did not describe correctly the name of 2ND LIEUT. HUNTLEY, a parishioner.

During the past month we have had letters from many of our lads. SIGNALLER HALLSWORTH wrote from India on Aug. 9th. He has been staying in the hills at Ghora Dhaka having been sent there from Peshawar, where the weather was about 118 in the shade and caused an attack of fever. He adds: 'A few weeks ago a heat wave came over Peshawar, when the glass reached 124 degrees in the shade. About 30 died in the station—four from my battery from the terrible heat. I am so glad I was out of it ... The last part of my journey to Ghora Dhaka had to be taken on "tats" (mountain ponies). It was about 17 miles and was the most exciting and most beautiful ride I have ever had. The scenery is wonderful. The air up here is beautiful and cool, laden with healthy scent from the huge pines which cover the sides of these pretty hills. We are about 10,000 feet above sea level ... Please convey my kindest regards to my friends at St Michael's.'

The lads in France write hopefully of the prospect of peace. L-CPL CHAS. WILLATT sends his 'kindest regards to his friends.' PTE K.V. DUNCAN in a letter from Salonika, written on Sept. 3rd, says that he believed Walter Ray, who was just out of Hospital was on his way to

Blighty. Karl himself is hoping to come soon. 'Fancy', he says, 'it will be three years in November since I left home. Time does fly.' SERGT COTTON, also in Salonika, is expecting leave, but we are afraid owing to what is now taking place all leave will be stopped. We heard in the middle of last month that PTE ROBERT WALKER had been gassed about a month before, in one of the attacks of the Sherwoods in France. He is now in Hospital in England and says he is going on satisfactorily. He wrote on Sept. 21st: 'As soon as I got gassed I went blind for a week and I also lost my speech, but I am glad to say my sight has come back and my speech is coming back. Please remember me to Miss Cantrill and all the boys.' We wish him a speedy recovery.

NOVEMBER 1918

1 October: British and Arab forces occupy Damascus.
5 October: German positions on Hindenberg Line
cleared by Allied forces.
8 October: British forces begin assault on Cambrai and Le Câteau.
14–20 October: Allied Courtrai offensive.
17–24 October: British Selle offensive.
30 October: Allies sign armistice with Turkey.

Captain Robert A. Barker

It seems but yesterday that Captain Barker was at home on leave and we rejoiced to see him looking so well and cheerful, and now within three weeks of his return to the front in France we learn that he has given his life in the service of his country. It appears that he died of wounds received in action on Sunday, Oct. 13th. Captain Barker was confirmed at St Michael's in the year 1909, and subsequently became a Server at the Altar and a Sunday School Teacher. In 1914 he went into residence at St Catharine's College, Cambridge, but in the autumn volunteered for service, being wounded at the battle of the Somme in 1916, and again in August this year. He won by his gallant conduct the Military Cross though it had not been actually given to him by the King. The letters received by his mother from officers and men of his regiment show the esteem in which Captain Barker was held by those with whom he was closely connected when on active service. These letters will be a source of comfort to Mrs Barker and her surviving son, though they must feel acutely the great loss which they have sustained. We give extracts from some of the letters: His C.O., Lieut.-Col. T.W. Daniels, who knew him at Cambridge, wrote, 'Robert has been with me many months, and not only was a gallant soldier, but a most charming companion. He was undoubtedly the most popular officer I had. He was sniped on Oct. 13th at about 10 a.m., and died in the evening. He has been buried in the Military Cemetery at Montigny. I cannot adequately express my sorrow: he was one of those whom I cannot replace. The whole battalion desires to express its deepest sympathy with you in your terrible loss.' The Chaplain says: 'He was wounded in the abdomen and spine on Oct. 13th, and brought to this 53rd Field Ambulance, when every attention was given him. I saw him after he had been dressed. He asked me to write to you. He said "Tell mother, I'm wounded, and I'll write when I can: that's all." I am very sorry to have to tell you that he died the same evening. His last words were, "I suppose I shall pull through." I buried him this (Monday) afternoon and a cross will be put over his grave as soon as practicable by his Regt.'

Captain Brandt wrote: 'He was one of my best friends out here. We were very often together, and got to know each other very well: with always a smile on his face and so good natured, he was always ready to do any little job cheerfully.' The last extract is from a letter written by Pte G. Norman, who had been his servant. 'I was not with him at the time he died, but I came down the line with him to the dressing station and he did not seem to be in much pain. He was hit by a sniper in his side and one of the runners that was with him got killed. I am very sorry to lose him because he has been very good to me. I have been his servant now about nine months, and he was liked in the battalion by all the officers and men.'

2nd Lieutenant C. Eric Hardy

Just before going to press we heard, with deep regret, that 2nd Lieut. Hardy, one of our communicants, had been killed in action on Oct. 24th. Mr and Mrs Hardy will have the sincere sympathy of their many friends at St Michael's. The following letter has been received from the Major in his Regiment: 'I am deeply grieved to tell you your son was killed in action yesterday, Oct. 24th. He led his four guns into action very bravely and had done some extremely good work when he was instantly killed by machine-gun fire. I brought his body out, together with a brother officer who fell at the same time, and, followed by all the officers of the Company, the Colonel of the Battalion, other officers, N.C.O.s and men who knew him, we paid him our last respects and laid him to rest in a hero's grave. I cannot tell you the gloom it has cast over the whole Battalion, the loss of your son, he was very popular and liked by everyone and his men would follow him anywhere. My bravest officer, very capable in all his work, and in the mess he always kept us cheerful under all circumstances. As a loss to the Company he can never be replaced, and my personal loss is even greater, for he was my favourite officer. My Company join me in tendering to you their deepest sympathy in your great loss. Your sacrifice is a terrible one and the loss to the wide circle of his friends will be very keenly felt. Exceedingly brave and untiring in all his work it can truly be said of him, he fought and fell a great hero and the Company has lost the best officer it ever had. Again, extending to you my deepest sympathy.'

Our Soldiers

During the past month amongst those of our lads on leave we have seen L-CPL A. PALMER, L-CPL C. WILLATT, L-CPL F. FLETCHER, PRIVATES A. BUCK, A. GARTON and J. LOWE, all seemed well and hearty, looking forward to an early termination of the war. Letters have been received from several men, one from DRIVER JAS. AULT shows how the lads look for letters from home. He wrote from France on Oct. 15th, he had previously been home on leave from Salonika: 'Just a few lines to let you know where they have sent me to this time, I am now out in France in a camp for the treatment of this Malaria Fever. It is a very pretty part, but we find it very monotonous at night time, we must not grumble however for we are much better off than we were out in Salonika for many things. There are quite a number of boys I know here, many of them, having been in my own unit. We were taken to a Service on Sunday but it was nothing like the services we have at home in the Old Church. To-day some of the boys received a letter for the first time since we came out, you should just see the boys when the mail comes up, my word!, there is a rush and how downhearted a fellow is if there is not any for him.' TROOPER K.V. DUNCAN wrote on Oct. 4th from Greece: 'I have been in Hospital with the "flue" and am now in a Convalescent Camp, I hope to get back to the boys in a month. Along with me is another of our fellows who has just returned from leave so I have all the latest Derby news ... What do you think of the war news out here? quite a surprise to everyone, even the troops. About four days attacking on our front and Bulgaria packed up. Just my luck to have to go into Hospital. I managed the first day's trek and then had to give in.'

We hope that our friends will not think that an Armistice, if it takes place, will mean the immediate return of the boys. It will be a long time before they all reach home and we shall need to send those New Year's Gifts we may be quite sure.

DECEMBER 1918

2–11 November: British Sambre offensive.
8 November: British take Maubeuge.
11 November: Allies sign armistice with Germany.

The Armistice

We shall never forget Monday, Nov. 11th, the day on which we commemorate St Martin, the Soldier Saint of France, for then the fighting ceased and a prospect of righteous peace was assured. It is a matter for great thankfulness, that generally the thought of God and His goodness was in the minds of the people. For all the Churches were filled with congregations at night to offer thanksgiving. At St Michael's the service was at 7 p.m., when the Church was quite full. We give an outline of the Service: Hymn 166, then the Vicar said a few words as an introduction and read the Hymn of Praise and Thanksgiving after Victory in the Form of Prayer to be used at Sea; after hymn 298, "Praise my Soul the King of Heaven", Prayers of Thanksgiving were said, and the service concluded with the Te Deum, the whole lasting about 45 minutes. On Sunday, Nov. 17th, the Special Form of Thanksgiving was used and all the services, which were well attended, were of a festal character.

Our Men at the Front

We have had fewer letters than usual during November and probably the reason is that the men are on the move and have no time for writing, those who have sent letters are rejoicing in the thought of a speedy return to Blighty, but we fear it will be some months before they reach home. We heartily congratulate SERGT HARRY E. COX, one of our choir men, who is at Salonika, on being awarded the Serbian Military Virtue Medal, he says 'it is really a very nice gold medal, there are only four other people in the British Army who have got it.' We hear that

LIEUT. T.A. WRAGG is on his way home, we shall hope to see him at Christmas and quite restored to health. ORD. TELEGRAPHIST F. ALBERT SMITH sent an interesting letter from the Mediterranean, from the Submarine in which he serves, he says: 'I am having a very good time out here. I cannot say exactly where, but I am East, enjoying my new surroundings very much. My first trip in the submarine was full of interest and wonder to me. Everything was A1. I cannot describe being submerged, in fact there is very little difference except the air gets very thick, you could cut it with a knife, this makes one feel very drowsy, but after a short while on the surface the boat gets cooled down once more.' The Vicar intends to call a meeting of the Church Council to consider the question of a memorial for our heroic dead. He will be pleased to receive any suggestions as to the form it should take.

JANUARY 1919

6 December: British forces occupy Cologne

Our Soldiers and Sailors

As our men are generally on the move we have not received many letters lately. Those who have written are looking forward to coming home early in the New Year, being, as many say, 'sick and tired of a soldier's life' now that the need for action is past. We must give extracts from one letter, written in November, by PTE W.G. SANDERSON, from Syria: 'We have been right through the thick of it. Unfortunately I have lost some good friends, who have made the great sacrifice. May they rest in peace. It has been a most marvellous advance and if those at home could see some of the roads they would be astonished at Transport being able to go over them. Well, you will be interested to know that I was in Nazareth on our Festival (Sept. 29th), and although it was quite impossible to attend or attempt to hold a service owing to the fact that we were on the heels of the enemy and still chasing him, I had a few moments of quiet thought and knew at 9.30 a.m., by our time here (7 in Derby), the Holy Sacrifice would be offered and special prayers for us who are away. I can quite truly say that the prayers offered for me must have been the means of saving my life from what seemed certain death near the Sea of Galilee ... I have bathed both in that sea and also in the river Jordan, and visited and spent some time in Damascus, which is a fine Eastern City, but very dirty. The people are a lazy lot—in fact I will

give you an instance I saw myself—a person died in the street (quite a
common sight) just in front of a house and the people would just stride
over the corpse rather than move it, and would let it lie all day ... I hope
it will not be long before I am home again with you at St Michael's'.

The New Year's gifts to our men should reach them early in January.
A post-card photo of the interior of the Church and the following letter
accompanied each gift: 'My dear — , It is under very different circumstances from those in 1917 that I write this year. For we are now
rejoicing that peace seems to be assured and we are hoping that before
very long you will be once more in the old Town and in the old Church
of St Michael. We have prayed for you there and now, with our prayers,
we offer our thanksgiving to God for you and for our country, not
forgetting those who have given their lives to defend us and are gone to
be with their Saviour in Paradise. We send you this little present of
money as a token of our regard, trusting that you may be able to
purchase some little souvenir, to remind you of your association with the
forces of the King which, with our Allies, have so valiantly fought and
gained the Victory. With all good Wishes from myself and many friends
at St Michael's. I remain your true friend, Harry R. Rolfe, Vicar'. Full
particulars of the number of gifts sent and a balance sheet will be
published next month.

FEBRUARY 1919

The New Year's Gifts

We are not able this month to publish the Balance Sheet of the fund for
sending gifts to our Sailors and Soldiers, as there may be a little more
money to come in. But we have already received more than enough to
cover all expenses. About 80 gifts were sent and we have received 67
acknowledgements—we hope to get the rest during February. The
following extracts from letters are fair samples of the remainder:

HM Submarine E2, Dec. 31st: 'Today I received your letter, 10/- note
and card of the Church, for which, Vicar, I thank you and the good
people of St Michael's very much indeed. It is very nice to be remembered like this when one is so far away from home; and I ask you to
accept yourself and to convey to all my friends at St Michael's my very
best wishes for a bright, healthy, and happy New Year. I hope to be
home early in February.' ALBERT SMITH.

Bruhl, Germany, Jan. 3rd: 'Many thanks to you and my friends at St

Michael's for the Christmas Greetings and present which I received quite safely yesterday. Christmas has not been a bright one for the inhabitants of this town—very little for them to eat. I am staying here indefinitely, and I am not sorry either, because it is a good size town and owns a Cinema, which is allowed to open every few days for our benefit. The people are treating us well and they are quiet'. BRIAN FROGGATT.

St Ville, Germany, Jan. 6th: 'I have received the registered letter and its contents quite safe to-day, and I must thank you and the many friends at St Michael's very much indeed for the same. I am at a small place just inside Germany, near the Belgian frontier. I must say the country is fine, just like our Peak district'. A.E. BISHOP.

Vignacourt, France, Jan. 2nd: 'I was pleased to receive the kind letter and present from St Michael's, and I thank you all very much ... I visited a Cemetery just outside this village on New Year's Day. It brought many memories back to me of those I knew and who will not return to their dear ones, especially one—his name was Edward Keay, and we were close friends. We were here together last Easter, and went to Communion then. He died for his country by my side on May 28th. His brother was also killed about the same time ... The earth seems very peaceful now. It seems wonderful. No booming of guns, no chug! chug! of Boche machines overhead looking for a target for their bombs. I hope to be home soon'. F.W. COX.

Germany, Jan. 17th: 'Very many thanks for your most welcome gifts which safely arrived about a week ago. You must excuse me for not replying earlier, but nowadays we are continually on the move. However, we have at last settled down for a short period, so I'm taking the opportunity of thanking you and also our friends at St Michael's for the generous gift which I more than welcomed, and which I am sure will be greatly appreciated by all who receive it. Well, I am at last in Germany and at present we are billeted some twenty miles east of Cologne, so we are well over the border. We are treated with due respect by the civil population, and altogether it is not so bad as we anticipated, although there is a kind of haughtiness and suspicion about them, which suggests contempt. However, we don't mind that, so long as things are quiet ... The photograph of the Church is splendid and I thank you very much for it. You can little realise, dear Vicar, how we cherish such gifts, and I am certain that in years to come, if you chanced to ask me if I still had the photo. I shall be able to produce it'. A. BUCK.

MARCH 1919

Our Soldiers

As far as we can learn about 30 of our men have been discharged and returned home. We hope later on, when all have come home, to have a Social to welcome them. On the whole they look remarkably fit and well. Most of them return to former employments. One is horrified, however, to learn the manner in which some of them are sent back. One man assures the Vicar that he, with a large number of demobilised men, were sent the long, slow journey across France in cattle trucks during the severe weather in the middle of February, and that five of them died on the way. Surely some enquiry ought to be made into the truth of this.

Very few of our friends in Salonika have as yet reached home. LIEUT. WRAGG has come back sick with malaria; we sincerely hope that his health may soon be restored, and we trust that our lads who have been for years in and about Salonika will soon be back again. Many of them have had no leave for years. Below we append a Balance Sheet showing how the money has been expended for the New Year's Gifts.

Seventy-nine gifts were sent and seventy-two have acknowledged them with thanks; one has been returned; the replies of a few far away from England have not yet had time to reach us. Only three are uncertain and these are in France. Under present conditions it may not have been possible to deliver the letters, but we quite expect to learn of their reception later.

FEBRUARY 1920

Our Returned Soldiers

On Tuesday evening, Jan. 20th, a Dinner was given to the Discharged Soldiers belonging to St Michael's by the Vicar and Churchwardens, assisted by a few friends, members of the congregation. There are still some of our men in the Army, and several have left the town, whilst others were unable to come, but 70 accepted the invitation and sat down to an excellent repast provided by Mr Ramsden, at his restaurant in the Corn Market. Mr Churchwarden R. Hudson presided, and was supported by the Vicar, the Rev. E. Taylor, Messrs H. Cheetham, G.H. Baker, W.H. Warburton, L. Greensmith, C.E. Hardy and A. Willatt.

After dinner only one toast was given—'The King'—and the company settled down to enjoy a programme of songs, etc., provided by our Choirmaster (Mr T.A. Wragg), which was thoroughly appreciated by all present.

During the evening the Vicar (on behalf of the Congregation) gave a most hearty welcome to those who had safely returned to their homes. He mentioned that though the smallest parish Church in the town, no fewer than 146 of the men connected with it had responded to the call of King and Country—almost all as volunteers. With two or three exceptions, all had served abroad in various parts of the world, in Belgium, France, Greece, Palestine, Mesopotamia, India and East Africa, and had nobly done their duty, and the congregation had followed them with their sympathy and prayers. Thirty had made the supreme sacrifice, and the last to be added to the list was Mr Kenneth Stiven, who, wounded in 1917, had been recently obliged to go into Hospital again for an operation, which had ended fatally only the day before. He asked all to stand in silence as a mark of their sympathy and regard for all who had fallen. Besides the hardships common to all many had suffered from wounds, gas poisoning, sickness, etc. He concluded by offering good wishes to all who had done their duty in the war, and expressed the hope that they would continue to attend the Church.

Mr R. Hudson also made a few remarks, apologising for the absence of his co-churchwarden, Mr Arthur Cox. He endorsed all that the Vicar had said and expressed the hope that all who had come back would rally round the little Church, and take their part in helping the country they had fought and suffered for to be a home of peace, friendliness and freedom.

Cheers were given for the Vicar, the Church-wardens and St Michael's, and the singing of Auld Lang Syne and the National Anthem brought the evening to a close. All who were present expressed their pleasure at the happy time they had spent together.

BIOGRAPHICAL NOTES

In these notes month and year in bold type indicate where reference is to found in the parish magazine in the previous section. Military ranks are recorded as Rolfe gives them, though in all lists in the magazine absence of rank usually implies that the serviceman is a private or equivalent. Most of the available service information about servicemen in the magazine is to be found in the monthly letters section. Further biographical details given here are found in other sections of the magazine but are not necessarily recorded in the Letters. Additional details from other sources have been added where possible and the source noted.

Abbreviations: Listing on the St Michael's Roll of Honour is recorded here as *RH* with the theatre of war, discharged wounded, or died on active service added appropriately as in the March 1917 and August 1918 lists in the magazine; *Dis* for Discharged or Sick; *Departed* for died on active service; *E/EP* for Egypt and/or Palestine; *F* for France/Flanders; *G* for Greece; *GB* for Great Britain; *MI* for Mesopotamia and India; *POW* for Prisoner of War; and *Sailor*. Information from the Commonwealth War Graves Commission is noted as *CWGC* and that from the Public Record Office as *PRO*.

ABELL, LAURENCE (or LAW-RENCE) JOSEPH Pte 4309 1st/5th Batt. Sherwood Foresters (Notts and Derby Regt). **June 1915** Listed as serving. **Aug 1916** Wounded during first Somme offensive. **Dec 1916** Wounded 1 July 1916. Discharged. Arm 'almost useless at present'. **Mar 1917** RH/Dis. **Aug 1918** RH/Dis.

ADAMS, WILLIAM Formerly in the Sunday School. **Nov 1914** Listed as serving.

ALLEN, REGINALD Aug 1918 RH/GB.

ALLSOPP, FRED Formerly in the Sunday School. Pte, Gunner (so **Oct 1917**). **July 1915** Listed as serving.

March 1917 RH/GB. **Aug 1917** Letter 17 June 1917 from Durban, S. Africa. **Oct 1917** Letter 10 Aug 1917 from Mesopotamia, having taken four months to reach there. 'There is not a brick nor stone here—absolutely nothing but sand and tents'. Description of conditions generally. **Jan 1918** In hospital in Baghdad with dysentery but 'going on well'. **Feb 1918** No further news but probably still in Baghdad. **Mar 1918** No further news. **May 1918** Now in convalescent camp. **July 1918** Letter 11 April 1918 having just received Rolfe's New Year's parcel. References to church services etc. **Aug 1918** RH/MI. **Sept 1918** Letter from Mesopotamia.

ANNABLE, W. Formerly in the Sunday School. Pte **Feb 1919** At concert for wounded soldiers at Temple House, 15 Jan 1919.

ASHBY, HARRY Communicant. **Oct 1914** Listed as serving. Pte Grenadier Guards. **Sept 1915** Letter dated 13 Aug 1915, contrasting women harvesting close to the 'terrible conflict raging a few hundred yards away'. **Nov 1915** Listed as 'somewhere at the Front'. **Sept 1916** Letter 3 Aug 1916. Meeting John Whitaker (qv): note Ashby's tribute to stretcher-bearers. **Mar 1917** RH/F. **Sept 1917** Letter 15 August 1917 from hospital in Leeds. Wounded in thigh and arm at Ypres. Description of the incident.

AULT, JAMES Confirmed 28 April 1913. Driver. **Feb 1917** Letter from Salonika. Has been in hospital with an infectious disease contracted on board his troop-ship. Not allowed to visit the YMCA, bored, no books etc. **Mar 1917** RH/G. **June 1918** Letter from Salonika but not quoted. **July 1918** ditto. **Aug 1918** RH/G. **Sept 1918** Home on leave but suffering from malaria. **Nov 1918** Letter from France 15 Oct 1918 in a camp for the treatment of malaria. Ref. to importance of letters from home.

BAKER, ARTHUR Sgt (in **Aug 1918** RH) Could possibly be 10756, 1st Batt. The Sherwood Foresters. **Nov 1915** 'somewhere at the Front'. **Mar 1917** RH/GB. **Aug 1918** RH/MI.

BAKER, H. Sgt Possibly identical with preceding. **May 1918** Letter acknowledging New Year's gift.

BAKER, JOHN W. Could possibly be 14225, 10th Batt. Sherwood Foresters. **Nov 1915** 'somewhere at the Front'. **Feb 1916** Rank given as Drummer. Letter from France describing the desecration of churchyards. **Aug 1916** Missing in first Somme offensive. **Sept 1916** Note that Baker is seriously wounded and a POW. **Mar 1917**

RH/Wounded or Sick. **Aug 1918** RH/Dis.

BARKER, ROBERT ARNOLD 2nd Lieut, Lieut, Capt. (**May 1918**) 10th Batt. Sherwood Foresters (Notts. and Derby Regt). Confirmed at St Michael's in 1909; a server and taught in the Sunday School. Student at Cambridge in 1914 in preparation for ordination to the Anglican ministry. Son of Mrs E.J. Barker of Derby. Volunteered in autumn 1914. **June 1915** Listed as serving. **Nov 1915** 'somewhere at the Front'. **June 1916** Letter from France 24 May 1916. Church parade on Easter Day. Training in bombing. Marched 10 miles a day. Spent two months in trenches 'not been too bad' though he had a bullet through his trench coat. Harry Coulson in same village. **Aug 1916** Letter 15 July 1916 vividly describing taking an enemy trench at Fricourt. **Sept 1916** Wounded in arm, 'at home and doing well'. **Mar 1917** RH/GB. **May 1918** promoted Capt. Awarded MC. **June 1918** Letter 29 May 1918. Commands Company. Robert Walker his runner. **Aug 1918** quote from the *London Gazette* 29 July 1918 describing action leading to his MC. Rolfe notes that Barker has been wounded for the second time. Not serious. **Oct 1918** Home on leave. **Nov 1918** Died from wounds to abdomen and spine received from sniper-fire on 13 Oct 1918 at 10 a.m. three weeks after returning to the Front in France. Full obituary. Letter from CO. Buried in military cemetery at Montigny. Letter from chaplain. Letters from a friend, and from his soldier servant, Robert Walker.

Notes: 1. Robert Barker is buried in Montigny Communal Cemetery (Nord), France. Grave ref. C.3. The majority of the 30 battle casualties commemorated in this cemetery were killed in Oct 1918. They were buried by field ambulances and fighting units. *(CWGC)*

2. At the time of his death Capt. Barker's battalion was in a position east of the river Selle. He died from sniper fire coming from the village of Neuvilly (C. Housley, *A History of the 10th Battalion, Sherwood Foresters 1914–18* (1998) 69).

3. According to his family Robert Barker had also been Mentioned in Dispatches. *Source: Mrs D.E. Griffiths.*

BATES, FRANK Sgt **June 1916** Listed as serving (noted by Rolfe as a member of the congregation). **Mar 1917** RH/GB (Sgt here).

BESTRIDGE, JOHN Sept 1918 RH. A parishioner.

BESTRIDGE, SAMUEL Sept 1918 RH. A parishioner.

BEWLEY, ALEC WILLIAM HEBE Communicant. Lieut. 18th Batt. Sherwood Foresters (Notts. and Derby Regt) One of seven brothers who served, sons of Henrietta Bewley of 5 Queen Street, Derby, and the late H.T.L. Bewley. **Nov 1914** Had been secretary of Happy Home Union, and was working with the Boy Scouts. **Jan 1915** Also temp. Sunday School teacher. **Nov 1915** Although in Army, 'will not at present be moved to a distance' and so will advise new assist. scout-master. **Dec 1915** Harry Coulson's letter to the Scouts indicates that Bewley will seek a commission. **Feb 1916** Commissioned into 18th Batt. Sherwood Foresters. **Nov 1916** Letter dated 11 Oct 1916. Ill in hospital in London (Royal Free). Very graphic detailed description of the 'hell on earth' of trench warfare, also letter to the St Michael's Scouts. Now in 17th Sherwood Foresters. **Dec 1916** Still ill in England. **Mar 1917** relinquishing commission owing to ill-heath. Granted rank of honorary 2nd Lieut. Hopes to offer for active service later (see Scout report). RH/Wounded or sick. **Aug 1917**

Now a recruiting officer at Normanton Barracks, Derby (see Scout report). **Aug 1918** RH/GB.

BEWLEY, CECIL ARTHUR KIRKUS Communicant. L/Cpl, Cpl, Sgt, Derbyshire Imperial Yeomanry. **Oct 1914** Listed as serving. **Nov 1915** 'somewhere at the Front'. **Feb 1916** Reported to be in Greece in Joe Bewley's letter to their mother. **June 1916** Letter: ill in hospital in Salonika but improving. **July 1916** On way home via Malta. **Mar 1917** RH/GB Now Cpl. **Aug 1918** RH/GB. Now Sgt.

Notes: 1. Gordon Bewley, his son, records that while his father lay ill in a field hospital in Salonika 'German Zeppelins bombed the hospital, destroying most of the tented 'wards'. Many were killed and wounded—and my father's 'body' was removed to a temporary tented morgue. The following morning, a hospital worker walking through the body-crowded tent, noticed that my father's arm was moving feebly. He had already been certified as dead and was awaiting burial but was retrieved and sent home—so weak that his body was a 'skeleton with skin on it' (as my mother described him) and he had to learn to walk again, taking six months to be well enough to discharge'.

2. For the Derbyshire Yeomanry in Salonika see G.A. Strutt, *The Derbyshire Yeomanry War History 1914–1919* (Bemrose, Derby, n.d.) ch. 9–13.

BEWLEY, FRANK RICHARD PARKER Communicant. Sgt. **Nov 1914** Listed as serving. Army Pay Corps. Rolfe noted that five of Mrs Bewley's sons were in the Army, and one in the Army Pay Corps! **Mar 1915** further notice to his enlistment. **Mar 1917** RH/GB. **Aug 1918** RH/GB.

Note: Frank Bewley stayed in the Army until 1923.

BEWLEY, GEORGE HENRY NORBLAD Communicant. Pte, Sherwood Foresters, later transferred to the RFC. **Oct 1914** Listed as serving. **Nov 1915** 'somewhere at the Front'. **Mar 1917** RH/F. **Aug 1918** RH/GB.

Note: G.H.N. Bewley married Maud Maddock at St Michael's on 3 Sept 1915.

BEWLEY, JOSEPH CHARLES LAYBORN Petty Officer Motor Mechanic F/463. **Oct 1914** Listed as serving. **Feb 1915** Letter, Petty Officer and driver in No 1 Squ. A Section, Royal Naval Air Service. Description of cars with revolving turrets. Possibility of enemy coastal raids. **Sept 1915** Now in renamed Armoured Car Division serving with Gen. Louis S. Botha in South West Africa. Letter dated 30 July 1915 giving account of action resulting in capture of Windhok and of German reactions to 'watercart' armoured cars. Note: photographs in edition 'some time back' of the *Daily Express*. **Nov 1915** 'somewhere at the Front'. **Feb 1916** Admiralty notice reporting illness (enteric fever). Letter 11 Dec 1915 giving account of hospital train etc. **Mar 1916** Report of his death from pneumonia following enteric fever. Tribute from his CO. **Mar 1917** RH/Departed. **Aug 1918** RH/Departed.

Note: When he died Joseph Bewley was serving with HMS *President* Armoured Car Sqdn (East Africa), Royal Naval Air Service. Died 5 Jan 1916 aged 27. Buried in Nairobi South Cemetery, grave reference II.B.12. During the first World War Nairobi was the headquarters of the King's African Rifles and became the main hospital centre for the East African Campaign. *(CWGC)*

BEWLEY, OSCAR RALPH SEPTIMUS Communicant. Trooper, Derbyshire Imperial Yeomanry. **Sept 1914** Listed as serving. **Nov 1915** 'somewhere at the Front'. **Feb 1916** letter 18 Jan 1916 from Cairo, reporting e.g. a

'Derby boys' reunion. Has been ill from dysentery and jaundice contracted in the Dardanelles (evidently his previous posting). **July 1916** Home on leave and now rejoined regiment. **Mar 1917** RH/G. **Nov 1917** Met T.A. Wragg (qv). **Aug 1918** RH/G.

Note: For the service of the Derbyshire Yeomanry in Salonika see under Cecil Bewley, Note 2.

BEWLEY, THEODORE LYLE Sergeant-Dispenser, 1st N.M.D, Field Ambulance, RAMC. **Oct 1914** Listed as serving. RAMC (so **Oct 1917**). **May 1915** Letter about a field hospital. **Sept 1915** Letter referring to front-line field stations and stretcher-bearers etc., and to Col. Wraith. **Nov 1915** 'somewhere at the Front'. **Feb 1917** Letter 10 Jan 1917 from France. **Mar 1917** RH/F. **Oct 1917** Gassed 'but going on satisfactorily'. **May 1918** Letter received but not quoted. Rolfe says that this is from Sgt J. Bewley but this must be an error. **Aug 1918** RH/F.

Notes: 1. The RAMC depot for the 1st Reserve North Midland Field Ambulance was at 91 Siddals Road, Derby. In Oct 1914 Major E. Arnold Wraith issued a public appeal for electric torches to aid the search and treatment of the wounded at night (*Derby Daily Telegraph*, 20 Oct 1914).

2. **Nov 1914** Letter to Mrs Bewley from Keeper of His Majesty's Privy Purse re her six sons joining the Army. Mrs Henrietta Bewley lived in Queen Street, Derby. A seventh son, A.W.H. Bewley, enlisted in 1916.

3. **Nov 1916** *The Daily Graphic* (2 Nov 1916) carried a photograph of the 10 serving Bewley brothers and sisters as did the *Derbyshire Advertiser* (3 Nov 1916). The three sisters, all of whom became nurses (SJAB VAD), were Florence Ellen Bewley, Edith Mercy Bewley and Gertrude Mary Bewley.

BISHOP, ALBERT E. Pte, 1913–14

Sunday School football team. **May 1918** Letter received but not quoted. **June 1918** ditto. **Aug 1918** ditto. RH/F (first name from this list). **Feb 1919** Letter of thanks for gift 6 Jan 1919 from St Ville, Germany near Belgian frontier.

BISHOP, GEORGE Pte, **Jan 1916** Letter 20 Dec 1915. **Mar 1917** RH/F (first name from this list). **Aug 1918** RH/F.

BLADON, JAMES Sgt. **Aug 1918** RH/F.

BLAND, REGINALD Brother-in-law of Wilfred Burrows. **Nov 1914** Listed as serving.

BRIDGETT, GEORGE Mar 1917 RH/GB. **Aug 1918** RH/F.

BROOK(E)S, FRED W. Pte. Confirmed 28 April 1913. **Mar 1915** Listed as serving. **Jan 1916** Letter 18 Dec 1915. Note on conditions in the trenches: '... all mud and water ... bath-all-day-long kind of stunt ...' etc. **Mar 1916** Letter 3 Feb 1916 mentions being wounded by a sniper (see also Longdon **Feb 1916**) Contents of parcel from St Michael's. **Oct 1916** In hospital in Stockport with trench fever. **12/16** Recovered and returned to regiment. **Mar 1917** RH/GB. **Aug 1917** Letter from hospital in France 7 July. Wounded 'but not very badly'. Describes incident. **Nov 1917** Letter 28 Oct. In hospital in Cheshire. Bad dislocation of right knee from falling in the trenches. **Aug 1918** RH/GB.

BROWN, JOSEPH Sept 1918 RH. A parishioner.

BROWN, WILLIAM June 1915 Listed as serving. **Mar 1917** RH/Dis. **Aug 1918** RH/Dis.

BROWNE, FRANK Oct 1914 Listed as serving. **Jan 1915** Was Sunday School teacher and assist. Scout Master. **Nov 1915** 'somewhere at the Front'. **Aug 1916** Wounded in first Somme offensive. **Mar 1917** RH/F.

Apr 1918 In England for officer training. Cadet. See also Scout report.

BUCK, ARCHIE Pte **Aug 1915** Listed as serving. **Oct 1916** Seriously wounded in France. **Mar 1917** RH/F. **Aug 1918** RH/F. **Oct 1918** Home on leave. **Nov 1918** ditto. **Feb 1919** Letter of thanks for gift 17 Jan 1919. Billetted 20 miles east of Cologne. Comments on the attitude of the population to the occupying soldiers.

BUCK, F. Pte **Oct 1918** Home on leave.

BURROWS, WILFRED. Formerly in the Sunday School. Pte 6th Seaforth Highlanders. **Nov 1915** Listed as serving. **June 1916** letter from France 21 May 1916. Has written to Rolfe before, but not quoted. Describes shellfire and trench warfare. Mentions Herbert Fletcher's death by mine explosion. Tribute to battalion chaplain. Mentions Charlie Willatt's transfer to Royal Engineers. **July 1916** Note that he has been seriously wounded in France and is in hospital in London. Letter 13 June detailing his injuries. He was wounded at Vimy Ridge. **Jan 1917** Discharged from Army wounded. **Mar 1917** RH/Dis. **Aug 1918** RH/Dis.

Notes: 1. Wilfred Burrows' son John recalls that his father told him that he was wounded as the result of a prank. A friend placed an empty tin on his bayonet and raised it above the trench parapet and rattled it. Immediately a barrage was sent over by the Germans causing Wilfred Burrows' injuries.

2. Wilfred Burrows married Grace Annie Bland, sister of Reginald Bland, on 4 June 1918. They lived at 40 Gerard Street, Derby.

BURROWS, W.R. L-Cpl. **Mar 1917** RH/GB. **Aug 1918** RH/GB.

Note: A family of this name lived at 4 St Michael's Lane.

BUTLER, FERDINAND Sept 1914 Listed as serving. **Mar 1917** RH/GB.

Aug 1918 RH/F.

BUTLER, HARRY Possibly 102819 1st Batt. The Sherwood Foresters. **Nov 1915** 'somewhere at the Front'. **Mar 1917** RH/GB **Aug 1918** RH/F.

CANTRILL, CHARLES Nov 1914 Listed as serving.

CHOLERTON, RALPH Communicant. **Oct 1914** Listed as serving. **Mar 1917** RH/I. **Aug 1918** RH/MI.

CLARK(E), ARTHUR Mar 1917 RH/GB. No 'e' in surname in this list. **Aug 1918** RH/F.

COCKER, HARRY Pte, L.Cpl No. 202101 2nd/5th Sherwood Foresters (Notts. and Derby Regt). Possibly brother of Joe Cocker. Formerly in the Sunday School. **June 1916** Listed as serving (noted as member of congregation). **Mar 1917** RH/GB. **May 1917** Killed in France, 4 April 1917 aged 22 (23 according to CWGC). **Aug 1918** RH/Departed.

Note: The son of Joseph and Elizabeth Cocker of 44 Erasmus Street, Derby, Harry Cocker is buried in Vadencourt British Cemetery, Maissemy, grave reference IV.A.7. Maissemy is a village 5 km NW of St Quentin and 2 km N of Vermand. *(CWGC)* Maissemy was taken by British forces in 1917. Harry Cocker was killed at Le Verquier. *Source: Sherwood Foresters Museum.*

COCKER, JOSEPH ('JOE') 800731. Described variously as Trooper, Gunner, and Driver. 230 Bde. R.F.A. (T.F.). 1913–14 Sunday School football team. **June 1915** Listed as serving. **Nov 1915** 'somewhere at the Front'. **Apr 1916** Wounded, no particulars. **Mar 1917** RH/F. **July 1917** Has been in Derby on leave. Styled 'Gunner'. **Oct 1917** Now Driver. Awarded MM in an action at Bully Grenay 13 July 1917. Full account of the action. **Mar 1918** expected home soon to receive MM. **Aug 1918** RH/F. **Sept 1918** Letter. Date of action on which he won MM given

here.

Note: A Joseph Edward Cocker married Ada Jones at St Michael's on 10 Oct 1920.

COLLARD, ARTHUR Pte Communicant. 1913–14 Sunday School football team. **Oct 1914** Listed as serving. **Nov 1915** 'somewhere at the Front'. **Mar 1917** RH/F. **July 1918** Letter received but not quoted. **Aug 1918** RH/F.

COTTON, H.C. Sgt. (There may be confusion with next entry. Sgt G. A. Cotton enlisted in 1914 and was also serving in Salonika. No mention of G.A. Cotton on RH in **Aug 1918**). **Mar 1917** RH/G. Here listed as Sgt C. Cotton. **Mar 1918** Letter of thanks for New Year's gift. Note ref. to food parcels. Name given here as is Sgt C.Cotton. **Aug 1918** RH/G. **Oct 1918** Letter from Salonika from 'Sgt Cotton' expecting leave, though note Rolfe's comment about leave being stopped. See also Karl Duncan's letter in **Nov 1918**.

COTTON, GEORGE A. Sgt. Confusion with H.C. Cotton? **Nov 1914** Listed as serving. **Mar 1916** Cpl. Letter from Salonika. Mentions often passing the road to Mars Hill (Acts 17). Soon to be prepared for Confirmation and visit of a bishop. **Oct 1916** Letter from Salonika. Mentions heat and flies, blisters, 'terrible sores'. Mentions 'Mr Ram, our Chaplain' who has 'like the rest of us, gone very thin'. Note: Rolfe's ref. is to A. Cotton. **Mar 1917** Letter 30 January 1917 from Salonika (Rolfe here has C.A. Cotton). No listing as G.A. Cotton in **Mar 1917** RH. **June 1918** Letter from Salonika but not quoted. Now Sgt. **Aug 1918** see note above under H.C. Cotton.

COULSON, HENRY BARTON ('HARRY') Communicant. Pte No 267259. 10th Sherwood Foresters (Notts. and Derby Regt) though at the time of his death Harry Coulson was serving with 1st/6th Batt. Northumberland Fusiliers (see **Dec 1916**). **Jan 1915** Had been Sunday School teacher, member of the Men's Institute and was assist. Scout Master, 'Company Scout', and signaller. **Oct 1914** Listed as serving. **Nov 1914** Letter from Shoreham. 'Comrades Corps' forming 4th Coy, 12th Batt., 10th Sherwood Foresters. **Aug 1915** Note of Coulson's leave in Derby on 17 July and of his letter of appreciation that the Scout's band gave him 'a hearty send-off' (see Scouts report). **Sept 1915** Letters dated 13, 23 and 29 Aug 1915, from Belgium describing trench warfare. The latter written from the trenches. The last letter describes 'the very unsatisfactory arrangements made by the Chaplain of his Regiment, as regards services for Church of England men'. **Oct 1915** Letter (undated here) in Aug describing life while his coy. is in reserve. Definition of a 'Whiz-bang'. Further references to a 'Jack Johnson', and to 'a coal-box'. **Nov 1915** Listed as 'somewhere at the Front'. **Dec 1915** Letter to the Scouts from 'A Dug-out in the trenches, Belgium' Oct. 27. **Jan 1916** Letter, 20 Dec. 1915. Vivid description of being shelled. **Mar 1916** visits Scouts when home on leave. **Apr 1916** Letter received by Rolfe but not quoted. **June 1916** Letter from Robert Barker. Coulson in same village acc. to Rolfe. **Aug 1916** Wounded during first Somme offensive, before Fricourt. Letter describing effects of British barrage etc. Vivid description. **Sept 1916** Letter to St Michael's Scouts. **Oct 1916** Letter to St Michael's Scouts. **Dec 1916** Returned to France from leave. Now with 6th Northumberland Fusiliers. Letter dated 18 Nov 1916 describing being buried twice in one day by shellfire. Terrible trench conditions. **Mar 1917** Letter from France. Parcel did not arrive (see refs. to this earlier in

Mar 1917). Moving description of Christmas Day holy communion service. Another letter 20 Feb 1917; on signalling course. **Mar 1917** RH/F. **Apr 1917** Letter 18 March 1917 from France to the Scouts. **May 1917** letter from France early in April. Had visited a village church where he noted a picture as memorial to British soldiers buried in the cemetery. Also letter to the Scouts, 23 April 1917. **Feb 1918** married Ada Cecilia Buxton on 3 Jan 1918. See Scout notice and parish register. **May 1918** killed 12 April 1918. Struck by shell. **June 1918** The Scout troop was detached from St Michael's after Harry Coulson's death. See Scout report. **July 1918** Baden-Powell's letter to Ada Coulson. **Aug 1918** RH/Departed.

Notes: 1. Harry Coulson was the son of Henry Charles and Annie Coulson and the husband of Ada Cecilia Coulson of 8 Derwent Bank, Duffield Road, Derby. He was aged 26 when he died. He is commemorated on the Ploegsteert Memorial, Panel 2. This Memorial stands in Berks Cemetery Extension 12.5 km S. of Ieper, Belgium. (*CWGC*)

2. On his death Lieut. Lewis Craddock wrote to Ada Coulson: 'Just a few lines to tender you my deepest sympathy at your recent great loss at the death of your husband Signaller H.B. Coulson. At the time of his death he was doing excellent work, being with a forward wireless station which had been forced to move several times. It was entirely due to the men on the station that communications were re-established so rapidly. It was during one of these moves that a shell struck the house in which the station was working, and caused the death of your husband and one of his comrades ...' (*Derby Daily Telegraph,* 29 April 1918). This understandably reticent letter conceals the fact that Harry Coulson has no known grave. This report also carries a note of

the choral eucharist at St Michael's on Sunday 28 April at which Harry Coulson was remembered.

COX, FRED W. Second initial given in letter in **Feb 1919. Mar 1917** RH/GB. **Aug 1918** RH/F. **Feb 1919** Letter of thanks 2 Jan 1919, from Vignacourt France for gift from St Michael's. Visit to a war cemetery and memories of a fallen friend who 'died for his country by my side on May 28th. His brother was also killed about the same time ... The earth seems very peaceful now. It seems wonderful'.

COX, HENRY ('HARRY') E. Communicant. Given as E.H. Cox and Sgt in **Mar 1918.** Formerly in the choir. **Sept 1914** Listed as serving. **Apr 1916** Letter received by Rolfe but not quoted. **June 1916** Letter from Salonika describing unexpected and unforgettable Easter Day holy communion service. Name given as E.H. Cox here. **Mar 1917** RH/G. **Mar 1918** Letter of thanks for New Year's gift. **Aug 1918** RH/G. Listed as Henry E. Cox. **Sept 1918** Letter from T.A. Wragg. Cox is now RQMS at GHG in Salonika. **Dec 1918** Awarded Serbian Military Virtue Medal, one of only five in British Army to receive it.

CROSS, WILLIAM Nov 1915 'somewhere at the Front'. **Mar 1917** RH/G. **Aug 1918** RH/G. **Oct 1918** Home on leave.

CURD, JOHN June 1915 Listed as serving. Note: A family of this name lived at 13 Darley Lane, Derby.

CURZON, HARRY DCM. Communicant. Sgt 7820 2nd Batt., King's Royal Rifles, Army middleweight boxing champion. **Sept 1914** Listed as serving. **Dec 1914** Letter dated 23 Nov 1914. Had widowed mother who was regular communicant at St Michael's. Rolfe notes that Curzon had been promoted Cpl and then Sgt 'for conspicuous bravery in the field'. His mother

believed that he would be awarded the VC (in fact the DCM **Feb 1915**). **Jan 1915** Letter dated 18 Dec 1914, describing trench warfare. **Feb 1915** Awarded DCM for action on 31 Oct and 7 Nov 1914 in first battle of Ypres. Citation. **Mar 1915** Public presentation. Had been in hospital in Winchester injured (not wounded in action apparently). **Mar 1917** RH/GB. **Aug 1918** RH/GB.

Note: *Derby Daily Telegraph* (3 Feb. 1915) carries a detailed account of the actions for which Curzon won the 'King's Military Medal', second only to the VC. There is no record of the institution of this medal. The DCM is the second highest award for gallantry. The paper also notes that Curzon was promoted 'sergeant-in-the-field' (a rank, the report says, that could only be reduced by Royal consent). At the time of these actions Curzon's battalion was attached to the 2nd Infantry Brigade of the 1st Division, BEF. His mother lived at 48 Henry Street, Derby.

DEAN, ALBERT ARMITAGE (second name initial variously given as 'E.' or 'H.' in the magazines and as 'E.' in *Derby Daily Telegraph*. Second name given here as in the database of Sherwood Foresters Museum). 2nd Lieut., Lieut. **Oct 1914** Listed as serving. Given as Albert H. (in error for 'A.'?). **Jan 1915** Had been a Sunday School teacher. **Mar 1917** RH/GB. Given as 2nd Lieut A. Dean. **July 1917** Has been wounded, but not seriously. Has been on leave in Derby. Given as Lieut A.E. Dean. **June 1918** Wounded 'some time ago' (21 April 1918?, see note 1 below). Has gone to stay with Revd W.R. Johnson in Cornwall. Name given as Lieut A. Dean.

Notes: 1. Almost certainly this is Albert Armitage Dean who enlisted in the ranks of the Royal Fusiliers in 1914 and saw service in France. 2nd Lieut.,

4th Batt. The Sherwood Foresters, 5 Aug 1916. Joined 9th Batt., 26 Feb 1917. Wounded 9 May 1917 at Hermies. Joined 1st Batt. 20 Aug 1917. Acting Capt., 3 March 1918. Wounded 21 April 1918. Lieut., 5 Nov 1918; Capt., 27 October 1926. Saw service in India becoming Dept. Director Ordnance Clothing Factories and Department of Supply of the Government of India during the Second World War. Retired in 1947. Was secretary of the Regimental Association in the 1950s based in Derby. Died 19 Aug 1973. *Source: Cliff Housley, Sherwood Foresters Museum.*

2. According to *Derby Daily Telegraph,* 25 April 1918, Capt. A.E. Dean, eldest son of A.E. Dean, secretary and manager, Railway Servants' Orphanage, Derby, was 'wounded in recent severe fighting in France' and was on his way to hospital in Oxford. He enlisted in the Public Schools Battalion of Royal Fusiliers early in the war and went to France in 1915. In 1916 sent to England to complete his training for a commission and then attached to Sherwood Foresters. Had been wounded 'nearly a year ago in the fighting on the Somme'.

DOWLER, FRED Pte **Mar 1917** RH/GB. **Sept 1917** Letter 10 August 1917. Description of night fighting as a member of a machine-gun team. **May 1918** recovering from effects of gas attack. **July 1918** Letter from France 7 June 1918. Moving letter with a further reference to gas warfare. Mentions Harry Coulson and Jim Gleeson (qv). **Aug 1918** RH/F (first name from this list).

Note: Fred Dowler lived in Arthur Street. (*Derby Daily Telegraph,* 30 April 1918, report of him being gassed.)

DOWNMAN, BERNARD VINCENT RIDOUT 2nd Lieut 9th, attached 13th Batt. Sherwood Foresters (Notts. and Derby Regt). Brother of Theodore F.C. Downman. **Oct 1916** Killed on 21 Sept 1916 (here given as 22 Sept). 20 years of age. Intended to be ordained. **Nov 1916** Note of the manner of his death (on 21 Sept in this note) with 'his Bible by his side', adding a verse by Downman. **Mar 1917** RH/Departed. **Aug 1918** RH/Departed.

Notes: 1. Bernard Downman was the son of Frank Percival and Elizabeth Agnes Downman, then of 3 Dunsford Place, Bath. A native of Derby. Aged 20 when killed. Buried in Bouzincourt Communal Cemetery extension, Somme, France. Grave reference I.H.8. This cemetery was used not only for burial from the Field Ambulances but also for the interment of many soldiers killed in action and brought back from the line. *(CWGC)* Bernard Downman was killed in the trenches south of Thiepval. *Source: Sherwood Foresters Museum.*

2. The Revd F.P. Percival was licensed as an assistant priest at St Michael's, Derby and was subsequently diocesan organising secretary for the Church of England Temperance Society. Left Derby Feb 1917 to take charge of a mission district in Horfield, Bristol.

DOWNMAN, THEODORE FRANK CYRIL 2nd Lieut, Lieut. 5th Batt. Sherwood Foresters. Brother of B.V.R. Downman (qv). **Mar 1915** Listed as serving. **Aug 1916** Missing in first Somme offensive. **Sept 1916** Now a POW. **Mar 1917** RH/POW. **June 1918** Released and now in Holland. **Aug 1918** RH/POW (but see **June 1918**).

DUFFY, TOM Pte **Mar 1915** Had been member of St Michael's Men's Bible Class. First of the St Michael's men to be wounded. Letter 7 Feb 1915. J.C. Hill with him in trenches. Letter 13 Feb 1915: Now in Netley hospital having been wounded by shell-fire at the village of Voilaines, near La Bassée, near Ypres; has a bed for the first time since he left Derby. **Mar 1917** RH/F. **Aug 1918** RH/F.

DUNCAN, ARCHIBALD W. ('ARCHIE') Choirman and Sunday School member. Pte A Coy, 6th Seaforth Highlanders. Enlisted 1915 (so **Dec 1916**) **Sept 1915** Listed as serving. **Sept 1916** Reference to Archie Duncan in letter from Fred Fletcher (qv). **Dec 1916** Letter early in Nov 1916 describing waterfilled trenches. Killed in action 13 November 1916. See letter from CO of his coy. **Jan 1917** Killed in same action in which W.H. Walkerdine was wounded (see his letter). See further note from Lieut. Wragg, the St Michael's Choirmaster, about Archie Duncan. **Mar 1917** RH/Departed. **Aug 1918** RH/Departed.

Note: No 3292 Signaller Pte A.W. Duncan of 1st/6th Batt. Seaforth Highlanders was the son of Frederick William and Edith Duncan of 115 Osmaston Road, Derby. Killed Sunday 13 Nov 1916 aged 21. Buried in Mailly Wood Cemetery, grave reference I.C.5. The cemetery is on the outskirts of the village of Mailly-Maillet 9 km N of Albert. The cemetery was begun to bury thirteen men of the Seaforth Highlanders killed 25 June 1916. The 1st (Highland Division) buried there many of their dead from the capture of Beaumont Hamel in Nov 1916. It is clear that Archie Duncan was killed in this action. *(CWGC)*

DUNCAN, KARL V. Trooper No 75677, 1st Derbyshire Yeomanry (Corps of Dragoons), Salonika Forces, Greece (**Sept 1917**). Sec. 1913–14 Sunday School football team. Home address 115 Osmaston Road, Derby. **June 1915** Listed as serving. **Nov 1915** 'somewhere at the Front'. **Mar 1916** Letter 12 Feb 1916 from Salonika, describing countryside and muddy conditions; Greeks wearing sacks for footwear etc. **Apr 1916** Letter received by

Rolfe but not quoted. **May 1916** Letter received 7 April 1916 from Salonika. Vividly describes patrolling the dividing line. Describes voyage from Egypt, mud, mules, 'the peculiar looking Greeks', 'had Church every Sunday' (chaplain: Revd Edward J. Powell from Nottingham), the Balkan war etc. **Sept 1916** In hospital in Malta with malaria. **Oct 1916** Letter 11 Sept 1916. In convalescent camp in Malta. Is with Walter Ray and Arthur Smith. Details extent of illness due 'bodies buried no distance in the ground' and to 'Greek method of doing away with dead cattle'. Holy Communion 'very nice indeed'. **Feb 1917** in hospital in Malta for a second time with malaria. Letter dated 10 Jan 1917. **Mar 1917** RH/G. **June 1917** Letter: in St Andrew's Hospital, Malta. **Aug 1917** Letter from Malta 22 June 1917. Expects 'we shall finish where Norman Powell was wounded' though 'there is nothing official' (circumlocution to avoid censorship?). Describes the life in a convalescent camp near beaches and 'larking in the sea'. **Sept 1917** Letter 22 Aug 1917 from Salonika. **Nov 1917** met T.A. Wragg (qv). **June 1918** Letter received but not quoted. **July 1918** Letter from Salonika 28 May 1918. 'very quiet'. Mentions that Walter Ray has malaria, 'just a relapse—which one looks upon quite undisturbed'. **Aug 1918** letter. RH/Greece. **Oct 1918** Letter from Salonika 3 Sept 1918: Walter Ray should be on his way home having been in hospital. **Nov 1918** Letter 4 Oct 1918 'from Greece'. Been in hospital with 'flue' and now in convalescent camp. Hopes to return to regiment in a month. Ref. to offensive which led to Bulgaria 'packing up' after four days (Bulgaria signed armistice 29 Sept 1918 following Allied breakthrough on 15 Sept).

Note: For the Derbyshire Yeomanry in Salonika, see G.A. Strutt, *The Derby-*

shire Yeomanry War History 1914–1919 (Bemrose, Derby, nd) ch. 9–13.

EDWARDS, BEN Sept 1915 Listed as serving. **Mar 1917** RH/F. **Aug 1918** RH/F.

ELSMORE, E. Pte 2nd Batt. Sherwood Foresters. **July 1917** POW. recipient of food parcel from Sherwood Foresters POW committee, noting his full POW address in Hanover, and requesting letters to be sent to him. Mother, Mrs Glover, lived at 71 Yates Street, Derby. He received 3 food parcels each month for the first 6 months, each valued at 7*s*.

ELVIDGE, ARCHIBALD J. Communicant. Cpl 36920 'B' Bty, 88th Bde, Royal Field Artillery. Confirmed 28 April 1913. **Oct 1914** Listed as serving. **Jan 1915** Letter describing Bulford camp, Salisbury Plain. Promoted Bombardier. **Nov 1915** Promoted Cpl. Killed by shellfire. **Mar 1917** RH/Departed. **Aug 1918** RH/Departed.

Note: Killed Sunday, 3 Oct 1915, aged 25. Son of George and Bertha Ellen Elvidge, 11 Pear Tree Road, Derby. Buried in Le Touret Military Cemetery, Richebourg-L'Avoue, Pas de Calais, France. Grave reference: II.H.27. *(CWGC)*

EVERINGTON, THOMAS (WALTER) Sgt. Confirmed 28 April 1913. Possibly the Thomas Walter Everington who married Zuradah Joyce 26 Dec 1915. **Dec 1915** Listed as serving. **May 1916** Letter received but not quoted. **Mar 1917** RH/F (first name from this list). **Aug 1918** RH/F.

EYRE, HENRY (HARRY) Communicant. **Oct 1914** Listed as serving. **Nov 1915** listed as L-Cpl. and wounded. **Mar 1917** RH/Dis. Rank given as Sgt here. **Aug 1918** RH/Dis. Listed as Sgt.

FETTERPLACE, SAM Sgt 9019 2nd Batt. Sherwood Foresters (Notts. and Derby Regt). **Apr 1915** Confirmed

in 1901 and had been in choir before enlisting several years previously. Killed 21 Feb 1915. **Mar 1917** RH/Departed. **Aug 1918** RH/Departed.

Note: 1. Sam Fetterplace is commemorated on the Ploegsteert Memorial, Panel 7, in the Berks Cemetery Extension 12.5 km S of Ieper, Belgium. The Memorial commemorates men who have no known grave. *(CWGC)* Aged 28 *Source: Parish register.*

2. Born in Cleethorpes, Lincs. Killed in the trenches at Houplines, Belgium. *Source: Sherwood Foresters Museum.*

FLETCHER, CALEB Communicant. Sapper. **Sept 1914** Listed as serving. **July 1915.** Letter dated 10 June. Mention of Bishop of London's visit to the troops in France, Easter 1915 (see also **May 1915**). Graphic letter: 'I could not help wondering whether there could be a God to allow such things to occur. And then I remembered that this is a "holy war" ... ' (referring to bishop's Easter sermon). **Nov 1915** 'somewhere at the Front'. **Mar 1917** RH/F. **Aug 1918** RH/F.

FLETCHER, FRED Pte, L-Cpl Argyle and Sutherland Highlanders. **June 1916** Listed as serving (noted by Rolfe as a member of the congregation). **Sept 1916** Letter dated 13 Aug. Description of experiencing shell-fire. Ref. to meeting Archie Duncan and attending the Church Hut with him. Total lack of Church of England chaplains. **Feb 1917** Letter dated 31 December 1916. **Mar 1917** RH/F. **Aug 1918** RH/F. **Nov 1918** Home on leave. Now L-Cpl.

FLETCHER, HERBERT AUGUSTINE Pte No 3291 6th Batt. Seaforth Highlanders. **June 1916** Letter from Wilfred Burrows (qv) mentions Herbert Fletcher's death by mine and that he was buried in the cemetery of the village in which they were billetted.

Note: Herbert Fletcher was the son of James and Annie Fletcher, Railway

Terrace, Derby. Killed Thursday, 28 April 1916 aged 21. Buried in Maroeuil British Cemetery, grave reference: II.D.10. Maroeuil is in the Department of Pas-de-Calais, 6 km NW of Arras. *(CWGC)*

FOSTER, ARTHUR Confirmed 28 April 1913. Pte **Sept 1915** Listed as serving. **Sept 1916** Seriously wounded in thigh and in hospital in Manchester. **Dec 1916** Now improving 'after a very trying time'. **Aug 1917** Discharged from Army wounded. **Aug 1918** RH/Dis.

FOSTER, ROBERT Nov 1914 Listed as serving.

FOSTER, WILLIAM Aug 1918 RH (listed as a sailor).

Note: There are 45 men with this name on the naval roll in the PRO. As William may not have been his first Christian name it has so far proved impossible to trace his service record.

FOY, WILLIAM EDWARD Former member of the Sunday School. Pte 200283 1st/5th Batt. Sherwood Foresters (Notts. and Derby Regt) **Sept 1914** Listed as serving. **Nov 1915** 'somewhere at the Front'. **Sept 1916** reported missing. **Oct 1916** No news. **Nov 1916** No news. **Dec 1916** Believed killed. **Mar 1917** RH/Departed. **Aug 1918** RH/Departed.

Note: William Foy died 1 July 1916, the first day of the Battle of the Somme. He has no known grave and is commemorated on the Thiepval Memorial, Panel reference: Pier and Face 10C 10D and 11A. *(CWGC)* He was killed at Gommercourt. *Source: Sherwood Foresters Museum.*

FOX, BENJAMIN Mar 1917 RH/I. **Aug 1918** RH/MI.

FOX, FRANK Mar 1917 RH/GB. **Aug 1918** RH/F.

FRITH, CUTHBERT Mar 1917 RH/GB. **Aug 1918** RH/F.

FROGGATT, GEORGE BRIAN Pte. Baptised 26 Jan 1915 with his two brothers and confirmed with them 16 March 1915. Lived at 59 Agard Street, Derby. **Aug 1918** RH/GB. **Oct 1918** Home on leave. **Feb 1919** Letter of thanks, 3 Jan 1919, for Christmas/New Year's gift, from Bruhl, Germany noting that this had been a poor Christmas for the inhabitants of this town: 'very little for them to eat ... The people are treating us well and they are quiet'. He says that 'I am staying here indefinitely'.

GARTON, ARTHUR WILLIAM Confirmed 28 April 1913. Pte **Dec 1914** Listed as serving. **Nov 1915** 'somewhere at the Front'. **Mar 1917** RH/G. **June 1918** Letter received from Salonika but not quoted. **Aug 1918** RH/G. **Nov 1918** Home on leave.

GEARY, WILLIAM Sept 1918 RH. A parishioner.

GLEESON, GEORGE JAMES ('JIM') Sgt 24827 8th Batt. North Staffs Regiment. **June 1916** Listed as serving (noted by Rolfe as a member of the congregation). **Aug 1916** Former acting Scoutmaster. **Oct 1916** promoted Cpl. **Mar 1917** RH/GB. **May 1918** Now Sgt. But 'nothing has been heard ... for some weeks—his friends are naturally very anxious'. **June 1918** killed by shellfire on 17 April 1918 (should be 18 April) less than two weeks after landing in France. Letter from CO. Buried in the field owing to the 'extremely critical' situation. His grave on southern slope of Kemmel Hill ('now in enemy hands'). Story in a 'recent edition' of *Derby Daily Telegraph* under 'A Hero of Kemmel Hill'. **July 1918** Letter from Fred Dowler 'Well do I know where [Jim Gleeson] fell and the churchyard where he is buried', and 'at one time a most beautiful spot.' It seems that Jim Gleeson's body was reinterred. **Aug 1918** RH/Departed.

Note: Jim Gleeson was killed on Thursday 18 April 1918 aged 28. He was the son of Mrs M.A. Gleeson of 41 Back Parker Street, Derby. Buried in Voormezeele Enclosure No. 3, Ieper, West-Vlaanderen, Belgium. Grave Reference XIV.H.22. *(CWGC)* The place of his burial indicates that Jim Gleeson was killed during the German Lys offensive which began on 9 April 1918. The village of Ieper and its cemeteries were captured by German forces after very heavy fighting on 29 April. It may be that Jim Gleeson was killed in the action preceding this.

GOODCHILD, WILLIAM FRANCIS HENRY Pte 4666 1st/5th Batt. Sherwood Foresters (Notts. and Derby Regt. Confirmed 28 April 1913 (order of Christian names given in register). **Nov 1915** listed as serving. **Oct 1916** Letter 15 Sept 1916 from the front in France. Has met Harry White. Has been patrolling though 'my nerves have not been very good, they have not been right since July 1st. We had a terrible time then' (first day of the Somme offensive). 'We seldom have a Chaplain long, but they all seem nice fellows'. **Feb 1917** Died Jan 1917. Letter dated 7 Jan 1917, cheerfully describing the mud. **Mar 1917** Confirmed killed in action 21 Jan 1917. **Mar 1917** RH/Departed. **Aug 1918** RH/Departed.

Note: William Goodchild was the son of William James and Elizabeth Elen (sic) Goodchild. Killed in the trenches at Souastre aged 21 and is buried in Foncquevillers Military Cemetery, Row 1, Block G, Grave 28. Order of Christian names given as Francis William Henry. *Source: Sherwood Foresters Museum.*

GREENLAY, W. Capt. of the 1913–14 Sunday School football team. **Nov 1915** Listed as serving. **Mar 1917** RH/GB. Now Cpl. **Apr 1917** In hospital in Birkenhead. Letter from Étaples, France, 19 March 1917. **Jan 1918** Believed to be discharged unfit for active service. **Aug 1918** RH/Dis.

GREENSMITH, BASIL Nov 1914 Listed as serving. Note: A family of this name lived at 73 Wilmot Street, Derby.

GREENSMITH, JOHN Nov 1914 Listed as serving.

GREENSMITH, GEORGE Nov 1914 Listed as serving. Pte **Aug 1916** wounded during first Somme offensive.

HACKFORTH, Revd JOHN EDMONDS SWITHUN July 1915 Article defending soldiers against charge of immorality, and questioning the substance of the story of 'Angel of Mons'. **Mar 1917** Became Army chaplain, initially based in Derby and continuing to assist at St Michael's. **Apr 1918** Article about Forces' chaplains.

Note: John Edmonds Swithun Hackforth, Schol. Episc. Manc. 1909; Hon. C.F. 1920; deacon 1911, priest 1912; assist. curate, St Margaret, Hollinwood 1911–14; St Michael, Derby 1915–17; TCF 1916–19; chapl. HM Detention Barracks, Derby, 1917–20; P.C. of Chaddesden, Derby 1919–33. Perm. Off. dio. Chichester, 1939.

HALLSWORTH, FRED Gunner, later Signaller. Formerly in the Sunday School. **Mar 1917** RH/GB. **Feb 1918** Now in India. **Mar 1918** Letter telling of his journeys in India. **May 1918** Letter acknowledging New Year's gift. **Aug 1918** Letter from India. RH/MI. **Oct 1918** Letter from India 9 Aug 1918 reporting deaths from heat in Peshawar. Now Signaller. Fine descriptions of life in the hills at Ghora Dhaka.

HALLSWORTH, LAURENCE Communicant. Pte then Sapper. A family of this name lived at 6 High Street. **Sept 1914** Listed as serving. **June 1915** letter dated 12 May 1915. Graphic description of an aerial dogfight, and of a land-mine exploding etc. **Nov 1915** 'somewhere at the Front'. **Aug 1916** Letter 4 July 1916 giving vivid first-hand description of advancing towards enemy positions under heavy fire on the first day of the Somme offensive, only to withdraw. **Feb 1917** on leave and married Daisy Louisa Hughes on 20 January. **Mar 1917** RH/F. **Aug 1917** Letter to churchwarden R. Hudson (of whose Bible Class Laurence Hallsworth had been a member), 1 July 1917, adding further graphic details to his letter in **Aug 1916**. **Aug 1918** RH/F.

HARDY, CHARLES ERIC (first initial not 'G.' as in **Nov 1918**) Communicant. Trooper (**Mar 1917**). 2nd Lieut., Lieut. 19 Batt., Machine Gun Corps by **Aug 1918**. **Sept 1914** Listed as serving. **Nov 1915** 'somewhere at the Front'. Pte **June 1916** Letter to his parents from Salonika, 24 April 1916 describing enemy aircraft sorties, fishing for chub with bent pins, 'Easter communion on Good Friday'. Vivid descriptions of Greek peasants ('like gypsies') etc. **Mar 1917** Letter from Salonika (having been home on leave). RH/G. **Aug 1918** RH/F. Now 2nd Lieut. **Nov 1918** Killed in action 24 Oct 1918. Obituary quoting letter from his coy. CO giving account of the action in which he was killed by machine-gun fire.

Notes: 1. Eric Hardy was the son of Charles Edward Andrews Hardy and Edith Mary Hardy of 69 Otter St, Derby. Born in Geraldton, Western Australia. The CWGC notes that he also served in Egypt, Gallipoli and Salonika. When he was killed he was a 2nd Lieut. with 19 Batt., Machine Gun Corps. Killed Tuesday 23 Oct 1918 aged 24. Buried in St Aubert British Cemetery, grave reference I.B.12. St Aubert is a village in the Department of the Nord 13 km E of Cambrai. It may be that Eric Hardy was killed in the same offensive as Robert Barker: the Pursuit to

the Selle (9–12 Oct 1918) and its aftermath. *(CWGC)*

2. From the evidence of his account of the Easter holy communion service held on Good Friday 1916 in Salonika it seems that Eric Hardy had initially been a Territorial serving with 1/1st Derbyshire Yeomanry.

HARDY, GORDON Lieut. **Nov 1916** Wounded in arm during the Somme offensive. In hospital in London. **Dec 1916** Improving. **Mar 1917** RH/Wounded or Sick. Listed here as 2nd Lieut. **Dec 1917** returned to duties in Derby. **Aug 1918** RH/GB.

HARRISON, BERT Communicant, formerly in the Sunday School. A family of this name lived in St Michael's Lane. **Sept 1914** Listed as serving. **Nov 1915** 'somewhere at the Front'. **Mar 1917** RH/F.

HARRISON, RICHARD Communicant. **Sept 1914** Listed as serving.

HARRISON, TOM Sept 1918 RH. A parishioner.

HERBERT-STEPNEY, HERBERT Nov 1914 Listed as serving.

HERBERT-STEPNEY, GUY Nov 1914 Listed as serving.

Note: There is no record of Herbert Herbert-Stepney in the records of The Sherwood Foresters. Major G.S. Herbert-Stepney, 13th Batt. Sherwood Foresters, disappears Army List May 1917. Col. C.C. Herbert-Stepney had a very distinguished war record. Capt. C.E. Herbert-Stepney, Adjt 13th Batt. Sherwood Foresters, disappears Army List May 1918. *Source: The Sherwood Foresters Museum.*

The Herbert-Stepneys are listed by Harry Rolfe in **Nov 1914** among those 'whose friends are closely connected with St Michael's' and 'whose names we would also wish to record and remember in our prayers'. There seems to have been no personal connection at this time between this family and St

Michael's.

HEWITT, ALFRED Mar 1917 RH/Dis. **Aug 1918** RH/Dis.

HEWITT, ALFRED Sept 1918 Name added to the RH. Parishioner.

HICKTON, WILLIAM Sept 1918 Name added to the RH. A parishioner.

HILL, JAMES C. ('JIMMY') Communicant. **Sept 1914** Listed as serving. **Dec 1914** Letter dated 20 Nov 1914. Now Cpl. Photo in *Daily Mirror,* 7 (should be 6) Oct 1914 'as one of a British outpost on the look out for the enemy' with a friend holding Hill's cap aloft to attract enemy fire. **Jan 1915** Postcard, 13 Dec 1914. Now Sgt. **Feb 1915** Letter dated 14 Jan 1915. **Mar 1915** With Tom Duffy, narrowly escaped being wounded. **Apr 1915** Letter dated 16 March 1915. Graphic account of battle. Heavy losses: 'It's nothing else but murder, but I suppose we should do the same to them'. Now resting at Béthune. **Nov 1915** 'somewhere at the Front'. **Mar 1917** In France. Promoted CSM Instructor. RH/F. **Aug 1918** RH/F. Note: A family of this name lived at 141 Bridge Street, Derby.

HIVES, JOHN June 1916 Listed as serving (noted by Rolfe as member of the congregation).

HOOSE, WILLIAM June 1916 Listed as serving.

HOPE, RICHARD Nov 1914 Listed as serving.

HORTON, WILLIAM EDWARD Pte 202487, 1st/5th Batt. Sherwood Foresters (Notts. and Derby Regt). **Apr 1917** Added to **Mar 1917** RH. Died following serious wounds sustained in the 'big push' (German main withdrawal on Western Front 4 March–5 April 1917) leaving a wife and two young children. **Aug 1918** RH/Departed.

Note: William Edward Horton was killed on Tuesday 14 March 1917 aged 37. He was the son of George S. and Frances Horton, and husband of Gertrude L. Horton of 1 Keys Street, Nottingham Road, Derby. Buried in Warlincourt Halte British Cemetery, Saulty. Grave Reference: VI.D.3. *(CWGC)* He died of wounds received, possibly, in the Gommercourt sector. *Source: Sherwood Foresters Museum.*

HUDSON, PETER Sept 1914 Listed as serving. Communicant. A note in **Oct 1915** says that his mother lived at 30 Rivett Street. **June 1915** badly wounded in the head. Further refs. to this in **Oct 1915** and **Nov 1915**. Visited by Rolfe in King George's Hospital, Stamford Sreet, London. **Apr 1916** now discharged, with pension. 'He seems fairly well, except at times'. **Mar 1917** RH/Dis. **Aug 1918** RH/Dis.

HUGHES, JOHN ALLAN Formerly in the Sunday School. **Sept 1914** Listed as serving. **Mar 1917** RH/Sailor. **Aug 1918** RH/Sailor.

Note: John Allan Hughes joined HMS *Victory II* as a Stoker 2 on 7 February 1913. *Victory II* was a shore establishment at Crystal Palace and a training depot for the Royal Navy. He served throughout the war in HMS *Donegal, Carnarvon, Birmingham, Excellent, and Cleopatra,* returning to *Victory II* for periods of up to two months on four occasions. Demobilised 1 May 1919 with the rate of acting Leading Stoker. Born 31 Oct 1894, occupation before naval service given as machine hand. *Source: PRO.*

HUNT, GORDON Communicant. **Sept 1914** Listed as serving. **June 1915** Letter giving vivid description of effects of a gas attack at 10 miles distance. **Nov 1915** 'somewhere at the Front'. **Apr 1916** Letter, 17 March 1916, describing the occupation of a German dug-out. **Mar 1917** RH/F. **Aug 1918** RH/F.

HUNTLEY, JOSEPH 2nd Lieut.

According to **Oct 1918** his name 'not described correctly' in **Sept 1918**. In **Oct 1918** given merely as '2nd Lieut. Huntley, a parishioner'. **Sept 1918** Name added to **Aug 1918** RH.

Note: Joseph Huntley was commissioned in the Sherwood Foresters but after training immediately attached to the Royal Flying Corps as an observer. Date of transfer 16 Aug 1918. *Source: Sherwood Foresters Museum.*

HUTLEY, GEORGE Formerly in the Sunday School. **Sept 1914** Listed as serving. **Nov 1915** 'somewhere at the Front'. **Mar 1917** RH/F. **Aug 1918** RH/F.

INNOCENT, HAROLD L-Cpl. **Mar 1915** Listed as serving. **Mar 1917** RH/I. **Aug 1918** RH/GB.

Note: A family of this name lived at 141 Leacroft Road, Derby.

JACKSON, HARRY Communicant. **Sept 1914** Listed as serving. **Mar 1917** RH/Dis. **Aug 1918** RH/Dis. Note: these last two entries may be duplicates of the next.

JACKSON, HARRY June 1915 Listed as serving.

JESSOP, HERBERT Mar 1917 RH/GB. **Aug 1918** RH/F.

JOHNSON, JOHN Apr 1917 Added to **Mar 1917** RH. **Aug 1918** RH/F.

JOHNSON, Revd WILFRED RYAN Nov 1912 Had been assistant curate at St Michael's for seven years to Oct 1912. **Aug 1917** Added to RH. In the Notices section of the magazine Rolfe added: 'Mr Johnson wished to go out to the fighting line, either as a Chaplain or as an assistant in the R.A.M.C., but he did not get appointed. He writes to say that he expects shortly to go away with the Ambulance Convoy, sent out by the London Committee of the French Red Cross for service with the French Balkans' Army. He will be technically a French soldier', but see Johnson's letter in **Mar 1918**. **Oct 1917**

Letter 7 Sept 1917. In the Balkan mountains writing during a break in his duties as a mess orderly. **Mar 1918** Letter saying that '... I'd never tried to enlist in the British Army and now what I'm in is the Red Cross work of a Voluntary Ambulance convoy. My period of service is up next month'. This to contradict 'that newspaper paragraph' (unidentified). **June 1918** See Lieut. A.A. Dean's entry. Johnson now returned from Balkans to his benefice in Cornwall (see below).

Note: Wilfred Ryan Johnson, Univ. London 1893, B.A. 1896; Sarum Theol. Coll. 1903; deacon 1903, priest 1904; assist. curate St John the Divine, Chatham 1903–5; St Michael, Derby 1905–12; dio. chaplain to Bishop of Truro 1912–15; Rector of St Ervan, St Issey, dio. Truro 1915–54; Proc. Conv. Truro 1929–45; Preb. of Bodmin in Preb. Church of St Endellion, 1946.

JONES, ARTHUR June 1915 Listed as serving. **Mar 1917** RH/GB. **Aug 1918** RH/GB.

KING, GEORGE JOHN Formerly in the Sunday School. **Nov 1914** Listed as serving. **Nov 1915** Listed as killed in action. **Mar 1917** RH/Departed. **Aug 1918** RH/Departed.

Note: George John King, Rifleman No. 9970, 3rd Batt. King's Royal Rifle Corps. Killed Sunday 10 May 1915 aged 27. Son of Caroline Ann King, 1 Darley Lane, Derby, and the late Albert King. Commemorated on the Ypres (Menin Gate) Memorial, Panel 51 and 53. *(CWGC)*

KNIGHT, GEORGE Sept 1918 Name added to the **Aug 1918** RH.

LAMBTON, GEORGE WILLIAM Communicant. Brother of J.H. Lambton. **Sept 1914** Listed as serving. **Nov 1915** 'somewhere at the Front'. **Mar 1917** RH/Sailor. **Aug 1918** RH/Sailor.

Note: SS 115516 George William Lambton enlisted 17 March 1914 and posted to HMS *Victory II* as a Stoker 2 (although his service number does not carry the K prefix letter which normally identified stokers). *Victory II* was a shore establishment at Crystal Palace and a training depot for the Royal Navy. He served for a short time in HMS *Crescent* and throughout the war in HMS *Agincourt*, returning to *Victory II* on two occasions. Demobilised on 14 April 1919 with the rate of Leading Stoker and immediately transferred to the Royal Fleet Reserve. Served for 12 years from 14 March 1914. Occupation before he joined the Navy given as moulder. Date of birth 5 Sept 1895.

LAMBTON, JOSHUA HENRY Communicant. Brother of George. Pte 1476. 1st/5th Batt. Sherwood Foresters Notts. and Derby Regt). **Sept 1914** Listed as serving. **Nov 1915** 'somewhere at the Front'. **Feb 1916** Letter noting that his comrades' thoughts 'are with the One above when there is any danger' and of the 2nd Sherwoods singing three hymns 'before they went over the parapet' at Hooge. **May 1916** letter from France 26 April. Vivid description of a field war cemetery, seen on Good Friday having come from the trenches. **Aug 1916** Missing in first Somme offensive. **Sept 1916** No news. **Oct 1916** No news. **Nov 1916** No news. **Dec 1916** Missing believed killed (here referred to as H. Lambton). **Mar 1917** RH/Departed. **Aug 1918** RH/Departed.

Note: Henry Lambton was killed on Saturday 1 July 1916, the first day of the Battle of the Somme. He has no known grave and is commemorated on the Thiepval Memorial, Somme, France: Pier and Face 10 C, 10 D and 11 A. *(CWGC)*

LANDER, JOHN T. Mar 1917 RH/GB. **Aug 1918** RH/F.

LEAHY, STEPHEN Sept 1918 Added to **Aug 1918** RH. A parishioner.

LEESON FRED Pte **Mar 1917** RH/E. **Aug 1918** RH/EP. **Oct 1918** Home on leave.

LEIGHTON, FRANK R. Gunner. **Mar 1917** RH/GB. **Oct 1917** Wounded in arm in Flanders and now in hospital in Leicester. **Nov 1917** 'going on nicely'. **Aug 1918** RH/GB (first name from this list).

LINDSAY, The Hon. and Revd EDWARD REGINALD Had worshipped at St Michael's when stationed in Derby and 'made friends with the Vicar'. He had enlisted as a Pte in R.G.A and was at this time a Bombardier. **Sept 1917** Letter 16/17 August 1917. **Feb 1918** Letter ref. sending money to servicemen.

Note: Edward Reginald Lindsay, Magd. Coll. Oxford B.A. 1898, M.A. 1902; Cudd. Coll. 1902; assist. curate, St Matthew's, Bethnal Green 1902–6; N. Hagbourne 1909–12; Archbishop W. Canada Mission, dio. Qu'Appelle 1912–17; vicar, Birdsall, Yorks. 1919–23.

LLOYD, E. First name possibly Edward. **Dec 1916** Badly wounded.

LLOYD, WALTER EDWIN Member of R.A. Hudson's Bible Class. Pte **Mar 1917** RH/F. **Apr 1918** Killed in action in 'the great German attack which began a fortnight ago.' (This was the final German offensive on the Western Front against the British 5th Army on the Somme and the French on the Aisne. It commenced on 21 March 1918). Lloyd was badly wounded and taken to hospital in Southampton. **Aug 1918** RH/Departed. first name given as Walter here.

Note: Walter Edwin Lloyd, Pte 40062, King's Own Scottish Borderers transf. to (446176) Labour Corps, was the son of John and Caroline Amy Lloyd. He died on Friday 30 March 1918 aged 39 and is buried in Derby (Nottingham Road) Cemetery, grave reference: 12317.

LONGDON, THOMAS EDWIN Confirmed 16 March 1916. Member of the 1913–14 Sunday School football team. L/Cpl, Sgt, Cadet. Regiment not given until he joined the Army Service Corps, see **Apr 1917. Mar 1915** Listed as serving. **Feb 1916** Letter 16 January 1916, mentioning Fred Brooks being wounded by a sniper; our pilots being 'too daring'; being under shell-fire at HG etc. Vivid descriptions. **Apr 1916** Letter received by Rolfe but not quoted. **May 1916** Letter from France 19 April. Not had opportunity to go to Church. **July 1916** Letter from France in early June, describing effect of heavy shelling ('I did cry'). Vivid descriptions of an air-raid. 'We are still expecting something to happen' (reference to first Somme offensive). **Aug 1916** Letter received describing his experience in graphic detail, but not quoted for lack of space. **Sept 1916** Letter early in August describing his experience of the Somme offensive: 'terrible valley of death'. Vivid description of being shelled. Note: 'running the gauntlet [of enemy fire] to get things signed'. Longdon was on HQ staff. (See letter in *The Times*, 11 Nov 1998, recording a similar experience.) Further letter 31 Aug received from Rolfe but not quoted. **Oct 1916** promoted Sgt. **Dec 1916** Letter early in Nov. Arrived back (from leave?) and chased his regiment around by cattle truck until 22 Oct. Went into action for the third time the next day in 'the great push' (final offensive of the first Battle of the Somme). Vivid description of much worse conditions than he has experienced before: 'I am one mass of mud'. Interesting description of one of the first tanks, described as 'wonderful new war machines'. **Feb 1917** Letter describing contents of Christmas parcel (so also Fletcher) and Christmas/New Year 'rough and ready' celebrations. **Mar 1917** RH/F. **Apr 1917** Letter 18

March 1917. Has been 'in the line' for seven weeks. Changed regiment to the ASC. Now chief clerk to the Brigade. Will be 20 on 15 April. **July 1917** Has been in Derby on leave. **Apr 1918** In England for officer training. **Aug 1918** Qualifying for service in tanks (see **Dec 1916** above). RH/GB.

LOWE, HENRY ('HARRY') Formerly in Sunday School. Drummer (so **Jan 1916**), then L/Cpl. No. 2215, 5th Batt. Sherwood Foresters. Field ambulance man and stretcher-bearer. Brother of John and Herbert. **Nov 1914** Listed as serving. **Nov 1915** 'somewhere at the Front'. **Jan 1916** Letter 20 Dec 1916 expecting to be moved to Egypt but convinced that the war would soon be over. **Aug 1916** Killed on first day of Somme offensive. See letter from Laurence Hallsworth **Aug 1916**. **Mar 1917** RH/Departed. First name given here as Harry. **Aug 1918** RH/Departed.

Notes: 1. L/Cpl. Lowe was the husband of Mrs H. Lowe of 2 Museum Row, Mansfield Road, Derby, and brother-in-law of Arthur Ollerenshaw. Killed on the first day of the Battle of the Somme, 1 July 1916, by sniper fire in the neck while rescuing a wounded officer in Gommercourt Wood. Aged 38. Buried in Foncquevillers Military Cemetery, grave reference: I.L.52. *Sources: Miss B.M. Lowe and CWGC.*

2. 'Stretcher Bearers who went out with the Battalion were our good friends the Band. It is difficult to express in cold print the work done by this devoted section and their successors ... Can men leave a more imperishable memory?'. *5th Battalion, The Sherwood Foresters War History 1914–1918* (Bemrose, Derby, 1930), p. 215.

LOWE, HERBERT Communicant. Pte 1/1st Derbyshire Yeomanry. Brother of John and Harry. **Sept 1914** Listed as serving. **Nov 1915** Listed as killed (in the Gallipoli landings, aged 20, though see note 1 below). **Mar 1917** RH/Departed. **Aug 1918** RH/Departed.

Notes: 1. Herbert Lowe, Pte 1691, Derbyshire Yeomanry, was the son of Mary Jane Lowe, of 29 Drage Street, Derby. Killed Friday 21 Aug 1915 aged 21. Commemorated on the Helles Memorial, Panel 17. *(CWGC)*

2. Herbert Lowe and his brother John were together in the landings at Suvla Bay. They were pinned down under fire. They made a dash for safety, Herbert going in one direction and John in another. Herbert was shot and killed but John escaped. *Source: David Lowe.*

3. The final British assault at Suvla Bay began on 21 Aug 1915. Herbert Lowe was one of 10 members of the regiment to be killed that day out of 27 who lost their lives 21–28 Aug. Full account in G.A. Strutt, *The Derbyshire Yeomanry War History 1914–1919* (Bemrose, Derby, nd, *c.* 1920–5), pp. 23–46. At this time the Derbyshire Yeomanry were part of the Notts. and Derby Mounted Brigade, 2nd Mounted Division.

LOWE, JOHN Formerly in the Sunday School. Drummer, 1/1st Derbyshire Yeomanry. Brother of Harry and Herbert. Married to George Wheatcroft's sister Susan. Probably the 'Drummer Lowe' who, while on leave, trained the Scout band to lead the St Michael's Whitsun Walk in 1916 (so **June 1916**). **Nov 1914** Listed as serving. **Nov 1915** 'somewhere at the Front' (in Salonika).

LOWE, JOSEPH Married Nellie Whitaker 25 December 1913. Had been secretary of the St Michael's Men's Institute. **Mar 1917** RH/GB. **Aug 1918** RH/F. **Nov 1918** Home on leave.

Note: No known connection with Herbert, Harry and John Lowe.

A family of this name lived at 3 Alexandra Street.

MARSHALL, JOHN Aug 1918 RH/GB.

MARSHALL, JOHN WILLIAM Confirmed 16 March 1915 (first names from this list). **Dec 1915** A Scout (Second). Listed as serving (see Scout report. First names reversed in the Notices section of the magazine). **Mar 1917** A note in the Scouts' report says that he had 'already seen service in France and is waiting until he is 18 years of age to join up again'. He had evidently volunteered well under age in 1915 and had been discharged. **Aug 1918** RH/GB.

MARSHALL, REGINALD ALBERT Former Troop Leader of the St Michael's Scouts. One of this name confirmed 28 April 1913 (first names from this list). Lived at 33 Jackson Street (**Oct 1916**). Pte, Rifleman (so **May 1918**). **May 1917** Listed as serving and added to RH. **Sept 1917** Visited Scouts and presented with a badge. **May 1918** Letter received but not quoted. **July 1918** ditto. **Aug 1918** ditto. RH/F. **Sept 1918** Wounded and now in hospital in Newcastle-on-Tyne.

MART, FRED Communicant (so **Nov 1917**) Pte, L/Cpl. **Mar 1915** Listed as serving. **Mar 1917** RH/GB. **June 1917** Letter 20 May from France noting birds singing during 'firing and shells'. **Nov 1917** In hospital in Rochdale following wounding near Ypres. Letter 20 Oct 1917. Vivid description of his experiences. **Aug 1918** RH/GB.

MARTIN, BENJAMIN Sept 1918 Added to **Aug 1918** RH. A parishioner.

MARTIN, WILLIAM Sept 1918 Added to **Aug 1918** RH. A parishioner.

MASON, ROBERT Sept 1918 Added to **Aug 1918** RH. A parishioner.

MAWSON, JAMES HENRY Pte **Feb 1916** Letter thanking Rolfe for a parcel and a prayer card with a hymn which 'we often sing ... out here'. **Mar 1917** RH/F. **Aug 1918** RH/F.

MERRY, GEORGE Sgt then

(officer) Cadet **Dec 1914** Listed as serving. **Mar 1917** RH/GB. **Apr 1918** In England for officer training. **Aug 1918** Officer cadet qualifying for 'the Air Service' (from 1 April 1918 the RAF) RH/GB.

Note: A family of this name lived at 10 Queen Street, Derby.

MIDGLEY, JAMES Able Seaman. (styled 'A/B' in **Apr 1918** and 'A.B.J. Midgley' in **Feb 1917**. Probably serving as an infantryman with the Royal Naval Division. **Feb 1917** Letter 8 Jan 1917 from France. With parcels, Rolfe sent cards with his photograph and the patriotic song, *Don't Worry* ('Pack up your troubles etc.'): see **Mar 1917**. **Apr 1918** Badly gassed and sent to hospital in Kent. Letter: He 'just missed being taken prisoner to make roads in Germany'. Effects of gas include temporary blindness. See also letter from Robert Walker in **Oct 1918**. **Mar 1917** RH/F. **Aug 1918** RH/GB.

Note: There is no James Midgley on the main naval roll in the PRO. There is F21687 William Edwin Midgley born in Derby 28 Jan 1877, formerly a fabric worker. His rate is given as AM 2 (probably an air mechanic). Although the dates of his service match those of James Midgley it is unlikely that they are the same man.

MORETON, WILLIAM A. Nov 1914 Listed as serving.

MORLEY, THOMAS Sept 1918 Added to **Aug 1918** RH. Parishioner.

MULLEN, JAMES Sept 1918 Added to **Aug 1918** RH. Parishioner.

MULLEN, TOM Sept 1918 Added to **Aug 1918** RH. Parishioner.

MURPHY, AUSTIN Sept 1918 Added to **Aug 1918** RH. Parishioner.

NIX, WILLIAM J. Pte. **May 1917** Listed as serving and added to RH. **Aug 1918** RH/GB.

NORTON, FRANK Mar 1917 RH/GB.

NORTON, LESLIE Lieut. (so **June 1918**). Brother of Percy. **Nov 1915** 'somewhere at the Front'. **Mar 1917** RH/F. **June 1918** at home suffering from shell shock. **Aug 1918** RH/Dis.

NORTON, PERCY CHAPMAN 2nd Lieut., later Lieut., R.F.C.; Communicant. Brother of Leslie. **Nov 1917** Missing 'on offensive patrol over the German lines ... He was seen to fall, and there is hope that he may prove to be a prisoner in German hands.' **Dec 1917** POW: confirmed in news to his friends. **June 1918** 'seems to be in fairly decent quarters' (see Leslie Norton's entry). **Aug 1918** RH/POW.

Note: Percy Chapman belonged to 54th Squadron. He was flying a Sopwith Pup (Sopwith Scout), serial number A7347, when he was brought down 13 Oct 1917 and captured near Dixmunde (Dixmoindern on his casualty cards). He was a prisoner of war at Karlsruhe and was eventually repatriated. *Source: Royal Air Force Museum, Hendon.*

OAKLEY, ALEX Aug 1918 RH/F.

OAKLEY, CHARLES Pte RAMC. His mother lived at 3 St Michael's Lane. **Nov 1917** Killed in action by a bomb 25 Sept 1917 aged 19. **Aug 1918** RH/Departed.

Note: Charles Oakley, Pte 417414, 2nd/2nd (North Midland) Field Amb., RAMC, died Monday 25 Sept 1917. Buried in Bridge House Cemetery. grave reference: B.2. The cemetery is situated 5 km NE of Ieper town centre. 'Bridge House' was a farmhouse 1.6 km S of St Julien. The cemetery was made by the 59th (North Midland) Division at the end of Sept 1917. Most of the graves are of soldiers killed in the Battle of Polygon Wood (Third Battle of Ypres, known as Passchendaele), 26–28 Sept 1917. *(CWGC)*

OLLERENSHAW, ARTHUR Sgt 5th Batt. Sherwood Foresters. **July 1917** His children attended St Michael's Sunday School. Wounded early in June.

Letter from his chaplain 18 June describing treatment of wounds.

Notes: 1. Brother-in-law of the Lowes (married to their sister Lizzie). He was severely wounded in the shoulder and was discharged in 1917. He was probably aged about 38 on discharge. He witnessed the death in action of his brother-in-law Henry Lowe and was deeply affected by what he saw. *Source: Miss B.M. Lowe.*

2. Arthur Ollerenshaw was wounded in the action fought by the 5th Batt. before Lens described in *5th Battalion, The Sherwood Foresters. War History 1914–1918* (Bemrose, Derby, 1930), pp. 107–25. He was in 15th Platoon, D Coy, and, in at least one action (before Commercourt on 12 March 1917) he led the platoon (ibid., p. 104).

PALMER, A. Bombardier, then L/Cpl. **May 1918** Letter received but not quoted. **July 1918** ditto. **Aug 1918** RH/F. **Nov 1918** Home on leave.

PARRY-JONES, EDWARD Nov 1914 Listed as serving. **Nov 1915** Capt. 5 Batt. S. Wales Borderers (Pioneers). Letters 30 September and 24 October 1914 describing trench warfare. **Sept 1916** Reported wounded. **Mar 1917** RH/Wounded or Sick. **Aug 1918** RH/GB.

PARRY-JONES, OWEN Capt. RAMC. **Nov 1914** Listed as serving. **Aug 1916** Letter to his family describing first days of the Battle of the Somme. **Nov 1916** Killed by a shell in France early in October (but see correct date below). The RAMC Roll of Honour says that he died as a result of wounds. **Mar 1917** RH/Departed. **Aug 1918** RH/Departed.

Note: Capt Owen Guy Parry-Jones, RAMC att. 3rd Batt., Suffolk Regt., was the son of Maurice Parry-Jones MD of 4 Full Street, Derby. He was killed on Thursday 29 Sept 1916, aged 29. Buried in Puchevillers British Cemetery, grave reference III.B.II. The 3rd and 44th Casualty Clearing Stations came to Puchevillers just before the opening of the Battle of the Somme on 1 July 1916. *(CWGC)*

PATRICK, JOHN Mar 1917 RH/F. **Aug 1918** RH/F.

PERCIVAL, WILLIAM Confirmed 16 March 1915. **Oct 1918** 'added to our Roll'.

PLANT, REGINALD Communicant. **Sept 1914** Listed as serving. **Nov 1915** 'somewhere at the Front'. **Mar 1917** RH/Sailor. **Aug 1918** RH/Sailor.

Note: J21863 Reginald Daniel Plant, born 31 July 1897 in Derby, occupation van boy (crossed out and Group No 34 Motor Car Driver substituted) joined HMS *Ganges* as a Boy 2 on 9 Jan 1913. Ordinary Seaman 31 July 1915, and served in HMS *Hawke, Conqueror, Cyclops, Orion, Endymion, Centurion, Eagle,* and *Repulse* and a number of shore establishments throughout the war. He was transferred to the list of Stokers on 12 May 1919, with the number K56777. His final posting, as Stoker 1, was to HMS *Vindictive* 20 Aug 1928, though his length of service is given as 12 years from 31 July 1915. Date of birth 31 July 1897. *Source: PRO.* Brother-in-law of Wilfred Burrows.

PLANT, WILLIAM Communicant. **Sept 1914** Listed as serving. **Nov 1915** 'somewhere at the Front'. Driver (so **May 1918**). **Mar 1917** RH/GB. **May 1918** Letter received but not quoted. **Aug 1918** ditto. RH/F.

POWELL, ALBERT ROBERTSON Rank given here as Sgt but Cpl both in the RAMC Roll of Honour and by CWGC. RAMC. Choirman. Only brother of Norman Powell. **Dec 1914** Listed as serving. **Mar 1917** RH/GB.**May 1917** Recently gone to France. Letter, Easter Day 1917, from the trenches, but 'mostly open fighting now, we use anything for cover'. No church services 'up the line'. **Sept 1917** Ref. in Fred Wright's letter 5 Aug 1917 that he has not seen Sgt Powell. **Dec 1917** Killed in action in France 22 Oct. Parents dead. Uncle as next-of-kin received news. Copy of the notification of his death. Rank as Sgt given there. **Aug 1918** RH/Departed.

Notes: 1. Cpl Powell, No. 417353, 1st (North Midland) Field Amb. RAMC, was killed Sunday 22 Oct 1917. He is buried in Sucrerie Cemetery, Ablain-St Nazaire. Grave Reference: I.B.23. Ablain-St Nazaire is a village 13 km N of Arras. *(CWGC)*

2. The depot of 1st Reserve (North Midland) Field Ambulance, RAMC was at 91 Siddals Road, Derby. OC Major E. Arnold Wraith. See Note 1 under entry for Theodore Lyle Bewley.

3. The family lived in St Michael's Lane. *Source: Frank Lowe.*

POWELL, WILLIAM NORMAN R. Communicant. Only brother of Albert Powell. Former St Michael's Scouts Patrol Leader. **Apr 1915** Confirmed 16 March 1915, and joined Leicester Regiment 17 March 1915. Age 15, see Scout report in **May 1917. Mar 1916** L/Cpl. Wounded in action in Persian Gulf. **Apr 1916** Two letters received. 7 Feb 1916, wounded in hands and head. In hospital in Amarah, Mesopotamia. 20 Feb 1916 from another hospital describing improvement in his condition, a concert, the hospital etc. **June 1916** Sent to Bombay but now in a military hospital in Cairo. Doing well. **July 1916** Report of his death from wounds in Cairo, with moving letter from the hospital chaplain, J. Baghot de la Bere. 3rd Batt. Leicesters here. He was 16 when he died, see Scout report, **May 1917. Aug 1916** Letter from Robert Baden-Powell. **Mar 1917** RH/Departed. **Aug 1918** RH/Departed.

Notes: 1. Norman Powell, Pte 17332, 2nd Batt. Leicestershire Regt, died Tuesday 24 May 1916. He is buried in Cairo War Memorial Cemetery, grave reference F.71. The principal military hospital was in the Citadel in Cairo. *(CWGC)*

2. First name from the list of those recently confirmed **Apr 1915.**

PRICE, THOMAS E. Dec 1915 Listed as serving.

RAY, WALTER   Oct 1916 first mention in letter from Karl Duncan (see his entry). **Mar 1917** RH/G. **July 1918** See letter from Karl Duncan. Ray has malaria: 'just another relapse—which one looks upon quite undisturbed'. **Aug 1918** RH/G. **Oct 1918** See letter from Karl Duncan with ref. to Walter Ray.

REDFERN, JACK Apr 1916 Letter from a friend said that he had been wounded earlier but had now been killed by a sniper. Here said to be L/Cpl.

Notes: 1. J. Redfern, Pte, No. 11904, 2nd Batt. Sherwood Foresters (Notts. and Derby Regt), was the son of Mr and Mrs G. Redfern of 20 Grove Place, Darley Lane, Derby. Killed Wednesday 9 March 1916, aged 25. Buried in Lijssenthoek Military Cemetery, grave reference V.B.15. The cemetery is located 11.5 km W of Ieper (Flanders) town centre on the road between Ieper and Poperinge. Lijssenthoek 'lying close behind the extreme range of enemy shell-fire, was a natural position for clearing hospitals'. 10,000 1914–18 casualties are buried here. *(CWGC)*

2. Jack Redfern joined the 1st Batt. Sherwood Foresters on 7 Dec 1914, serving with D Coy. On 19 Jan 1915 he was wounded by rifle fire in the trenches at night while repairing trench breastworks at Richebourg. Evacuated home 17 Feb 1915 and, on recovery, was posted to 2nd Batt. Died of wounds resulting (probably) from shell-fire.

Source: Sherwood Foresters Museum.

ROBINSON, PERCY Nov 1915 'somewhere at the Front'.

ROBINSON, CYRIL Ordinary Seaman attached to Army (see **Aug 1917**) Wireless operator with Royal Flying Corps. Telegraphist (so **Oct 1917**). Brother of Joe. **Mar 1917** RH/F. **July 1917** Letter. Significant comment about attendance at church services. He is often the only one present. Notes 'rigorous censorship'. **Aug 1917** Letter, 19 July 1917, to R. Hudson, churchwarden. Ref. to censorship. Effect on ears of wearing headphones for long periods. Was in field ambulance hospital. Ambulance train. Now in hospital in Boulogne. 'I long for the sea, to which I properly belong'. **Sept 1917** Letter 4 Aug 1917. Now in No. 12 Convalescent Camp, Boulogne Base. Has had trench fever and neurasthenia. **Oct 1917** Letter in September. Ref. to J.E. Staley, CF, who had met Cyril Robinson (qv). **May 1918** discharged from service suffering from shell shock. **Aug 1918** RH/Dis.

Note: There appears to be no Cyril Robinson on the main naval roll in the PRO. Under RNR there is 22178/DA Cyril C. Robinson, rate DH (Deck Hand?), and under RNVR BZ/5511 Cyril Robinson, rate AB. It has not been possible to translate these references into a service record which would give place of birth.

ROBINSON, JOE Royal Garrison Artillery. Sgt. **Sept 1917** First mentioned in letter from Cyril Robinson, his brother. 'He was made a Bombr, and a Corporal one day and 10 days after was made a Sergeant. He is now in Italy'.

ROBSHAW, BEN Mar 1917 RH/F. **Aug 1918** RH/F.

ROE, ARTHUR Communicant. Gunner. **Sept 1914** Listed as serving. **Sept 1915** Seriously wounded on 29 Aug. Note of his bravery. **Oct 1915** Now in hospital in Brighton. Letter dated shortly before he was wounded describing shelling of his battery and death of a close friend. Visited by Rolfe. **Apr 1916** Letter 16 March 1916 from convalescent home describing wound to arm. **June 1916** 'fairly well' but in hospital in Sussex. **Mar 1917** RH/Dis. **Aug 1918** RH/Dis.

ROSE, ARTHUR Mar 1917 RH/F. **Aug 1918** RH/F.

SANDERSON, WILLIAM G. Pte. (first name as **Aug 1918**) **Mar 1918** Letter from 'somewhere in Palestine ... in the region of very important operations'. Tribute to 'our Navy for the safe escorting of Transports'. **May 1918** Letter. Still in Palestine. Detailed description of visits to the holy places in Jerusalem. **June 1918** Letter 24 April 1918. **Aug 1918** RH/EP. **Sept 1918** Letter 29 July. Here L/Cpl but Pte in **Jan 1919**. **Jan 1919** Letter from Syria in November. Here styled Pte in error? Letter with some detail of the area and of the rapid advance of the Allied forces (Turkish offensive in Palestine checked 13 July 1918. Collapse of Turkish resistance in Palestine 22 Sept. British and Arab forces occupy Damascus 1 October 1918).

SARSFIELD, W. Pte Grenadier Guards. **July 1915** '... an old scholar (i.e. Sunday School) whom the Vicar had lost sight of'. Letter dated 21 June. Ref. to many former members of St Michael's Sunday School. This letter seems to have been written from the trenches during an enemy bombardment. **Nov 1915** 'somewhere at the Front' **Feb 1917** Killed Dec. **Mar 1917** RH/Departed. **Aug 1918** RH/Departed.

Note: William Sarsfield, Pte 17916, 1st Batt. Grenadier Guards, was the husband of Evelyn Sarsfield of 8 Drewry Lane, Derby. Killed Friday 9 Dec 1916, aged 30. Buried in A.I.F. Burial Ground, Flers, grave reference V.A.7. The burial ground is 2 km N of Flers

(Somme). The original military cemetery was greatly enlarged after the Armistice to include British and French graves from the battlefields of the Somme. *(CWGC)*

SHARP(E) HAROLD Mar 1917 RH/F. Without 'e' in this list. **Aug 1918** RH/F.

SHARP(E) RICHARD (without the 'e' in **May 1917**) Pte **May 1917** recently enlisted and 'added to our Roll'. **Aug 1918** RH/F.

SHIPLEY, TOM Oct 1918 First mention as 'added to our Roll'.

SKINNER, EDWARD Oct 1918 First mention as 'added to our Roll'.

SIMPSON, L. EARDLEY Capt. **Mar 1915** Listed as serving.

SMITH, ALBERT June 1915 Listed as serving. **Mar 1917** RH/F. **Aug 1918** RH/F.

SMITH, ARTHUR June 1915 Listed as serving (or the next entry). **Nov 1915** Listed as killed. **Mar 1917** RH/Departed. **Aug 1918** RH/Departed.

Note: It has been impossible to trace Arthur Smith in the CWGC commemorations.

SMITH, ARTHUR This may be William Arthur Smith. **June 1915** Listed as serving (or previous entry). **Oct 1916** With Karl Duncan (see his letter). **Mar 1917** RH/G.

Note: an Arthur Smith was a member of the 1913–14 Sunday School football team .

SMITH, ERNEST Nov 1914 Listed as serving.

SMITH, FRANCIS ALBERT Ordinary Telegraphist (so **Aug 1918**). Former choir boy (so **Aug 1918**). Confirmed 28 April 1913. **Aug 1918** Has volunteered for service as a telegraphist on a submarine in the Mediterranean. Letter 20 July 1918. On course in 'Wireless Instruments' in Portsmouth. To be based in Malta. RH/Sailor. **Dec 1918** Letter from submarine in Mediter-

ranean where when submerged 'the air gets very thick, you could cut it with a knife, this makes one feel very drowsy ...' **Feb 1919** Letter of thanks 31 Dec 1918 for New Year's gift of 10s. and giving his ship as HM Submarine *E2*.

Note: Albert Smith was in the Royal Navy Volunteer Reserve and joined the Submarine Service 9 Sept 1918. HMS *E2* was commissioned 9 July 1913 and carried a complement of three officers and 27 ratings. Its commander during Albert Smith's service was Lieut. Philip H. Bonham-Carter. *E2* was paid off into reserve in Malta, Dec 1918. Albert Smith was demobilised 19 Feb 1919. *Source: The Royal Navy Submarine Museum, Gosport.*

SMITH, HAROLD Noted by Rolfe as member of the congregation. **June 1916** listed as serving. Sapper. **Mar 1917** RH/GB. **May 1918** Letter received but not quoted. **Aug 1918** RH/F. **Oct 1918** Home on leave.

SMITH, WILLIAM ARTHUR This may be the Arthur Smith on the **Mar 1917** RH/G. **Aug 1918** RH/F.

SMITH, PERCY Aug 1918 RH/GB.

STALEY, Revd JAMES EDWIN Oct 1917 Met Cyril Robinson (qv) having enlisted as an Army chaplain.

Note: James Edwin Staley, Fitw. Hall Camb. B.A. 1907, M.A. 1911; deacon 1909, priest 1910, assist. curate, St John Baptist, Peterborough 1909–13; St Michael's, Derby 1913–14; chapl. HM Prison, Bristol 1914–17; assist. curate Bishopston 1916–17; TCF 1917–18, hon. CF 1918; assist. curate St Saviour, Woolcott Park, Bristol, 1919–20; Vicar of St Thomas Ap., Eastville, Bristol 1920–1931; Rector of Stapleton, 1931–47; chapl. Bristol Mental Hospital 1939-43; Hon Canon, Bristol 1945; Perm. Offic. Dio. Bristol 1947.

STEVENS, JAMES THOMAS ('JIM') Confirmed 28 April 1913. Pte. **Apr 1917** Listed as serving. **Oct 1917**

Gassed (and now bronchitis). Letter describes action in the third battle of Ypres. **Nov 1917** 'going on nicely'. **Aug 1918** RH/GB. **Oct 1918** Home on leave.

STIVEN, KENNETH CUMMIN Communicant. **Oct 1914** Listed as serving. **Mar 1917** RH/F. **Apr 1917** 2nd Lieut. Seriously wounded, 'apparently by accident' in France. **July 1917** Improving. Has been in Derby on leave. **Dec 1917** Discharged owing to his wounds. **Aug 1918** RH/Dis. **Feb 1920** Died from an operation consequent on his wounds on 19 Jan 1920, aged 24. *Source for date and second Christian name: Parish Register.* Added by Rolfe to the list of those who 'had made the supreme sacrifice'.

STONE, FRANK Mar 1917 RH/GB. **Aug 1918** RH/GB.

STUART-WILLIAM, LAURENCE Nov 1914 Listed as serving.

SWORDS, JOHN Sept 1918 Added to the **Aug 1918** RH. Parishioner.

THOMAS, EVAN OWEN Cpl. No 38403. 3rd Batt. South Staffs. Regt. **June 1915** Listed as serving. **May 1916** Letter 13 April 1916 from France. 'If folks at home only knew what the men out here go through'. Graphic description of life in trenches. 'The rats upset me more than the enemy'. **June 1916** Letter from France 10 May 1916. After trenches in 'Rest billet' 'but I can assure you it is wrongly labelled, as there is more humbug than rest to be found here'. Arrived in this billet on Good Friday and left for the trenches on Easter day. Vivid description of trench life and warfare. Letter 31 May. He is ill and in hospital. **July 1916** Hospital in Bristol. Letter 17 June 1916 importantly noting clearance of base hospitals 'which to my mind points to some forward movement about to be made shortly', a clear ref. to the Somme offensive in July. Interesting ref. to 'the

compulsionists' and the contrast with 'the man who had volunteered to do his bit' and 'the one beautiful spirit' of Tommies. **Mar 1917** RH/I. **Feb 1918** accidental death by gas poisoning while sleeping in a hut, Forest Hall, Newcastle-on-Tyne, 19 Jan 1918. Expecting discharge having been invalided home 'some weeks ago'. **Aug 1918** RH/Departed. First name given here.

Note: Evan Thomas was the husband of Edith Annie Thomas of 16 Keep Street, Derby. Buried in Derby (Nottingham Road) cemetery. Grave reference 8802 (c). *(CWGC)* Aged 43 *Source: Parish Register.*

THOMPSON, REGINALD Nov 1915 Listed as serving. **Mar 1917** RH/Sailor. First name given in this list. **Aug 1918** RH/POW.

Note: In the naval records in the PRO the only Reginald Thompson who was serving in or by 1915 is K28935 Reginald Thompson, a stoker 2nd class, born in Miles Platting, 29 Dec 1877. He was a fireman before enlisting in Portsmouth. He joined HMS *Victory* II 3 Nov 1915. *Victory II* was a shore establishment at Crystal Palace and a training depot for the Royal Navy. The period of his engagement given as from 3 Nov 1915 ' - Hostilities'. His service record is ambiguous and difficult to interpret. He served only until 16 April 1916 when he is said to have 'Run Victory 14/4/16'. This indicates that he was AWOL for 30 days or more. If this Reginald Thompson had been a POW it is likely that this would have been written in his records. If this is the Reginald Thompson listed in the St Michael's parish magazine it may be that Rolfe was told that he was a POW as a cover up for the fact that he was AWOL. There is an additional note in his service record: 'Garth Caelle 19 Aug 17 S 165'. The meaning of this is unknown.

THORNLEY, ALBERT Former Sunday School teacher. **Sept 1915** Listed as serving.

THORNTON, ALBERT Nov 1915 'somewhere at the Front'.

TIMSON, ARTHUR GEORGE Confirmed 28 April 1913 (Christian names reversed in the list of those confirmed). Formerly in the Sunday School, and 'leader' of the Wolf Cubs. **Mar 1917** RH/GB.

Note: A family of this name lived at 10 Wide Yard, St Michael's Lane, Derby.

TIMSON, JOHN Sept 1918 Added to the **Aug 1918** RH. Parishioner.

TIMSON, SAM Sept 1914 Listed as serving. Parishioner.

TOY, W. June 1915 Listed as wounded.

TURTON, JOHN HENRY Confirmed 28 April 1913. Pte. **May 1917** Listed as serving and added to 'our Roll'. **June 1918** Letter received but not quoted. In France and at the Front. **July 1918** Letter received but not quoted. **Aug 1918** RH/F.

WAINWRIGHT, F. Aug 1918 RH/GB.

WALKER, ROBERT Former St Michael's choirboy. Possibly Samuel Robert Walker, confirmed 28 April 1913. **Mar 1917** RH/GB. **June 1918** See Robert Barker's letter. Walker is his runner and 'a very stout fellow in the line too'. **Aug 1918** RH/F. **Oct 1918** Gassed in France in September 'in one of the attacks of the Sherwoods'. Letter 21 Sept from hospital in England. Effects of gas as temporary loss of speech and temporary blindness. Cf. letter from J. Midgley in **Apr 1918.**

WALKER, TOM Mar 1917 RH/GB. **Aug 1918** RH/F.

WALKERDINE, WILLIAM H. (BILLY) Sunday School teacher. Pte. **Dec 1915** Listed as serving. **Dec 1916** Seriously wounded in Somme offensive.

Probably now in England. **Jan 1917** In hospital in Edmonton. Letter 10 Dec 1916 detailing his wounds and very graphic description of 'going over the top' to take Beaumont Hamel. 'Now the whole thing seems a dream' (an identical comment to that of Robert Barker: see his entry **Aug 1916**). He notes that Archie Duncan was killed 'in that push'. **July 1917** Satisfactory. Has been in Derby on leave. **Aug 1918** RH/GB. (First name from this list).

Note: During the First World War the family home was 'Glenthorne', Thornhill Road Derby. W.H. Walkerdine was born on 18 May 1887. He went to school in Vernon Street. He was killed in a road accident in Derby, 20 Nov 1963. *Source: John Walkerdine.*

WARBURTON, HARRY Communicant and formerly in the choir. Lieut. then Capt. 'Of the Canadian Forces' (i.e. Canadian Expeditionary Force) (**Nov 1917**). **Mar 1917** RH/GB and here listed as Capt. **Nov 1917** Lieut. In hospital with shell shock and trench fever. Letter 17 October 1917 describing his experiences going over the top. He was injured in 'a premature with one of my guns' which blew off the legs of all four of the gun crew. **Aug 1918** RH/Dis and 'in Canada'. Listed as Capt.

WATERFIELD, ARTHUR Sept 1918 Added to **Aug 1918** RH. Parishioner.

WESTON, HENRY Aug 1918 RH/F. **Oct 1918** Home on leave.

WESTON, TOM, Formerly in the St Michael's band before enlisting in the Hussars. Had been in Hussars six years and one year in reserves. Pte. **Apr 1915** Killed in action 4 March 1915. **Mar 1917** RH/Departed. **Aug 1918** RH/Departed.

Note: Thomas Weston, Pte 712, 19th (Queen Alexandra's Own Royal) Hussars. He was the son of Mrs E. Weston,

45 Bath Street, Derby. Killed Wednesday 4 March 1915, aged 29. Buried in Wulverghem-Lindenhoek Road Military Cemetery, grave reference III.F.II. The cemetery is located 13 km S of Ieper (Flanders) town centre on the road connecting with the main road from Ieper to Kemmel. The cemetery was originally a dressing station cemetery. *(CWGC)*

WHEATCROFT, GEORGE. Formerly Sunday School and football team (see **June 1917**). His sister Susan was married to John Lowe. Pte. **June 1915** Listed as serving. **Mar 1916** Letter 24 Feb 1916 to his Sunday School teacher, Miss Iliffe. In hospital in Liverpool following an accident/enemy action in Alexandria. Two weeks in hospital ship and ten hours on the train. **Apr 1916** 'going on well'. **June 1916** 'nearly convalescent'. **July 1916** Visited by Rolfe in convalescent hospital in Blackpool. **Mar 1917** RH/F. **June 1917** Killed early in May in France 'in the great battle then going on'. **Aug 1918** RH/Departed.

Notes: 1. George Frederick Wheatcroft, Pte 242479, 1st/6th Batt., Sherwood Foresters (Notts. and Derby Regt) and formerly (2625) Derbyshire Yeomanry, was the son of Lemuel and Harriet Wheatcroft, 36 Roman Road, Chester Green, Derby. Killed Sunday 23 April 1917, aged 20. Commemorated on the Arras Memorial, Bay 7. *(CWGC)*

2. He was killed in action at Fosse 3 De-Lievine, Arras. *Source: Sherwood Foresters Museum.*

WHEELER, H.J. Sept 1918 Added to **Aug 1918** RH. Parishioner.

WHEELDON, J. Formerly in the Sunday School. Pte. **Feb 1919** At concert for wounded soldiers at Temple House, 15 Jan 1919.

WHITAKER, JOHN ('JACK') Communicant and former choirboy. Brother of Sam. Pte Grenadier Guards. Stretcher Bearer. **Sept 1914** Listed as serving. **July 1915** Letter dated 8 June 1915. Description of a three-day 'charge' etc. **Nov 1915** 'somewhere at the Front'. **Sept 1916** Meeting Harry Ashby (see letter from Ashby). Note tribute to Army stretcher-bearers in this letter. **Mar 1917** RH/F. **June 1917** His work 'very severe'. Warm tribute to Rolfe. **Nov 1917** Killed in action. Moving tribute in letter from his chaplain, 27 Oct 1917. **Aug 1918** RH/Departed.

Note: John Whitaker, Pte 17264, No. 3 Coy., 1st Batt. Grenadier Guards, was the husband of Lilian M. Whitaker of 54 Wolfer Street, Derby. Killed Thursday 12 Oct 1917, aged 26. Commemorated on the Tyne Cot Memorial to the Missing, panel 1914. The Memorial is located 9 km NE of Ieper (Flanders) town centre. *(CWGC)*

WHITAKER, SAMUEL RICHARD ('SAM') Communicant. Brother of Jack. Sapper, Royal Engineers, transferred to the Royal Corps of Signals. **Sept 1914** Listed as serving. **Dec 1914** Letter 22 Nov 1914 telling of his gratitude for his Christian upbringing at St Michael's. **Jan 1915** Letter 16 Dec 1914, is at HG, notes trench warfare. **Nov 1915** 'somewhere at the Front'. **Mar 1917** Letter 2 February 1917 from Salonika ref. improvised places for worship. RH/G. **June 1917** Letter from Salonika comparing Easter dates. **Aug 1918** RH/G.

WHITE, HARRY 1913–14 Sunday School football team. Pte. **July 1915** Listed as serving. **Nov 1915** 'somewhere at the Front'. **Oct 1916** Serving in France (see letter from William Goodchild). **Mar 1917** RH/F. **Oct 1917** Wounded in arm and leg. In hospital in Bradford. Letter describes the permanent loss of use of his arm. Wounded at Lens. **Nov 1917** 'going on nicely'. **Dec 1917** Discharged owing to wounds. **Aug 1918** RH/Dis.

WHITE, SIDNEY Formerly in the Sunday School. **Sept 1915** Listed as serving. **Nov 1915** 'somewhere at the Front'.

WHITEHEAD WILL(IAM) Former choirboy. Sgt. **June 1915** Listed as serving. **Dec 1916** Reported missing, feared killed in the Somme offensive. **Mar 1917** RH/Departed. **Aug 1918** RH/Departed.

Notes: 1. Lance-Sgt William Whitehead, No. 26324, 'C' Coy., 16th Batt. (Chatsworth Rifles) Sherwood Foresters (Notts. and Derby Regt), was the son of William and Elizabeth Whitehead of Ilkeston, and husband of Sarah Louisa Whitehead of 87 Manchester Street, Derby. Killed Monday 10 Oct 1916, aged 24. Buried in Connaught Cemetery, Thiepval, grave reference X.G.8.

2. He was killed when attacking the Schwaben Redoubt near Thiepval. *Source: Sherwood Foresters Museum.*

WHITEHURST, RICHARD Mar 1917 RH/GB. **Aug 1918** RH/F.

WILLATT, CHARLES ('CHARLIE') Formerly in the Sunday School. **Nov 1915** Listed as serving. Pte, 6th Seaforth Highlanders. Transferred summer 1916 to Royal Engineers. **Apr 1916** Letter 9 March, describing training in France. **May 1916** Letter from France 9 April. First experience of being under fire, and in trenches, Church attendance while fully armed etc. **Apr 1917** Added to **Mar 1917** RH. **June 1916** Letter from Wilfred Burrows (qv) saying that Charlie Willatt had been transferred to Royal Engineers. **June 1918** Letter received but not quoted. Now L/Cpl. **July 1918** ditto. **Aug 1918** RH/F. **Oct 1918** Letter received. **Nov 1918** Home on leave.

WOOD, SAMUEL Former member of the Sunday School and of Robert Hudson's Bible Class. Pte. **Nov 1914** Listed as serving. **Dec 1915** Letter vividly describing his rescue from the hospital ship *Anglia* when it struck a mine off Boulogne 17 Nov 1915. Now in hospital in Leicester.

WOODWARD, ERNEST Sept 1918 Added to **Aug 1918** RH. Parishioner.

WOOLLEY, CHARLES L. Nov 1914 Listed as serving.

WOOLLEY, JOHN Sept 1918 Added to **Aug 1918.** Parishioner.

WOOLLEY, TOM Nov 1915 'somewhere at the Front'. **Mar 1917** RH/Dis. **Aug 1918** RH/Dis.

WRAGG, THOMAS A. Choirmaster. Lieut., Prob. Derbyshire Yeomanry. **June 1915** Listed as serving. **Jan 1917** In a tribute he says that he trained Archie Duncan. **Mar 1917** RH/GB. **Aug 1917** Posted 'somewhere in the East'. **Nov 1917** Letter from Salonika where he had met Karl Duncan 'his late Choirboy, who had grown almost beyond recognition' and also Oscar Bewley. **May 1918** Letter from Salonika. **June 1918** Letter received but not quoted. **July 1918** ditto. **Aug 1918** RH/G. **Sept 1918** Letter in August. Has met Sgt Harry E. Cox one of his choirmen (qv). **Dec 1918** On way home. **Mar 1919** Home with malaria.

WRIGHT, FRED RAMC (Possibly Frederick Thomas S. Wright, confirmed 16 March 1915). **June 1915** Listed as serving. **Mar 1917** RH/GB. **Sept 1917** Slightly wounded. Letter 5 Aug 1917 describes the incident. The vicar had obviously written to him as he replies, 'No, I have not seen Sergt Powell.' **Aug 1918** RH/F.

THE SERVICEMEN:
LISTS AND STATISTICS
IN THE PARISH MAGAZINE

In September, October and November 1914 Rolfe printed a 'First list of 'Soldiers and Sailors belonging to St Michael's'. This is arranged in sections designated thus:

> Communicants
> Sunday School
> Closely connected, defined in November 1914 as those 'whose friends are closely connected with St Michael's [whom] we would also like to record and to remember in our prayers'.
> Parishioners, i.e. those living in the parish but apparently not worshippers at St Michael's and not included in any other category.

There were 60 on the initial lists of those joining the Army and the Navy given in September, October and November 1914. Of these 33 were communicants including two servers, three Sunday School teachers and one choirman. Additionally, a further eight had been in the Sunday School. Two parishioners are listed. Those 'closely connected' to St Michael's through friends number 17. Of this original list Rolfe numbers communicants and former members of the Sunday School as 33 (in October 1914). Although I say 'former', throughout the War Rolfe never assumed that a man was not still a member of the Sunday School or a Scout or a member of a Bible class. Like very many others Rolfe assumed in September 1914 that the war would end very shortly (see, for example, the reference in September 1914 to the postponement of the Mission).

Rolfe adds to the September 1914: 'Many others have been commended to our prayers'. It is very probable that these men were named and added to subsequent lists.

In subsequent lists each of these editorial designations was dispensed with, though throughout the war Rolfe, when he quoted letters or when he gave news of servicemen, often noted that a man had been in the choir, the Boy Scouts, a Bible class etc. He also occasionally added statistical details. For example, by the end of the 1915–16 season 40 members of the St Michael's Institute (a young men's social club meeting each week-night) had enlisted. By the end of the war five had been killed (see September 1919).

In November 1915 Rolfe printed a 'List of our lads somewhere at the Front'. This is a second list of those included on what was subsequently called the St Michael's Roll of Honour (but in this case not including those on active service but stationed in Great Britain). It contains 44 names. Of these three were wounded and six men listed as 'Fallen in Battle'. However, Rolfe noted that there are 104 men 'serving King and Country' who were 'connected with St Michael's'. In addition, he noted that six had been killed and two wounded (a mistake for three) totalling 113 (this should be 114). The number in excess of this 44 (i.e. 60) were currently evidently serving in Britain.

In March 1917 Rolfe printed 'A List of Servicemen', now designated the Roll of Honour and referred to in the Biographical Notes as 'RH/GB/F etc.' This contains 129 names subdivided into theatres of war and those serving at home, those discharged as wounded or sick, prisoners of war, and 17 who had died. Two men, Herbert Fletcher and Jack Redfern were omitted from the list of the dead and therefore the true total should be 131.

In August 1918 an updated Roll of Honour was published. This contained the names of men 'connected with St Michael's Church' and is similarly sub-divided. The list of the dead includes those who, like Joe Bewley, died of disease while on active service as well as those killed in action. In September 1918 additional names were added of those whose homes were in the parish. The references in the index of servicemen is to the complete list as at September 1918. The total of these two lists, including the dead, is 167. Rolfe gives the total of those he lists who were actively associated with St Michael's (omitting the additional names in September 1918) as 145 but the total is actually 144.

In February 1920 Rolfe stated that 146 men 'connected' with St Michael's had 'responded to the call of King and Country—almost all as volunteers', of whom 31 had 'made the supreme sacrifice'. These 31 comprise the 27 men who appeared in the list of those who had died on active service in the August 1918 list, together with the two men who were killed subsequently, Robert Barker and Eric Hardy. In February 1920 Rolfe added Kenneth Stiven who was discharged wounded in late 1917 (see December 1917) and died from an operation consequent on his wounds in early 1920. This would make 30, but does not include Herbert Fletcher and Jack Redfern. The whereabouts of the St Michael's memorial listing the names of those who had died on active service is currently unknown.

In the Biographical Notes above, containing all the servicemen who are mentioned in the magazines, there are 224 names. The discrepancy between this and the February 1920 calculation is probably due to Rolfe not counting as 'connected with St Michael's' men whose homes were not in the parish and were otherwise unconnected but nevertheless known to him (perhaps because they were relatives or friends of members of the congregation and he had been asked to pray for them). In addition the former assistant clergy at St Michael's who enlisted, and men like the Hon. and Revd E.R. Lindsay were omitted for the same reason.

It would be very unfair to expect complete consistency from Harry Rolfe. He was a very busy and committed parish priest in war-time, and he did ask that he be notified of corrections and omissions. However, this still leaves a significant number of men who had been closely connected to St Michael's (as, say, communicants or former members of the Sunday School) unaccounted for.

A number of men mentioned in the September, October and November 1914 magazine are not recorded in the Roll of Honour in either March 1917 or August 1918. These men were either communicant members of the congregation, had been members of the Sunday School, had friends who were 'closely connected' with St Michael's, or were parishioners. As these men were well-known to Rolfe why were they not listed subsequently? They include two groups:

Communicants or former members of the Sunday School
or parishioners on enlistment in 1914

Adams, William. November 1914. No subsequent list.

Ashby, Harry. October 1914, November 1915 and March 1917 but not August 1918.

Browne, Frank. October 1914, November 1915 and March 1917 but not August 1918.

Dean, Albert H. October 1914, not November 1915 but March 1917 but not August 1918.

Harrison, Bert. September 1914, November 1915 and March 1917 but not August 1918.

Harrison, Richard. September 1914. No subsequent list.

Lowe, John. November 1914, November 1915 but not March 1917 or August 1918.

Timson, Sam. October 1914. No subsequent list.

*Men who had friends or relatives belonging to St Michael's
and who were listed in November 1914 but not subsequently*

Bland, Reginald
Cantrill, Charles
Foster, Robert
Greensmith, B.
Greensmith, G. (Noted as wounded **Aug 1916**)
Greensmith, J.
Hope, Richard
Moreton, William A.
Smith, Ernest
Stepney, Herbert Herbert
Stepney, Guy Herbert
Stuart-William, Laurence
Wood, Samuel
Woolley, Charles L.

Though listed under this heading in 1914 it may be that these men were simply lost sight of as the war progressed unless attention was brought to them (as, e.g., the Parry-Joneses).

Jack Redfern (**April 1916**) is mentioned 'by a friend' in 1916 as having been wounded and subsequently killed by sniper fire but is not recorded on the Roll of Honour in March 1917 or August 1918. Herbert Fletcher was killed (**June 1916**) but is not on the Roll of Honour in March 1917 or August 1918. This may be because neither Redfern or Fletcher had any connection with St Michael's. Then why mention their deaths in the magazine?

The following additional names are mentioned in the magazine but do not appear on the updated Roll of Honour:

Annable, W. **Feb. 1919** (wounded: not known about until this time).
Baker H., **May 1918** but not on March 1917 or August 1918 lists.
Barker, R. omitted August 1918 list (clear error)
Bates, F., **March 1917** but not August 1918 list.
Buck, F., **Oct. 1918** on leave but not on August 1918 list.
Curd, John, **June 1915** enlisted but on no subsequent list.
Elsmore, F., **July 1917** POW but not March 1917 or August 1918 lists, perhaps because he had no connection with St Michael's.
Hives, John, **June 1915** enlisted. No subsequent list.
Hoose, William, June 1915 enlisted. Ditto.

Lloyd, E., **Dec. 1916** wounded, but not on March 1917 or August 1918 lists.

Marshall, J.W. Listed **Dec. 1915** but omitted March 1917.

Norton, F., **March 1917** but not August 1918 lists.

Ollerenshaw A., wounded **July 1917** but on no subsequent list.

Price, Thomas E. Listed **June 1915**, but no other list.

Robinson, J. **Sept. 1917** but on no subsequent list.

Robinson, P., **Nov. 1915** but no subsequent list.

Simpson, L. Eardley, **June 1915** listed but no other list.

Smith, Arthur, **March 1917** but not August 1918 list.

Timson, A.G., **March 1917** but not August 1918 list.

Thornley, A., **June 1915** listed (possible confusion with next)

Thornton, A., **Nov. 1915** but no subsequent list.

Toy, W., **June 1915** wounded but on no subsequent list.

Wheeldon, J., **Feb. 1919** noted as wounded, but not known about before.

White, Sidney, **Nov. 1915** but no subsequent list.

Willatt, C., **Aug. 1918** but nothing earlier.

The total of names not found on the lists and noted in the three lists above is 51. Rolfe lists 167 names in the Roll of Honour given in August 1918 and September 1918. Robert Barker was inadvertently omitted from the August 1918 list. Tom Shipley was 'added to our Roll' in October 1918. If we add to the total the four clergy (Hackforth, Johnson, Lindsay and Staley) deliberately not included on the updated Roll of Honour we have the 224 names mentioned in the magazine. There remain the possible confusions concerning Cotton, Arthur Smith and Thornton/Thorley.

INDEX

This is an index to the Introduction and the Letters, not the Biographical Notes, nor does it include persons for whom there is an entry in the Notes. Foreign place-names have been spelt in the manner most familiar to English readers and assigned to the territory in which they were situated during the First World War.